Indentured to Liberty

Indentured to Liberty

Peasant Life and the Hessian
Military State, 1688–1815

PETER K. TAYLOR

Cornell University Press

Ithaca and London

First published 1994 by Cornell University Press.

Library of Congress Cataloging-in-Publication Data
Taylor, Peter K. (Peter Keir), 1950–
    Indentured to liberty : peasant life and the Hessian military
state, 1688–1815 / Peter K. Taylor.
        p.   cm.
    Includes bibliographical references and index.
    ISBN 0-8014-2916-1
    1. Hesse-Nassau (Germany)—History. 2. Peasantry—Germany—Hesse-
Nassau.   3. Finance, Public—Germany—Hesse-Nassau—History—18th
century. 4. Hesse-Nassau (Germany)—Armed Forces—History—18th
century. 5. German mercenaries—History—18th century. 6. Hesse-
Nassau (Germany)—Rural conditions.   I. Title.
DD801.H57T39   1994
943'.41—dc20   93-41906

Printed in the United States of America

Contents

Illustrations

Figures

Maps

Preface

This book investigates some consequences of a military and financial relationship between England and the German state of Hesse-Cassel. Between 1688 and 1815 English kings frequently used trained military units from this German principality to fight both continental and colonial land wars. The Hessian Landgraves rented their armies through so-called subsidy treaties and thereby called on their rural subjects to defend the liberties and interests of Englishmen. Wealth acquired through these relationships financed the Landgraves' efforts to refashion their state and transform the society that supported it.

My primary focus is on the way members of peasant families in Hesse-Cassel experienced the new and more complicated forms of domination which grew out of the international trade in military units. Since my approach emphasizes connections between human groups, however, I have considered the practices of both the English and Hessian states when I deem them relevant to the lives of rural people and their encounter with the international military system. I have tried to shape my account in terms of the intentions of actors and with regard to the structural consequences of their actions and relationships.

My research suggests that we must broaden the historical context in which we understand what we have come to call the "German Problem." The peculiarities of German historical experience remain a major concern for intellectuals and popular writers alike. Among some historians of the past, writing about a "German Problem" grew out of the experience of the Hessian subsidy relationship with England. For

Germans and Americans, the most important instance of that relationship occurred between 1776 and 1784, when Hesse-Cassel contributed troops to put down the rebellion in the English colonies of North
America.

The political and social stresses entailed in providing a fully equipped
field army of 12,000 men to fight an ocean away called the very practice
of subsidy treaties into question and associated the treaties firmly with
issues of freedom and tyranny. Because the English state applied these
"mercenary" forces against Englishmen, the treaties drew considerable
criticism in England. As one of many denunciations demanded, "Let
not the historian be obliged to say that the Russian and German slave
was hired to subdue the sons of Englishmen and of freedom."[1] Disap-
pointing the political hope expressed here by Alderman Bull during a
1775 debate in the English House of Commons, Hesse-Cassel sent over
19,000 conscripted soldiers to put down the rebellion. The alderman's
connection between freedom and English subjects had long been encoded in commonplace phrases, and by the eighteenth century "English
liberties" had become a metaphor for rights under natural law in
Enlightenment political theory.[2] For example, Montesquieu defended a
"country" ordering of politics for France by contrasting English liberty
and oriental tyranny.[3]

As Bull seemed to fear, the ratification of the subsidy treaty between
England and Hesse-Cassel in 1776 gave rise to a historiography that
contrasted Anglo-American liberty with German tyranny. American
accounts of the Revolutionary War emphasized the use of German
troops to suppress liberty in the colonies, while German accounts
emphasized the petty oppression of the territorial princes who raised
them.[4] (The latter clearly celebrated the Prussian-Hohenzollern "liber-

1. Cited in Edward J. Lowell, *The Hessians and the Other German Auxiliaries of
Great Britain in the Revolutionary War* (New York, 1884), 30; for other examples from
America see Rodney Atwood, *The Hessians: Mercenaries from Hessen-Kassel in the
American Revolution* (Cambridge, 1980), 184.

2. Isser Wolloch, *Eighteenth-Century Europe, Tradition and Progress, 1715–1718*
(New York, 1982), 237–39; E. P. Thompson, *The Making of the English Working Class*
(New York, 1966), 77; Thomas Paine, *The Rights of Man* (New York, 1961), 270;
compare Edmund Burke, *Reflections on the Revolutions in France* (New York, 1961),
43–44.

3. Mark Hulliung, *Montesquieu and the Old Regime* (Berkeley, 1976); Paul John
O'Donnel, "State and Society: The Politics of Method in 'L'Espirit des lois'" (Ph.D.
diss., University of California at Los Angeles, 1981).

4. Lowell, *The Hessians*; Friedrich Kapp, *Der Soldatenhandel deutscher Fürsten:
Ein Beitrag zur Kulturgeschichte des 18. Jahrhundert 5* (Berlin, 1874); Phillip Losch,
Soldatenhandel (Marburg, 1976).

ation" of the subjects of these princes in the Second Empire.) After World War I, Anglo-American accounts that emphasized a German Problem continued to rely on the contrasts between English liberty and Germany tyranny. Tyranny and slavery became more closely associated with particular faults in the German character, culture, or historical experience. In many accounts, the aggressions during the world wars, the failures of the Weimar Republic, and the terrors of the Nazi era became symptoms of an authoritarian social and political psychology that gripped Germans as a result of "late" or "flawed" "modernization." The liberties contrasted with German tyranny, however, had lost their historical anchors and become abstract, universal values. Tyranny, too, eventually lost its base in particular eighteenth-century military and state practices and shifted ground to twentieth-century fears of totalitarianism. Yet, even after 1945, German historical and social analysts could pose the central question of German history as: "Why was Germany not England?"[5]

Today, with a reunified German nation-state at the center of a changed Europe, it seems particularly appropriate to reexamine the origins of the German problem. Removed from the relatively concrete contrasts of Alderman Bull, historians continue to ask why Germans have so frequently played the role of aggressor in international affairs, have sometimes failed to create and sustain parliamentary political institutions, and have sometimes reverted to social relations inconsistent with individual liberty and human love.[6] Although the incapacity to build human relationships not characterized by authoritarianism and the reifications of bureaucratic systems seems as much a general human problem as a German one, the Holocaust in central Europe rendered the horrors of these tyrannies peculiarly transparent. Because the immediate agents of horror were primarily German-speakers, it has become all too easy for those of us who live in cultures that have a more consistent parliamentary history and that do not bear the label of authoritarianism to avoid examining. The time has come to rethink the historical basis of the categorical contrasts between English liberty and German slavery and to study what encouraged Anglo-Americans to conceive their own historical experience in terms of a German "other."

5. Ralf Dahrendorf, *Society and Democracy in Germany* (New York, 1967), 16.

6. A. J. P. Taylor, *The Course of German History* (London, 1945), 8–9, Dahrendorf, *Society and Democracy in Germany*, 6–8; David Calleo, *The German Problem Reconsidered* (Cambridge, 1978); David Blackbourne and Geoff Eley, *The Peculiarities of German History: Germany and the World Order, 1870 to the Present* (Oxford, 1984); T. W. Adorno et al., *The Authoritarian Personality* (New York, 1950).

Historians have so separated English and German experience because they use a set of analytic tools that define nation-states, national communities, and national cultures as isolated entities formed by unrelated problems. Eric R. Wolf has warned against reifying analytic categories for "we create false models of reality by endowing nations, societies, or cultures with the qualities of internally homogeneous and externally distinctive and bounded objects," but we should remember "that human populations construct their cultures in interaction with one another and not in isolation."[7] Heeding his warning, I view German tyranny and English liberty as parts of intimately entwined systems.[8] In this spirit, one purpose of my work is to examine certain aspects of the German Problem as if they were woven into a general history of a European-dominated world in the eighteenth century.

Many postwar commentators have identified military institutions, particularly those of Prussia, as one prominent aspect of the political and social failures of Germans.[9] Some have explained this martial society as a response to geopolitical conditions that provided Germans with numerous threats to their existence and no easily defensible borders.[10] Following Eckhart Kehr, Hans Rosenberg and Otto Büsch have given us a thicker description of developing social militarism and autocracy in Prussia.[11] In particular, Büsch's account of militarism as institutions and practices that penetrated and altered social relationships at every level of Prussian society provided substantial inspiration for my investigation. Though Rosenberg and Büsch analyzed territoriality from within, they did not seek outside a German orbit for connections between Prussian autocracy, bureaucracy, and social militarism. By addressing Hessian conditions, I hope to extend their analysis

---

7. Eric R. Wolf, *Europe and the People without History* (Berkeley, 1982), 6–7.

8. This view may seem dangerously close to the exculpatory "others have not done much better (*Andere haben nichts viel besser gemacht*)," but this is not my intent. Rather, it is to use that insight as a tool for criticizing the Anglo-Saxon tradition and the way we construct liberty and tyranny conceptually and historically.

9. Otto Büsch, *Militärsystem und Sozialleben im alten Preussen, 1713–1807: Die Anfänge der sozialen Militisierung der preussich-deutschen Gesellschaft* (Berlin, 1962); Gordan Craig, *The Politics of the Prussian Army, 1640–1945* (New York, 1955); Gerhard Ritter, *Staatskunst und Kriegshandwerk* 4 (Munich, 1954–68).

10. Calleo, *The German Problem*, 206ff.; F. L. Carsten, *The Origins of Prussia* (Oxford, 1954).

11. Büsch, *Militärsystem;* Hans Rosenberg, *Bureaucracy, Aristocracy, and Autocracy: The Prussian Experience, 1660–1815* (Boston, 1958); Eckhart Kehr, *Der Primat der Innenpolitik* (Berlin, 1963).

beyond Germans and to shift focus away from Prussia, which has too long held center stage.

Despite the reputation of the Hohenzollern state, the fiscal and military institutions of the late Stuarts and the early Hanoverians developed more intensively and more effectively, and ultimately had more success.[12] And despite the Prussian reputation for military autocracy, military institutions played a more central role for territorial states whose armies proved fiscal resources rather than liabilities.[13] Hesse-Cassel, for example, had a ratio of soldiers to population which varied from 1:19 before the Seven Years War to 1:14 during the American War of Independence. Both ratios are more intense than those reported for Prussia, which ranged between 1:22 and 1:36.[14] Thus to examine British and Hessian military institutions as they entwined themselves in the global relationships of the first British empire is to open other contexts in which to examine the "German" problem of social militarism.[15]

The debts I have incurred in the preparation of this work are many and varied. None is deeper than that to Hermann Rebel. Without his initial direction and continuing intellectual stimulation, I might never have become interested in peasants, fairy tales, or draftees. My development as a scholar owes so much to conversations and written exchanges with him that I am sure that I borrow from him without fully realizing it.

Many people have helped me with sources for this work as well. Heide Wunder of the Gesamthochschule at Cassel provided me letters of recommendation and forums for my initial efforts at analysis. Christina Vanja contributed both encouragement and continued advice that was indispensable in finding my way through the archives at Marburg. Without her help large sections of this book simply would not have been possible. I also thank Inge Auerbach, Alfred Höck, and George

12. John Brewer, *The Sinews of Power: War, Money, and the English State, 1688–1783* (London, 1989), 29–30.

13. Hans Vogel and Wolfgang von Both, both *Landgraf Wilhelm VIII. von Hessen-Kassel: Ein Fürst der Rokokozeit* (Munich, 1964) and *Landgraf Friedrich II. von Hessen-Kassel: Ein Fürst der Zopfzeit* (Munich, 1973); and Charles W. Ingrao, *The Hessian Mercenary State: Ideas, Institutions, and Reform under Frederick II, 1760–1785* (Cambridge, 1987).

14. André Corvisier, *Armies and Societies in Europe, 1494–1789* (Bloomington, Ind., 1979), 123–24.

15. Brewer, *The Sinews of Power*, 41.

Thomas Fox for their help as archival guides. I acknowledge the cooperation of the Evangelische Pfarramt Hessens and especially the pastors of Oberweimar and Niederweimar in my use of the parish register of Oberweimar.

Numerous people have helped me convert archival work into a written account of the eighteenth century. I thank Professor Fox for helping find and correct counts from the parish register of Oberweimar. John Kolp and Andrew Federer held my hand as I learned computer data analysis and nominal record linkage. Help in polishing my clumsy prose and untwisting my labyrinthian thought processes came from Louis Rose, Rosalind Hayes, Henry Horwitz, David Sabean, and James C. Scott. Laurie Graham and Angela DeBello both went over the manuscript with fine-tooth combs.

Chapter 4 appeared previously as " 'Patrimonial' Bureaucracy and 'Rational' Policy: The Case of Hessian Recruitment Reform, 1762–1793," *Central European History* 22 (1989): 33–56, and is reprinted by permission of the publisher, Emory University. Substantial portions of Chapter 8 appeared originally as "Military System and Rural Social Change in Eighteenth-Century Hesse-Cassel," *Journal of Social History* 25 (Spring 1992): 479–504, and are published by permission of the journal.

In this day and age all research requires outside financial assistance, and I have benefited from the generosity of several institutions. First the University of Iowa provided both work and fellowship support while I was a graduate student there. I also thank Uhlrich Littmann, who administered the generous support of the German Fulbright Commission over the course of a sixteen-month research trip in Germany. A second six-week trip was financed largely by a faculty development grant from the College of Liberal Arts at Wright State University.

A special thanks goes to my wife, Kathleen Taylor, who not only provided a sounding board for my wilder ideas but bore my absences (mental, emotional, and physical) while I wrestled with this project. The love and support of my families (spouse and children, parents and siblings, and affinal kin) have given me a needed countermodel to the necessity I encounter in the past and present. No haven, they still provide the glimmer of hope without which no work may be done.

PETER K. TAYLOR

River Forest, Illinois

Abbreviations

Archives and Libraries

KaOw	*Kirchenarchiv Oberweimar/Niederweimar*
LbK	*Landesbibliotek Kassel*
LoC	Library of Congress
StaM	*Hessisches Staatsarchiv Marburg*

Archival Source Citations

abN	*alte blaue Nummer*
ALb	*alte Lokalbehörden*
B/	*Aktenbestand*
Br	*Begrabungsregister*
H/	*Handschrift*
Hr	*Heirathsregister*
K/	*Kadaster*
Kp	*Kirchenprotokolle*
Kr	*Konfirmationsregister*
mL	*monatliche Listen*
MRb	*Mass-und Rangirbücher*
Ms/	*Materialsammlung*
P/	*Protokolle*
R/	*Rechnungen*
Tr	*Taufregister*

Bound Printed Sources

HLO   *Sammlung Fürstliche Hessische Landesordnungen und*
        Ausschreiben
HSAK   *Hochfürstlicher Hessen-Kasselischer Staats- und Adressen*
        Kalender
KHM   Jakob and Wilhelm Grimm, *Kinder- und Hausmärchen*
        (Berlin, 1812).

Weights, Measures, and Currencies

Alb   *Albus*
Ar   *Acker*
Fg   *Frankfurtergulden*
H   *Heller*
Rt   *Reichstaler*
Sg   *Steuergulden*

Part I

The Interlocking Political Economies of the Subsidy System

This examination of the impact of England's military-subsidy relationship with Hesse-Cassel concentrates primarily on the costs paid by the Hessian rural population. Yet a full understanding of these costs as Englishmen and Hessians structured them requires an account of what moved people to fashion the subsidy system and the benefits that ensured its longevity. Only in this wider context can we give meaning to the suffering such arrangements entailed. Further, such an account helps establish historical agency and permits us to separate the voices of those who obeyed from the echoes of commands.

Though necessarily cursory, this section outlines the historical dynamic of English and Hessian involvement in the subsidy enterprise as it brought together peoples who practiced three different modes of production; capitalist, tributary, and kin-ordered. I have deployed the idea that "social formations" are sets of "articulations" (intimately intertwined relationships) between human groups practicing different "modes of production" because such theoretical language attends to connections between peoples across national boundaries without deflecting attention from either collaboration or conflict between and within these groups.[1] Using it allows me to place the subsidy enterprise in a context that highlights the ironic relationship between the pro-

---

1. See Eric R. Wolf, *Europe and the People without History* (Berkeley, 1982), 77ff., and Fredric Jameson, *The Political Unconscious: Narrative as a Socially Symbolic Act* (Ithaca, 1981), 34–46, 88–102, for concepts.

cesses of "rationalization" born of capitalism and bureaucracy and the promises of "liberty" encoded within the ideology of the English political system.[2]

To be sure, Hesse-Cassel and England used their subsidy relationship primarily to redeploy tribute-taking mechanisms. Unlike capitalists who take surpluses through market mechanisms as profit, tribute-takers monopolize the means of violence (armies and weapons) or the capacity to threaten its use (bureaucracies). Tribute-takers faced those who produced surpluses primarily as a lord directing a servant rather than as an employer dealing with an employee. According to Eric Wolf, systems of tribute tend to vary, some with highly centralized control and others with more localized centers of power — a difference often conceived as one between absolutism and liberty in the English context. Moreover, merchants also played a role in taking tribute by generating wealth in markets unbalanced by political intervention and then passing some of it back as taxes to those who enforced "mercantile systems."[3] Capitalist, worker, lord, servant, and merchant are the theoretical names that we apply to the flesh and blood characters of the following section.

On the north side of the English Channel the exchange of military protection and substantial amounts of money for Hessian service required Englishmen to refashion instruments of taxation and state finance and thus to create Europe's most dynamic fiscal-military state.[4] These new arrangements preserved at least the appearance of older forms of liberty for some Englishmen. Moreover, within the space of new bureaucratic, financial, and fiscal institutions, entrepreneurs created a new capitalist order out of older forms of mercantile business and at the same time promoted a newer vision of liberty based on a "free" market.

On the other side of the Channel, Hessian Landgraves used their patronage relationship with a growing world power to guarantee their own dynastic interests and to play a role out of proportion to their resources in international politics. Also, in responding to the English demands for troops, Landgraves from the time of Charles I (1670–

2. See Max Weber, *Economy and Society* (Berkeley, 1978), 2: 956–58, for "rationalization."

3. Wolf, *Europe,* 80, 83–88.

4. Here it is important to acknowledge my heavy dependence on the work of John Brewer, *The Sinews of Power* (London, 1989), xvii ff., without which the English side of my overview in this chapter would have been seriously shortchanged.

1730) through that of William IX (1785–1821) formed the subsidy relationship as a business partnership from which they hoped to gain wealth. Thus, their rudimentary state participated in a putting-out system in which they functioned as merchants subject to the fluctuations of a commodity market in trained military units. Responding to these markets they redeployed the structure of their tribute taking. On the one hand, they intensified their claims on the wealth and resources of their rural subjects. On the other, they centralized the institutions of state and subordinated local authorities to the system. Both in England and in Hesse-Cassel, the political and business aspects of the subsidy enterprise encouraged bureaucrats to "rationalize" their procedures and develop rudimentary forms of "modern" state institutions. Such tendencies, however, faced strong countervailing structures, and any "rationality" achieved by authorities remained only a partial synthesis that intensified both newer forms of reification and older forms of tyranny to which further sections of this book are devoted.

1 Liberty, Labor, and the English Military System, 1688–1815

When Colonel William Faucitt arrived in Cassel on 10 December 1775 to negotiate the subsidy treaty that inspired Alderman Bull's hyperbole about German slavery and English liberty, he extended a relationship which had begun almost eighty years earlier, during the Nine Years War.[1] The use of subsidy troops formed an important part of what D. W. Jones has called "a strategy of indirect supply."[2] English kings and their Parliaments constructed the English fiscal-military state after the Glorious Revolution of 1688, relying heavily on a strategy that exchanged English wealth for "foreign" troops and materials.[3] In the course of eighty years, the Hessians became the best and most consistent providers of these subsidy troops. The money from this enterprise became such a crucial aspect of Hessian state finances and the development of Hessian absolutism that the Hessian state formed a mirror image of its English opposite — a military-fiscal or mercenary state.[4] To create their military commodity, Hessian Landgraves used a "direct-

1. Friedrich Kapp, *Der Soldatenhandel deutscher Fürsten nach Amerika: Ein Beitrag zur Kulturgeschichte des achtzehnten Jahrhunderts* (Berlin, 1874), 48–58.
2. D. W. Jones, *War and Economy in the Age of William III and Marlborough* (London, 1988), 20–22, distinguishes between direct and indirect supply.
3. John Brewer, *The Sinews of Power* (London, 1989), xvii.
4. Charles W. Ingrao, *The Hessian Mercenary State* (Cambridge, 1987), coined the term "mercenary state" to denote that state in which armies become fiscal resources rather than liabilities. For symmetry, one might call the mercenary state a military-fiscal state.

supply strategy" that cut deeply into the productive sinews of the rural society they ruled.

Indirect supply developed from William III's commitment to a forward defense of the English Protestant succession, of Dutch Protestantism, and of the Dutch state against the aggressions of France's powerful and most Catholic king, Louis XIV. William believed that both a strong naval and a strong land effort were necessary. But he created his policy instruments at a time when political elites were committed to parliamentary co-dominion, to hatred of permanent standing armies, to a political culture of English "liberty," and to minimal taxation. The apparently incompatible motivations and strictures fostered Europe's most modern and efficiently bureaucratized fiscal and military administration. The system commanded elite acceptance and provided multiple benefits for many Englishmen because it touched production and labor relationships only indirectly through efficient fiscal and financial institutions.

Founding the English Fiscal-Military State

The foundations of the English indirect-supply system grew directly out of the settlements of 1688. Prior to the Glorious Revolution, England had not significantly or effectually involved itself in any major continental military operation since the Hundred Years War. Though the English state was more effectively centralized than many in Europe, its defense rested on its island status and on its navy rather than on its capacity to mobilize the cavalry and infantry necessary to compete in continental war and diplomacy.

This muted military system suited the needs and desires of English country gentlemen quite well. As the backbone of England's mixed monarchy, as fiscal objects, as administrative workhorses, and as a political elite they tended to regard more intensive and permanent military institutions as threats to their independent social position. After 1660 they also had the historical experience of Cromwell's New Model Army to remind them of the dangers to their liberty represented by a domestic standing army. The fear of the large permanent armed establishment that James II tried to create played a role in convincing members of Parliament that it was time to invite William of Orange and his wife Mary to take the throne in 1688.[5] A Catholic king might have been tolerable, but one armed at the expense of his leading Protestant subjects and not subject to the checks of a regularly sitting parliament was not.

Ironically, inviting William to the throne led directly to England's growing involvement in continental land wars against Louis XIV, and with that involvement came the construction of England's fiscal-military state. As Prince of Orange, William had long hoped to entwine England in the fight against French aggression and did not stop pursuing that end once installed on the English throne. William's task required a difficult political balancing act; those who installed him were likely to be the least happy with any military entanglements on the continent — because of both the costs entailed and the threats represented by a standing army. Nevertheless, William managed to lay the foundations of a permanent military establishment, and he convinced the Parliament to develop ingenious fiscal instruments to finance it by tying it to the defense of a Protestant succession. In the process, he also established, more firmly than before, Parliament's claim to co-dominion and its control and oversight of the purse strings of the state.

Like the growth of Europe's other fiscal-military states, England's may be charted by increases in military manpower, military expenditure, taxation, and debt. Between 1697 and 1784, the British army and navy increased its manpower reserves for wartime years by more than 60 percent to 190,506. This increase is the more striking because during the Nine Years War the army doubled its 1696 strength of 20,000. Expenditures, taxation, and debt climbed even more sharply than did the numbers serving the king under arms. Expenditures were up by nearly four times, reaching £20.3 million by the American War in 1776. Revenues climbed from £3.6 million to £12.2 million over the same period. Even more indicative of England's unique solution to fiscal military state-building, however, debt rose by almost fifteen times, reaching £242.9 million by 1788. These numbers represent a rough outline of England's eighteenth-century military revolution.

Over this span of a century England, which had been a purely marginal, largely seaborne power, climbed to a position at the pinnacle of European power politics. Only France, Europe's wealthiest and

5. J. R. Jones, *Court and Country: England 1658–1714* (Cambridge Mass., 1979), 254–55.

most populous kingdom, could challenge that position. Moreover, as long as England remained involved in continental military action, French challenges, even in concert with other European powers, had little success. The percentage of state revenues spent on military activity by England varied between 74 and 61 percent (excluding debt service), a figure roughly comparable to Prussia, somewhat less than Russian expenditures of 90 percent, and a good deal more than the 25 percent spent by France. An equally approximate comparative figure, England's ratio of military manpower to population size (1:36), puts her roughly on par with other continental powers by the beginning of the eighteenth century. For some kingdoms, Prussia for example, a similar ratio probably had more social impact than it did for England. It is clear, as John Brewer notes, "that despite quite a small population, Britain was nevertheless able to put a great many men in the field and on the high seas."[6]

The Ideological Constraints

In John Brewer's terms, the development of the English "sinews of power" is the more remarkable because late Stuart monarchs and their ministers created them in a political environment constrained by the discourse of a "country ideology."[7] This language virtually required that political argument be cast in terms of liberties, privileges, and rights of corporations and individuals.[8] For "country" politicians, administrative centralization remained an evil expedient and responsible government a necessity to be maintained at all costs. In a somewhat contradictory vein, the more extreme country ideologues cast the state, or any emergence of a class of bureaucratic specialists, or the growth of a professional military establishment which knew and obeyed without question the will of its masters, as threats to liberty and good governance.

Extremists such as John Trenchard did not win full victory in the political battles after the Peace of Ryswyck. Their resistance meant that William received only limited army funding, however, and that Parliament failed to reform the militia into an effective fighting force.

6. All numbers in these two paragraphs are from Brewer, *Sinews,* 30, 40, 42.
7. Ibid., 155–57.
8. Henry Horwitz, *Parliament, Policy, and Politics in the Reign of William III* (Newark, 1977), 222–24.

This combination of limitations virtually assured that English military effort remained for a long time dependent on foreign "subsidy" troops.[9] In structuring the debate, moreover, hardliners also continued to influence the shape of the English fiscal-military state. The political settlement of the 1690s which traded a large but largely absent and minimally intrusive military establishment for a highly rationalized, extractive, and debt-driven fiscal structure, nonetheless could be expressed in country terms. As one country gentlemen argued "A wise and good man will rather chuse . . . one half of his estate, with the liberty of his conscience" rather than see himself and his friends "sacrificed to the idol of arbitrary power" with the security of his liberty "only precarious and during pleasure."[10] Thus the fiscal-military state was an expedient arrangement in which Englishmen gave wealth to a professionalized civil administration, overseen by a regularly meeting parliament, under the provision that the army could not be turned to the arbitrary dispossession of English liberties. Englishmen avoided continental absolutism by subcontracting the defense of their liberties and privileges to Germans, Native Americans, and Africans.[11] German subsidy troops represented an effective alternative to a less expensive, but disorderly, militia or an efficient, but more oppressive, standing army.[12]

The Englishman's negative attitude toward a permanent military establishment and toward service in it extended beyond the political discourse of country gentlemen. General hostility to the military establishment helped make it expedient to keep the English army small and encamped away from England. Rarely larger than 15,000 men in peacetime, the standing army seemed never to be more than half there during even the deepest crises of the eighteenth century. When many troops did camp in England their powers over civilians remained severely restricted. Civil jurisdiction always took precedence over military, unlike most continental situations where disputes between soldiers and citizens became a tricky negotiation between civil and mili-

9. Ibid., 236; J. R. Western, *The English Militia in the Eighteenth Century: The Story of a Political Issue* (London, 1965), 89–95; Lois G. Schworer, *"No Standing Armies!" The English Anti-Army Ideology in Seventeenth-Century England* (Baltimore, 1974), 155–65, 188–92.

10. In Brewer, *Sinews*, 142.

11. Compare Wolf, *Europe and the People without History* (Berkeley, 1982), 166–70 and 210–12.

12. Western, *English Militia*, 109–11.

tary authorities. This difference meant that recruits could sue those who had recruited them. Only in dire circumstances did legal commentators allow for the declaration of martial law.[13]

Suspicion of the military extended to quartering practices as well. General Wade commented that Englishmen associated "the idea of Barracks and Slavery so closely together that, . . . they cannot separate them."[14] Sequestering soldiers from the "liberty-loving populace" would have removed an important check on the army as a tool of tyranny. However, normal continental practices, such as billeting troops on private citizens, commandeering private means of transport, or using facilities within towns without permission of those concerned, were labeled oppressive by Englishmen.[15] Soldiers thus had to pay for such services and frequently ended up staying in public inns. Even within England's borders a version of indirect supply held.

Conscription was another symbol of the tyranny of standing armies for most of the populace. For this reason the standing army remained primarily voluntary, though in the deepest of wartime crises, in the face of severe manpower shortages, the state did resort to involuntary military servitude. Whether in peace or war, authorities kept close watch on recruitment procedures. For example, enlisted recruits appeared before justices of the peace to swear to the free-will nature of their recruitment. Law confined impressment to "such able-bodied men as had not any lawful calling or employment" certified by local authorities.[16] Despite abuses, the civil liability of those in collusion with the recruitment process, including military officers, tended to be a strong deterrent to coercive practices. Naval impressment had an even worse reputation but press gangs limited themselves largely to sailors and operated mostly on the high seas.

The aversion of Englishmen for involuntary military service and to those men who volunteered to serve showed in the high percentage of military personnel who spent most, if not all, of their time outside of England. Since navies were at sea a good deal of the time and not in the realm, Parliament seemed to prefer "blue water strategies" and naval expenditures over land engagements on the continent. Although twice as expensive as soldiers, sailors were half as dangerous or visible. The

13. André Corvisier, *Armies and Societies in Europe, 1494–1789* (Bloomington, Ind., 1979), 123–24.
14. Brewer, *Sinews,* 48.
15. Corvisier, *Armies,* 116ff.
16. In Brewer, *Sinews,* 50.

foreign troops who followed English colors because their princes received subsidies threatened English liberties even less. D. W. Jones has estimated that during the Nine Years War foreign troops accounted for 41 percent of English military effort and that this rose to near 60 percent during the Wars of the Spanish Succession.[17] Although their cost rose substantially during the century, more than 14 percent of all British forces came from foreign lands. The cost of these troops still amounted to nearly one-third of wartime expenditures. Subsidy troops could be raised quickly, under conditions not subject to the same legal restrictions which bedeviled the English army, and most of the time could be billeted away from England either where they fought or on those who raised them. Between 1702 and 1763 total expenditures for subsidies reached £24.5 million.[18] The American war by itself added at least £5.7 million.[19] More than any other power in Europe, England resorted to this expedient of indirect supply of men, and thus more than any other power did England escape the military domination of political and civil society. England exported militarism by subcontracting military recruitment and training to foreign princes.

Fiscal and Administrative Change

The use of indirect-supply methods required the state to alter its financial strategies significantly. This radical change entailed increased levels of taxation, a shift in the burden of taxation away from land taxes and toward excise taxes, and, most important, the creation of a nationally funded debt. Along with the fiscal revolution came a bureaucratic one that rendered administration professional, independent of politics, and relatively free of peculation and venality.

P. G. M. Dickson has provided us an account of the fundamental revolution of using public debt to fund military efforts initiated by the English state.[20] The institutions of public credit created to help finance William III's wars with Louis XIV involved the separation of long-term from short-term debt, the creation of a market in government se-

17. Jones, *War and Economy*, 99.
18. Brewer, *Sinews*, 32.
19. Kapp, *Soldatenhandel*, 212.
20. P. G. M. Dickson, *The Financial Revolution in England: A Study in the Development of Public Credit, 1688–1756* (New York, 1967), 40–49, and elsewhere, is the basis of my account of the financial revolution.

curities, and the building of the Bank of England. Prior to 1688 only the scale of government borrowing separated the king's borrowing from that of Europe's nobles. Creditors who lent did so at high risk and only for the short-term. Long-term debt frequently became a matter of constant refinancing until accumulated principal and compounded interest could be paid off only by the sale of royal estates, or as Cromwell did, selling estates confiscated for political reasons. Consequently, the crown paid high interest rates (10 percent or more) because creditors had only fragile confidence in the king's ability to pay. If, in these respects, England's kings resembled their continental counterparts, then their frugality and the limitations put on them by Parliament protected them from the deeper crises faced by some continental powers.

Where William III could claim credit for laying the foundations of England's peculiar military establishment, responsibility for the shaping of the institutions of public credit may be laid to Parliament. Beginning in 1692, members of Parliament created long-term public debt by authorizing the subscription of a Tontine and single-life annuities which eventually raised more than £880,000. Parliament made the debt public by guaranteeing it and attaching payments to particular revenue sources including an excise on beer and duties on imported cider and brandy. Tontines fell out of favor rather quickly as a method of borrowing. Public lotteries which fed off current popular obsessions with gaming replaced them. Annuities played the major role in long-term state borrowing.

Parliament also established the Bank of England as another source of long-term credit. Begun as an outright loan of £1.2 million, the act of 24 April 1694 provided that lenders became incorporated as bank shareholders when half the amount was raised. Parliament guaranteed repayment through new customs and excises created the month before. The loan looked so secure that it took only ten days for enough shares to be sold to reach the incorporation level. The bank eventually sold more than the nominal amount of the loan and thus lent the treasury more than originally intended. Despite the state credit crisis of the late 1690s, the Bank of England had a sound footing and became a central element of state finance for many years to come.

A fiscal crisis in 1696–97, which required William to negotiate a peace, nearly caused the collapse of the new financial arrangements and nearly ended the new dynasty. These financial problems stemmed from the mismanagement of state short-term borrowing.[21] By 1697 people exchanging Exchequer tallies in the market discounted them by over 30 percent. Supposedly, short-term borrowing merely anticipated tax revenues on the books, but by 1697 tax funds assigned to repayment had insufficient funds to pay the money borrowed on them. Many of the taxes filling the funds expired in that year and disaster loomed. The crisis required the legislature to intervene and extend some of the taxes and put borrowing processes on a sounder and more controlled footing. Parliament converted some short-term debt to the long term by exchanging obligations for stock in the Bank of England or other joint stock operations with government charters. Through these measures the paymasters of this indirectly supplied fiscal-military state remained solvent.[22]

Another set of practices that unlocked the wealth of the nation for military and many other purposes developed out of this financial revolution. Called "stockjobbing" by hostile contemporaries, trading in government securities became a key aspect of the financing: holders of shares in the national debt could liquidate these resources by selling them to third parties. This practice alleviated some of the pressure to liquidate the debt itself.[23] Increased liquidity for lenders made it both financially and politically possible to extend long-term national debt into the future indefinitely at or above the amounts required for England's military success. It also meant that state borrowing would not again lock up wealth in nonliquid paper.

Cumbersome recording and accounting procedures in the Exchequer discouraged much official transfer of government securities, but, as one critic lamented, transferring government debt from the Exchequer to the Bank of England and other joint-stock companies promoted securities exchange or stockjobbing, which "would have been impossible to have carried on . . . if our Debts had . . . been paid at the Exchequer" as they used to be.[24] Dickson calculated that as early as 1704 nearly one quarter of the Bank of England's stock changed hands in a year and that more than the whole of the stock of the East India Company did so. These rates dwarf treasury exchanges, which rolled

21. Ibid., 343–48.
22. Ibid., 357.
23. Ibid., 457.
24. William Pultney in ibid., 467.

over at a 4 percent rate. Dickson points out that turnover tended to decline as the eighteenth century progressed although the number of transfers remained relatively constant and the capital available for transfer grew.[25]

The creation of public credit charged to specific funds filled by specific tax revenues guaranteed by the parliaments of William and Mary combined with increased military expenditures to change the structure of English taxation over the course of the eighteenth century. Not only did revenues rise by four times between the Nine Years War and the American war, but also the burden of taxation shifted away from land taxes toward excises and customs. Further, the maintenance of confidence in government credit required that fiscal administration be "rationalized." The 30 to 40 percent of English military expenditure covered by borrowing would not have been possible without efficient and trustworthy institutions of extraction.[26] The same administrative institutions enhanced other tribute-taking enterprises as well.

Until the studies of Peter Mathias and Patrick O'Brian, it had been commonplace to see eighteenth-century England as a land freer from the heavy hand of the fisc than other European kingdoms.[27] In dispelling this myth, their studies show that the percentage of national income devoted to taxes rose from 3.5 percent in the 1670s to 12 percent during the American war. The share of per capita income devoted to taxes rose from 16 percent in the second decade of the eighteenth century to 23 percent by the eighth decade. According to Brewer, Englishmen in the 1780s on average bore a tax burden 2.7 times the size of the one levied on their French counterparts.[28]

Also needing some qualification is the belief that the English landed elites taxed themselves more willingly than did other such groups in Europe. If the share of revenue born by the land tax was any indicator, their willingness to bear this burden declined over the eighteenth century. Brewer shows that before the watershed year of 1714, land taxes accounted for over half of state revenues.[29] After that date, they rarely accounted for more than 30 percent — shrinking to near 20 percent in the 1780s. Indirect taxes on commerce and consumption, including

25. Ibid., 466, 468.
26. Ibid., 10; Brewer, *Sinews*, 88–90.
27. Peter Mathias and Patrick O'Brian, "Taxation in England and France 1715–1810," *Journal of European Economic History* 5 (1976).
28. Brewer, *Sinews*, 89.
29. Ibid., 95–99.

excises on beer and leather, swelled to take their place. After 1740, excises usually accounted for four shares in ten of state revenues and rose as high as 55 percent in the 1730s. Customs played a middling role throughout the century.

The heavier burden of taxation required a more rational and efficient administrative machine to oversee the disbursement of monies collected. Before the revolution of 1688, England remained a bureaucratically underdeveloped realm.[30] Expansion began under Charles II and James II but accelerated significantly with the growth of revenue and of the military establishment. The number of officials increased by a factor of three or four during the eighteenth century. The structures created after 1688 remained largely intact until the nineteenth century. Hiring practices and business procedures in these offices became so routine that John Brewer has claimed that the excise administration "more closely approximated to Max Weber's idea of bureaucracy than any other governmental agency in eighteenth-century Europe." Administrators achieved this triumph not by sweeping the slate clean but rather by adding to existing structures, by working around older kinds of officials, or by accommodating them. Although structures performed rationally, they did not have a flow-chart pattern of organization as modern bureaucracies do. No large body of venal *officiers* stood in the way of better procedures as in France, and yearly sessions of Parliament "eager to root out malfeasance and reluctant to disburse monies without good reason," exercised a vigilant oversight impossible elsewhere in Europe. Parliamentary oversight did not eliminate peculation but contained it sufficiently to maintain the legitimacy of taxation.

The Benefits of English Fiscal-militarism

The massive English investment in fiscal-militarism had many unanticipated benefits for some Englishmen. Tax and credit policies of the new English state fostered interest-group politics led by the "landed" and "financial" interests. These same groups invested heavily in new forms of "capitalist" enterprises. While taxation and military aggressiveness threatened some commercial developments, it fostered others by opening colonial and foreign markets to English merchants. Finally,

30. Ibid., 64–70.

productive enterprises based on capitalist forms of organization found encouragement in credit policies that facilitated secure and long-term borrowing and in military personnel policies that limited disruptions to the labor market.

Brewer argues that the common belief that debt and taxes affected landowners most heavily went a long way toward creating a landed interest.[31] Landowners and others based this perception upon the land tax assessment of 1692 and the very real difficulties landowners had in the credit market once state borrowing increased heavily after 1693. The strength of this interest prevented any revision of land tax assessments and so the proportion of the total burden paid by the landed aristocracy declined gradually. But taxation and government borrowing did not affect all members of this group equally. Landlords who had commercialized production on their holdings had advantages over those who had not, particularly after 1750 when rents once again began to rise. Owners of commercialized holdings, because of greater productive efficiency, could borrow money more easily and more easily passed tax burdens on to tenants and laborers through higher rents and lower wages. Moreover, the new possibilities for credit arrangements (such as long-term annuities) made it possible for shrewd operators to hedge against inevitable fluctuations of the market. The government eventually had to spend some of its income not only on weaponry but on victualing the troops in England and thus provided another market for commercial farms. Finally, the expansion of civil administration and the growing availability of military positions gave landed elites respectable places for their younger male progeny. Perhaps this meant fewer claims on the patrimony and ultimately more investment in improvement. Thus, the fiscal-military state not only had room for a capitalist agricultural sector but favored it over sectors not yet so improved.

Financiers also benefited from the unlocked wealth of the fiscal-military state. Frequently government contractors and bankers underwrote state loans and served on the boards of the Bank of England, the East India Company, and the South Sea Company. Men like John Gore, who died at age forty-six with £160,000, made huge fortunes from their positions on boards of directors by administering provisioning and subsidy remittances on the continent. Their success attracted the fearful gaze of the public because some saw debt as a government

31. Ibid., 199–207.

plot to tie as many people as possible to the settlements of the 1690s. Critics charged that the financiers threatened both trade and agriculture by using up available credit and, further, by promoting war. It appears that rather than amassing new fortunes made at the expense of trade and agriculture, these men put to use a variety of forms of old money that new financial arrangements had unlocked and increased. Their elaboration of the instruments of credit made it possible for others to revolutionize productive relations.[32]

Mercantile groups benefited substantially as well. Though wars up to the Seven Years War hurt trade and increased the burden of taxation on commerce while they occurred, the success of English arms opened doors all over the world and defended British trading territories already held. Moreover, the decision to rely on indirect supply and foreign troops gave merchants the opportunity to function as remittance men for the English state.[33] The Exchequer used bills of exchange to pay the wages and subsistence of soldiers fighting in Europe. These payments required men who had reserves of foreign currencies as well as needs for sterling to complete the supply circle. Networks of Dutch and Huguenot bankers, as well as English textile merchants, frequently worked on contract with English paymasters. Payment of subsidies became part of this business in which English, Dutch, and Frankfurt banking houses all had a share.[34] The forward commitment along with indirect supply of men and material adopted by England strengthened the connections and provided opportunities for international finance and, eventually, international capital.

Adam Smith's book *The Wealth of Nations* attacked the blizzard of regulations, monopolies, licenses, and taxes restraining English merchants. This "mercantile" system and its regulations had been a creation partially necessitated by the burgeoning debt and tax bills of the fiscal-military state. Many of the successes in raising tax money had been the result of the extent to which the English economy had been commercialized. However, Smith believed that the successful rationalization of customs and excise collection threatened to deflect the spirit of industrial and economic innovation into the political arena. In

32. Wolf, *Europe*, 272; Peter Mathias, "Capital, Credit, and Enterprise in the Industrial Revolution," in *The Transformation of England: Essays in the Economic and Social History of England in the Eighteenth Century* (New York, 1979), 92ff.

33. Jones, *War and Economy*, 79–83.

34. Joseph Sauer, *Finanzgeschäfte der Landgrafen Hessen-Kassel* (Fulda, 1930), 26ff.

addition to these restraints, the frequent wars after 1688 contributed heightened risk, higher insurance costs, and inflationary pressures on consumer goods both as the result of enemy action and intensified taxation.

The English fiscal-military state did offer some important positive benefits to entrepreneurs. Despite the predominance of indirect-supply strategies, military spending provided an important economic stimulus to some industries and some areas of the country. Of course, most benefits accrued to weapons producers, metallurgists, and gunsmiths as well as seaport towns that had naval shipyards and did naval provisioning. Textile industries that supplied military uniforms, particularly those of West Riding, seemed to benefit especially well.[35] Even wartime losses, had to be made up, and therefore increased the volumes of business, so that we may assume the development of a substantial military-industrial economy.

Further, the elaboration of the instruments of credit played a substantial role in the development of early capitalist enterprise as well as in older putting-out industries. Eighteenth-century entrepreneurs who began England's early industrialization did not make large investments in fixed capital but did need long- and short-term credit in order to manage seasonal and conjunctural fluctuations in income and outflow. Low requirements for fixed capital meant early entrepreneurs, according to Peter Mathias, "did not need great personal wealth (implying large family resources) provided that they had a good enough reputation to command credit and access to a modicum of long-term capital." Kinship and its connections could satisfy a great many of these needs on the local level through dowries and inheritances but fortunes made in public securities by London and, later, provincial bankers seemed also to provide important sources of credit.[36] Silent partnerships with men of wealth and connections proved yet another route for capital to move into the hands of early captains of industry. Although government borrowing might have competed for wealth with early industrial enterprise, its massive participation in capital markets probably had the effect of regularizing the rules, and securing the flows of credit. Indirectly, it also provided the very means of financing small but growing local and regional business concerns. The disruption and

35. Jones, *War and Economy,* 169, 310, 311.
36. Mathias, "Capital, Credit, and Enterprise," 94–102.

endemic insecurity caused by the credit schemes of other states in Europe stand as instructive counterexamples.[37]

Employers also could find comfort in the peculiar pattern of English military effort which limited the possible damage that enlarged military forces had on labor markets. The conversion of English land tenures to economic rents and the consequently high proportion of English workers involved in nonagricultural and wage-earning pursuits had ordered the labor market in favor of employers by the beginning of the eighteenth century.[38] This large amount of unlocked labor may account for the relatively low labor costs experienced both by capitalist farmers and the rural textile industries. Such an edge early on might have been the result of low military development which meant armies had not competed heavily for able-bodied men. The edge may well have continued after the military intensification began in 1688 because of the substantial reliance on subsidized foreign troops. Even so, during war, as Brewer described, "the military acted as a sponge, mopping up much unemployment and underemployment among the laboring poor, to such an extent that conscription became a necessity at some point during every eighteenth-century war.[39] The increased costs of labor to merchants and capitalists would have been much higher if a substantial proportion (up to 44 percent) of all military forces had not come from outside England through subsidy treaties. Without such relief, English authorities might well have found themselves worrying incessantly about economic collapse resulting from high labor costs, as many central Europeans did.[40]

André Corvisier has distinguished sharply between European states

37. J. F. Bosher, *French Finances 1770–1794* (Cambridge, 1970); Julian Dent, *Crisis in Finance: Crown Financiers, and Society in Seventeenth Century France* (New York, 1973); Martin Wolfe, *The Fiscal System of Renaissance France* (New Haven, 1972); Hermann Rebel, *Peasant Classes: The Bureaucratization of Property and Family Relations under Early Habsburg Absolutism, 1511–1636* (Princeton, 1983); P. G. M. Dickson, *Finance and Government under Maria Theresa, 1740–1780*, vols. 1 and 2 (Oxford, 1987).

38. Wolf, *Europe*, 270; Maurice Dobb, *Studies in the Development of Capitalism* (New York, 1949), 221–54.

39. Brewer, *Sinews*, 49, 196.

40. Peter K. Taylor, "The Household's Most Expendable People: The Draft and Peasant Society in Eighteenth Century Hessen-Kassel" (Ph.D. diss., University of Iowa, 1987), 118–20; Otto Büsch, *Militärsystem und Sozialleben im alten Preussen 1713–1807* (Frankfurt, 1981), 156–59.

in which military authority predominated and those in which civil authorities held sway.[41] Prussia stands as his paradigm of the former and England of the latter. Corvisier would like to lay much of the responsibility for such differences on the intensity of military effort. As my discussion shows, however, intensity is not so important as kind. The English made no less intense a military effort than the Prussians, but rather relied to a much greater extent on an indirect supply of men and logistic means. Prussians overwhelmingly recruited, supplied, and paid for their own army, while the English raised wealth through various ingenious expedients and, to a much larger extent, paid others to raise, supply, or train military forces. This system permitted them to both maintain and defend their "liberties." The Prussian stratagem meant that military authority permeated society at every level and the Prussian state and society gained a reputation for being hostile to "liberty."[42] In such a society both wealth and labor remained locked up in tributary relationships. Had labor and wealth remained locked up in the English system, paying for a substantial military build-up would have been impossible without trampling on the very liberties the system protected. What is more, the instruments for unlocking wealth tended to encourage the further development of capitalist agriculture, industry, and labor relations — a new form of "liberty."

41. Corvisier, *War*, 119–225.
42. Büsch, *Militärsystem* xv, 163–70.

2   The Hessian State and the Developing Political Economy of Subsidies, 1600–1815

The English system of indirect supply created many markets outside England. European bankers and entrepreneurs responded to the opportunities of these markets, but the provision of troops through subsidy treaties fell mostly to the tributary overlords of German territorial states. These princes could dispose of large amounts of cash tributes and had legal rights in the persons of their subjects. This advantageous position allowed them to subordinate independent military entrepreneurs (mercenary captains and colonels) or to drive them entirely out of the market for troops which they had previously dominated.[1] To respond to changing opportunities presented by England and other states, territorial princes had to refashion the political economies of their domains. Hesse-Cassel was one such refashioned state, and one of the most successful.

The Subsidy Treaties of Hesse-Cassel

As instruments for the indirect supply of troops to English war efforts, subsidy treaties usually contained many provisions and specifications. Although some simply contracted for providing troops, most treaties took the form of a defensive alliance between princes who pledged

---

1. Compare Fritz Redlich, *The German Military Enterpriser and His Workforce: A Study in European Economic and Social History* (Wiesbaden, 1965), 2:274.

"true friendship" and the protection of one another's "interests."[2] The treaty between England and Hesse-Cassel, negotiated by Ernst Martin von Schlieffen and Colonel William Faucitt and signed on 15 January 1776, made provision for four different kinds of payments. First, levy money (*Werbegeld*) at the rate of £7 4s. 4 1/2d. per man for 12,000 men was to be paid by the exchequer in sterling to the Dutch banking house van Notten.[3] In addition to this recruitment money, the English contracted to pay a subsidy of £108,281 5s. per year for the duration of the war plus half that total for one year after the war. Van Notten handled these monies as well. The British also undertook to pay each Hessian soldier at British rates of pay. The payments, "subsistence" in English financial nomenclature, apparently went into company treasuries because Faucitt, the English negotiator, sought a clause guaranteeing that Hessian paymasters would actually disburse the full amount to each soldier.[4] Moreover, British paymasters complained that commanders in charge of pay lists frequently padded them.[5] Unlike the treaty signed with the duke of Brunswick at the same time, the Hessian treaty included no provisions for payment for killed and wounded soldiers. Hessian Landgraves had negotiated such provisions in the past. However, von Schlieffen managed to get Faucitt to concede to a clause guaranteeing early payment of subsidy arrears from the Seven Years War amounting to £41,820 14s. 5d.

In return, the English army received fully trained and equipped military units. Equipment included uniforms, personal weapons, field packs, as well as muskets and artillery pieces. The officers acquired uniforms and equipment on their own account from Hessian and other European sources, paying for them out of the unit treasuries.[6] Some items of their own uniforms and equipment, as well as food for the units, were charged by the officers to the "subsistence" of the men — that is, the amount was deducted from the men's wages. Units included infantry, grenadier, garrison, dragoons, and jägers. Of the lot, only

2. Friedrich Kapp, *Der Soldatenhandel deutscher Fürsten nach Amerika* (Berlin, 1874), 54; Redlich, *The German Military Enterpriser*, 2: 88–98; Rodney Atwood, *The Hessians: Mercenaries from Hessen-Kassel in the American Revolution* (Cambridge, 1980), 22; Edward Lowell, *The Hessians and the Other German Auxiliaries of Great Britain in the Revolutionary War* (New York, 1884), 19.

3. Lowell, *The Hessians*, 19; Joseph Sauer, *Finanzgeschäfte der Landgrafen Hessen-Kassel* (Fulda, 1930), 26.

4. Atwood, *The Hessians*, 27.

5. Kapp, *Soldatenhandel*, 58.

6. Redlich, *The German Military Enterpriser*, 2: 47–48, 54–55.

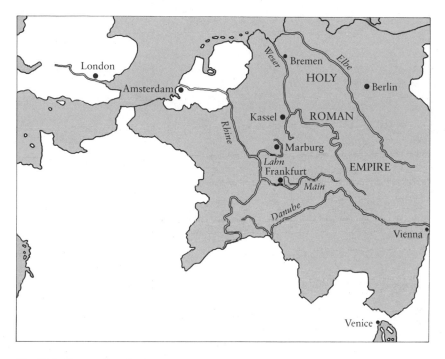

The Holy Roman Empire in 1762.

Table 1. The subsidy treaties of Hesse-Cassel

Year	Client	Number of troops	Face value Rt[a]
1677	Denmark	1,600	—
1678	Denmark	1,500	34,000
1684	Spain	1,500	14,870
1684	Venice	1,000	80,000
1687	Netherlands	3,400	14,870
1688	Netherlands	4,600	—
1694	England	—	10,000
1701	Netherlands	1,000	29,936
1702	Netherlands	1,000	—
1702	Netherlands	4,920	11,376
1703	England/Netherlands	9,000	21,000
1703	England/Netherlands	11,070	24,492
1707	England/Netherlands	11,070	120,845
1707	England/Netherlands	—	115,900
1708	England/Netherlands	9,000	100,000
1717	German Emperor	2,300	13,026
1726	England	1,200	543,478
1733	German Emperor	3,200	—
1736	England	4,000	—
1740	England	6,000	—
1742	German Emperor	3,000	324,000
1743	Prussia	3,000	—
1744	German Emperor	9,000	75,000 + 36,229/mo.
1744	Prussia	3,000	—
1745	England	6,000	—
1747	Netherlands	3,400	—
1755	England	12,000	258,620
1757	England	18,992	272,727/mo.
1759	England	12,000	272,727/mo.

garrison units came under suspicion for low quality because they were, in fact, concealed militia units made up of the least willing and smallest recruits. Treaties thus represented a substantial influx of money into Hessian realms, and a substantial outflow of men and material.

For the Hessian Landgrave, the treaty of 1776 proved the most lucrative of a series of treaties which began in 1677 and ran through 1815. See Table 1. Hessian Landgraves authorized at least thirty-eight different treaties in that 138-year span. They provided manpower for seven different powers: Denmark, Spain, the Republic of Venice, the States General of the Netherlands, the Habsburg Emperors, the King in Prussia, and England. Of the thirty-seven treaties, nineteen involved relations with England, eleven with the Netherlands, five with the

Table 1. *Continued*

Year	Client	Number of troops	Face value Rt[a]
1760	England	15,392	—
1776	England	12,000[b]	19,000,000[c]
1787	England	12,000	258,720[d]
1793	England	8,000	172,413[d]
1793	England	12,000	301,724[d]
1794	England	12,000	100,000 + 20,689/mo.
1809	Austria	10–12,000[e]	—
1815	England	7,500	280,000[f]

SOURCE: Phillip Losch, *Soldatenhandel* (Marburg, 1974), 7–14, unless otherwise noted. The monetary amounts represent what was contracted for rather than what was paid; there were few if any indications of how long treaties were in effect.

[a]European currencies other than Reichstaler were converted using rates of exchange available for Hamburg in John J. McCusker, *Money and Exchange in Europe and America: A Handbook* (Chapel Hill, 1978).

[b]This number of troops were to be supplied for the duration of the American war 1776–1783. Deserters and casualties were supposed to be replaced. Over the course of the war 18,970 troops served the British crown under Hessian auspices, according to Rodney Atwood, *The Hessians, Mercenaries from Hessen-Kassel in the American Revolution* (Cambridge, 1980), 254. Not all of these men necessarily came from Hesse-Cassel nor were all of them there and fighting at the same time.

[c]This estimate of the actual amount the Landgraves received as a result of the treaty of 1776 was made by Joseph Sauer, *Finanzgeschäfte der Landgrafen von Hessen-Kassel* (Fulda, 1930), 21.

[d]These figures are based on an exchange rate of 1.74 Danish Kroners per Reichstaler, the rate in 1755, which is certainly an underestimate given continuing inflation in the second half of the eighteenth century.

[e]A condition of this treaty, that the Austrians somehow liberate Hessian territory from Napoleon, made it doubtful that the treaty was ever executed.

[f]This figure is based on an exchange rate of .22 English pounds per Reichstaler—the rate in 1757.

Habsburgs, two each with Prussia and Denmark, and one each with Spain and the Venetian Republic. Thus, as Fritz Redlich has suggested, the market for trained military units had only a few buyers.[7]

As the eighteenth century wore on, Hesse's involvement in the market became more exclusively tied to its relationship with England. In fact, the English king even paid the Landgrave a retainer of £125,000 for several years after 1727 in order to have first claim on Hessian troops.[8] The fact that England remained in arrears in many subsidy payments also tended to force Hessians again and again into English

7. Ibid., 83.
8. Atwood, *The Hessians*, 14.

rather than other arms. Finally, during the reign of William VIII, the relationship with England became further complicated when the Land-grave requested that George II guarantee the succession of his son and the continuation of Protestantism in his domains.[9] By that point, the relationship seemed to be determined as much by English patronage as by market forces. How the Landgraves of Hesse-Cassel became en-twined in this business-client relationship is a complicated story which may best be unfolded as a narrative.

Foundations of the Hessian Mercenary State, 1567–1688

The history of Hessian involvement in providing indirect supply for English war efforts cannot be separated from the growth of Hesse-Cassel's peculiar form of petty absolutism.[10] The Landgraves began this process in the sixteenth century under the permanent dual con-straints of poorly endowed lands and the terms of the will of Phillip the Magnanimous (1520–1567). Phillip's bigamy, and his insistence that all four of his sons be settled at the expense of his domains meant that he divided his relatively large realms into four smaller pieces at his death. At that time the largest of these pieces, Hesse-Cassel, encom-passed 61,000 square kilometers with 175,000 people. None of the heirs could enjoy the influence that their father exercised in the early phases of the Reformation because none had sufficient resources to do so.[11]

The heir to Hesse-Cassel, William IV (1567–1582), played the hand dealt him by his father largely by turning inward and concentrating on creating a spartan and economically run state.[12] Though he did not rely heavily on the expedients of venality or on lien administration, as did France and Austria, he created a bureaucracy of non-noble domain

9. Hans Vogel and Wolfgang von Both, *Landgraf Wilhelm VIII. von Hessen-Kassel* (Munich, 1973), 77.

10. F. L. Carsten, *Princes and Parliaments in Germany from the Fifteenth to the Eighteenth Century* (Oxford, 1959).

11. Karl E. Demandt, *Geschichte des Landes Hessen* (Kassel, 1959), 182–84; Christian Röth and Karl von Stamford, *Geschichte von Hessen vom Tode Landgraf Philipps des Grossmütigen an mit Ausschluss der abgetrennten Lande* (Kassel, 1886), 284–88.

12. Demandt, *Geschichte des Landes Hessen*, 184.

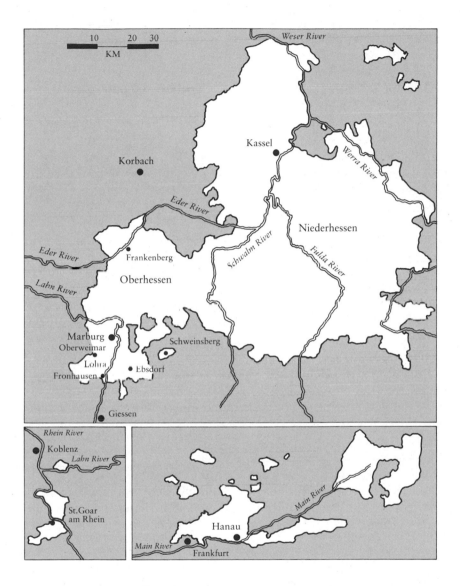

The territory of Hesse-Cassel in 1776. Based on "Hessen zur Zeit des Amerikanischen Unabhängigkeitskriegs," in Inge Auerbach et al., *Hessen und die Amerikanische Revolution: Eine Ausstellung des Hessischen Staatsarchivs Marburg* (Marburg, 1976).

managers.[13] The officials of the landgravial domain helped with William's crowning achievement, a proto-cadastral document entitled *The Economic State*.[14] This document for a long time simplified control over both local jurisdictions and the Landgrave's domains.

William IV stayed within the bounds of his meager income because of his purely defensive foreign policy. Despite his circumspection, he provided small amounts of military support in money and mercenary soldiers to the besieged Protestant House of Orange in the Netherlands. He increased his resources by recalling the escheated fiefs of Plesse and Schmalkalden. The efforts to husband and rationalize his resources have generally drawn favorable reviews from historians who chronicle state power.

The judgments on Moritz the Learned, his successor (1592–1627), have been considerably more ambivalent. Karl E. Demandt decried Moritz for spending his territory into a debt of a million-plus gulden even before the disasters of the Thirty Years War.[15] Moritz gave his court the splendor visible in other monarchical residences at the turn of the seventeenth century, but only at great cost to his territory. More important, he made the first attempts to carry out a military revolution within his own domains. He sought to construct a well-disciplined and trained militia that would permit a reduced use of expensive and unreliable mercenary forces.[16] Moritz became heavily involved in military operations because of long-standing religious and political ties to the House of Orange and because of increasing military obligations to the Upper Rhenish Circle. The defeat of his mercenary forces by the Spanish general Spinola at Rees in 1599 increased his ardor for a "direct supply" military strategy.

Moritz laid out his new theory of military strategy in 1601, in a manuscript of some 288 folio pages.[17] He wished to base the defense of Hesse-Cassel on trained peasants who would serve only parttime. The plan was radical because, in most military theory of the time, weapons

13. Kersten Krüger, "Frühabsolutismus und Amtsverwaltung: Landgraf Wilhelm IV. Inzipiert 1567 Amt und Eigenwirtschaft Amt Trendelberg," *Hessisches Jahrbuch für Landesgeschichte* 25 (1975): 117–47.

14. Ludwig Zimmerman, *Der Hessische Territorialstaat im Jahrhundert der Reformation* (Marburg, 1933).

15. Demandt, *Geschichte des Landes Hessen*, 192.

16. Gunther Thies, *Territorialstaat und Landesverteidigung: Das Landesdefensionswerk in Hessen-Kassel unter Landgraf Moritz* (Marburg, 1973), 16–19.

17. Ibid., 21–26.

technology remained the monopoly of professional mercenaries who alone learned the complexities of timing and tactics required to fight with halbards, pikes, muskets, cannons, and arquebusses. The disciplined, mass use of these weapons had rendered the feudal levy obsolete.[18] In defense of his plan, the Landgrave offered the classic criticisms of mercenary warfare based on units recruited and trained by independent military enterprisers: the expense, the disloyalty of the commanders, and the mutinous character of mercenary units.[19] He also recognized that the looting and banditry suffered by Hesse-Cassel at that time frequently originated with disbanded (*abgedankte*) mercenaries.

As a solution, Moritz envisioned an army of peasants highly motivated to defend home, hearth, and faith.[20] He planned biweekly training sessions of peasant soldiers in their villages with occasional mustering of larger units for three or four-day periods in order to achieve coordination on a broader scale. This army remained largely at home, feeding and equipping itself at its own expense. Giving officers salaries, he expected them to have professional experience.

Such an army had many benefits. Moritz estimated the cost at 21,000 gulden a year—considerably less than he paid for his current mercenary army. He thought that regular training would not only allow peasants to succeed against units of professional armies on the field of battle, but would also discipline them to a more godly (Protestant) home life. He also anticipated a substantial increase in his own authority because militia units could be used against freebooters and looters from the disbanded military units of other princes, as well as in police actions. Thus, he linked his direct supply strategy to a more regimented and orderly society certainly inconsistent with English notions of liberty.[21]

Hesse-Cassel failed to wean itself from its dependence on foreign mercenaries before the end of the Thirty Years War. The institution of Moritz's militia only meant the creation of a second army, increasing military expenses rather than reducing them. The state could no longer

18. Gerhard Oestreich, "Zur Heerverfassung der deutschen Territorien von 1500 bis 1800," in his *Geist und Gestalt des frühmodernen Staates, Ausgewählte Aufsätze* (Berlin, 1978), 290.

19. Thies, *Territorialstaat*, 32–34; Redlich, *The German Military Enterpriser*, 2:272–73.

20. Thies, *Territorialstaat*, 33.

21. Ibid., 34.

bear these new costs by careful management of domainal incomes and the traditional forms of taxation. Attempts to finance the new military structure lead directly to conflicts between the Landgrave and the Hessian Diet (*Landtag*), as it did in many German territories during the seventeenth century.[22] Gunther Thies has argued that the unwillingness of the Diet to support Moritz's reforms led to the disasters of the Thirty Years War, as well as to the huge burden of debt that Moritz passed on to his successor, William V (1627–1637).[23] To this we must add the unlikelihood that Sunday soldiers could be effective in the field against the better trained, battle-hardened professionals found in the armies of a Tilly or a Wallenstein. As a result, Hesse-Cassel suffered some of the worst damage of any territory during the conflicts of 1618–1648, with some areas experiencing population losses of up to 70 percent.[24] Moritz's early attempt at direct-supply military institutions failed because of military amateurism, insufficient financial means, and lack of political leverage.

The rebuilding of financial and military institutions proceeded slowly in Hesse-Cassel after the Thirty Years War. The Imperial Diet laid the legal foundations for reconstruction in the territorial estates in paragraph 180 of the *Reichstagsabschied* of 1654 and the emperor confirmed them in the *Wahlkapitulation* in 1658. These documents spelled out the formal obligation of territorial nobles (*Landsaßen*), subjects (*Untertanen*), and townsmen (*Bürger*) to defend the empire, but under the authority of their territorial prince. Territorial princes acquired the right to collect military taxes first asserted by military entrepreneurs such as Wallenstein during the years of war.[25] Military service obligations of various kinds became part of life for every territorial inhabitant.

Using this legal foundation, the Great Elector and his successors in Prussia built a standing army and financed it with a combination of traditional taxes, the new military land taxes, and rigorous domain management.[26] William VI (1637–1670) of Hesse-Cassel, however,

22. F. L. Carsten, *The Origins of Prussia* (Oxford, 1954), and *Princes and Parliaments*.

23. Thies, *Territorialstaat*, 234.

24. Günther Franz, *Der dreissigjährige Krieg und das deutsche Volk* (Stuttgart, 1979), 71–73.

25. Oestreich, "Zur Heerverfassung," 290–310; Fritz Redlich "Contributions in the Thirty Years War," *Economic History Review* 12 (1959–60): 247–54.

26. Carsten, *The Origins of Prussia*.

faced continued resistance to such expedients by his territorial Diet.[27] In limiting the Landgrave's army to three companies, the Treaty of Westphalia underwrote the power of the Diet. Nevertheless, the Landgrave negotiated a conversion of the feudal levy into a military tax (*Kontribution*). On occasion, the Diet allowed the Landgrave to collect Kontribution from his non-noble subjects for terms of six months, but such incomes always remained inadequate to the task of creating an instrument of foreign policy commensurate with the role Hessian Landgraves hoped to play in European dynastic politics.[28] The only internal pressure in this period came from populations of uprooted folk and released soldiers who, the Diet claimed, wandered through the region as a consequence of the late war.[29]

Faced with this set of limitations, the young Landgrave Charles I (1670–1730) chose subsidy treaties as an alternative method of financing the construction of a standing army. Following the advice of his mother, the Prussian princess Hedwig Sophie, he increased the army to a total of eighteen companies of infantry and four of horse.[30] Both political pressure from the emperor and the threat of impending bankruptcy convinced him to send a force of 1600 men to support the king of Denmark, Christian V, in his struggle against Sweden and Prussia in 1677.[31] The treaty came without the approval of the Diet, which had never shown any interest in an active foreign policy.[32] In extracting a payment of Rt 32,000 for these troops, Charles merely adopted an expedient that was increasingly popular among small territorial princes. The first prince to do so, Duke Johann Friedrich of Braunschweig-Lüneburg, had leased three regiments of his new standing army to the Republic of Venice during the 1660s.[33] Similar treaties had been a part of Hessian history since 1460 but the Landgrave had never used them to finance a standing army.[34]

27. Demandt, *Geschichte des Landes Hessen*, 202.

28. Ibid., 204; Günther Hollenberg, "Landstände und Militär in Hessen-Kassel," *Hessische Jahrbuch für Landesgeschichte* 34 (1984): 103; Carsten, *Princes and Parliaments*.

29. Hans Georg Böhme, *Die Wehrverfassung in Hessen-Kassel im 18. Jahrhundert bis zum siebenjährigen Krieg* (Kassel, 1954), 14.

30. Demandt, *Geschichte des Landes Hessen*, 202.

31. Hans Philippi, *Landgraf Karl I. von Hessen-Kassel, Ein deutscher Fürst der Barokzeit* (Marburg, 1976), 645.

32. Hollenberg, "Landstände und Militär," 105.

33. Redlich, *The German Military Enterpriser*, 2:95.

34. Hollenberg, "Landstände und Militär," 101.

The initial sally into the subsidy market as a direct supplier appeared to be somewhat of a disaster. Although the Landgrave received payment, the troops he sent in 1677, and again in 1678, suffered high casualty rates because of disease. These failures convinced the Landgrave to import the count of Lippe from Braunschweig to organize the management of his new subsidy-financed standing army.[35] The count convinced the Diet to extend the term of Kontribution to twelve-month periods and disassociated it from times of emergency.[36] Later, in the eighteenth century, terms extended to three years and the Diet lost the ability to reduce authorized amounts after 1704. The Diet retained the responsibility for apportioning taxes, but the landgrave's officials collected them. Because of shoddy collection procedures for the Kontribution, however, less than half the nominal amount agreed to by the Diet (Rt 388,000 per annum) ever came into the military treasury (*Kriegskasse*).[37]

Several expedients resulted. Many military units simply collected necessary taxes themselves in the form of goods and services which they charged against a village's Kontribution obligation. This arrangement was used for quartering troops as well. Before subsidies became regularized the military treasury borrowed cash from the domainal treasury (*Rentkammer*). What shortfall remained was made up by the Landgrave, who charged it to the accounts of the Upper Rhenish Circle. As subsidies began rolling in more frequently after 1684, the Landgrave's officials still treated his agreements as defensive alliances and did not inform the Diet of the payments involved. Thus, many past expedients designed to make up bureaucratic and military shortfalls remained in place long after the need for them diminished.[38]

On this foundation, the count of Lippe created a two-track direct-supply army that owed much to the influence of Moritz the Learned. However, the count made some important changes in structure that freed the Hessian military from independent military entrepreneurs, thus succeeding where Moritz had failed. The Hessian army of the 1680s relegated the Hessian militia to secondary role, although it followed the models provided by Moritz.[39] The militia's responsibilities included defense of Hessian borders and maintenance of domestic order and fell within the limitations imposed by the imperial legislation

35. Philippi, *Landgraf Karl I.*, 645.
36. Hollenberg, "Landstände und Militär," 103.
37. Philippi, *Landgraf Karl I.*, 647.
38. Hollenberg, "Landstände und Militär," 103.
39. Philippi, *Landgraf Karl I.*, 644.

of the 1650s. The standing army became the Landgrave's instrument of foreign policy. Since these troops technically joined the colors by voluntarily "selling their skins," their use in the Landgrave's subsidy business as auxiliary troops was entirely legal.[40] Apparently unable to bear the costs of recruiting outside Hessian territory, Hessian recruiters concentrated their attention on "masterless servants and loafers" in the territory.[41] In an effort to aid his own recruiters the Landgrave forbade any further foreign recruitment within Hessian borders.

Toward Profitability, 1688–1726

After 1688, the Landgrave began a long-term subsidy relationship with the General Estates of Netherlands; this flowed easily and naturally through the House of Orange into a similar relationship with King William III of England in 1694. These treaties meant more income, but they also placed more demands on the Hessian military and financial bureaucracies. Raising and financing the 11,000-man army envisioned by Charles and encoded in subsidy treaties proved to be more than the new administrative institutions could handle. Hans Philippi estimated that military expenditures over the period 1688–1698 amounted to six million Reichstaler. The Diet appropriated less than half of this amount in Kontribution. The rest came from English and Dutch subsidies and by the pawning of incomes of the Duchy of Schaumberg to Dutch moneylenders.[42] Eventually, the Diet permitted the Landgrave to redeem those incomes through a special bonus Kontribution.

After 1701, with new international tensions surrounding the Spanish succession, Charles felt further pressure to rationalize his fiscal and military institutions. The death of the count of Lippe eased the way to further centralization of tax collections and other military incomes. Taking management of these directly into his own hands, the Landgrave created a military commissary (*Generalkriegskommisariat*) which oversaw finance, accounting, recruitment, military justice, and war production.[43] Money and resources that had previously gone into company and regimental treasuries now flowed directly into the

---

40. Rainer Freiherr von Rosenberg, *Soldatenwerbung und militärisches Durchzugsrecht im Zeitalter des Absolutismus: Eine rechtsgeschichtliche Untersuchung* (Berlin, 1973), 89.

41. Chapter 3.

42. Philippi, *Landgraf Karl I.*, 651–52.

43. Ibid., 654.

Kriegskasse. This procedural change circumscribed some of the financial manipulations of captains and colonels who had been able to function as military subcontractors.[44] Payments once taken by regiments in kind were now demanded in cash and this change resulted in substantial unrest among the Landgrave's rural subjects. The need to raise cash required the kin-ordered households of the Hessian countryside to participate more frequently in the credit and commodity markets heavily controlled by the state.[45]

During the Wars of the Spanish Succession (1702–1713), the Hessian state crossed the line between fiscal-militarism and military-fiscalism and became what Charles Ingrao described as the mercenary state.[46] At this time, subsidies ceased to be an expedient to build an army; instead, the army became a resource necessary to provide the means to reform the state. Although at no time during this eleven-year span did the Landgrave's subsidy business become profitable in any strict sense of the word, the Landgrave nevertheless siphoned military monies out of the Kriegskasse for his own purposes.[47]

The office of military accounting entered subsidy monies in the accounts as extraordinary income, giving the Landgrave considerable personal discretion over its use. During the war, Charles diverted Rt 30,000 to purchase the lordship of Tilborg for his younger son, later Landgrave William VIII. Other funds he spent on grand parties at which he entertained foreign diplomats and generals. Further, he paid for the travel expenses of his own diplomats and generals as they pursued the possibility of more subsidy business. The practice began perhaps because subsidies came into the war treasury as hard cash while other treasuries and resources did not take the form of liquid assets.[48]

By the time peace came in 1713, the Landgrave's financial policies had rendered his military and state-building aspirations considerably less dependent on the Diet than they had been at the beginning of his

44. Redlich, *The German Military Enterpriser,* 2:77–87, for German proprietarial military management. Compare Prussian *Kompaniewirtschaft* in Otto Büsch, *Militärsystem und Sozialleben im Alten Preussen* (Frankfurt, 1981), 115, with the English in Alan J. Guy, *Oeconomy and Discipline: Officership and Discipline in the British Army* (Manchester, 1985), 2–4.

45. George Thomas Fox, "Studies in the Rural History of Upper Hesse" (Ph.D. diss., Vanderbilt University, 1976).

46. Charles Ingrao, *The Hessian Mercenary State* (Cambridge, 1987), 8–9.

47. Philippi, *Landgraf Karl I.,* 657.

48. Ibid., 657.

reign. Not only had he begun to use the liquid resources brought to him by foreign subsidies, but he had run up tremendous debts by pawning the incomes of his domain. This capacity for indebtedness — itself a source of independence — also became an argument used by the Landgrave to justify continuing to collect military income around Rt 670,000 per annum. Half of this he collected as Kontribution, the other half as subsistence and wage deductions which remained in regimental treasuries instead of going to the soldiers who had earned them. The Kriegskasse had twice the resources that it had in the 1680s, despite similar troop levels. And yet, the Landgrave remained dependent on the subsidy market because of the burden of postwar debt, which he defrayed through Dutch and English payments on their subsidy arrears. Had the Landgrave chosen to become independent of Dutch and English policy he would have risked the loss of at least some of the more than Rt 2.3 million these governments paid into his treasury between 1713 and 1724.[49]

The increased flow of wealth through military channels provided many opportunities for profit within the military command structure as illustrated for the 1770s in Chart 1 (see page 43). A 1726 audit of the war treasury's accounts, brought on by continuing complaints of financial abuse, documented the widespread practice of what Prussians knew as company management (*Kompaniewirtschaft*) and the English as proprietarial regiments.[50] Regimental and company commanders functioned as subcontractors for the Landgrave. On their own account, they recruited, equipped, and trained military units and then charged the costs to unit treasuries. Individual commanders exercised considerable control over the treasuries into which flowed recruitment bounties, wages, forage, and subsistence payments. Sometimes the payments came from foreign paymasters, sometimes from the Hessian Kriegskasse, and sometimes commanders themselves had to extract tax payments from peasant households. The Landgrave expected his commanders to be good managers and to cover the peaks and valleys in their unit's income with their own personal resources and credit. Unit commanders manipulated the resources of these treasuries to their own benefit and padded enrollment lists to acquire extra income. Financial controls over this process had been so weak in the first

49. Ibid., 656–57.
50. Redlich, *The German Military Enterpriser*, 2:46–56; Büsch, *Militärsystem*, 113–20; Guy, *Oeconomy and Discipline*, 2–4, for the British army.

decades of the eighteenth century that outright embezzlement became commonplace. Tax auditor (*Steuerrat*) Moeller, who oversaw the audit of 1726, argued that the only solution to abuses of the system included tighter and more rational budgeting and accounting procedures on the one hand and, on the other, increased subsidy incomes to reduce the temptation to cover shortages through peculation. Moeller further suggested that the subsidy business was natural, "necessary, and useful," particularly to the rural population of the territory whose military tax burden eased as a result of subsidy incomes.[51]

Years of Profitability, 1726–1760

Charles I made his first real profits from the subsidy business only with the last treaty of his reign in 1726. Philippi has estimated that the treaty with England and Kontribution collections brought military incomes up to Rt 6.9 million for the years between 1726 and 1730.[52] Expenditures amounted to only Rt 6.3 million because the army never left the territory while the treaty remained in effect and subsidy payments amounted merely to a retainer. Of the profit of Rt 600,000, Rt 117,000 was plowed back into additions to the standing army, raising its peacetime strength to some 12,000 men. Other discretionary funds went to finance the Landgrave's mistresses and to help purchase the Swedish crown for Charles's oldest son Frederick I (1730–51).

During the reign of Frederick I and William VIII (1751–1760), the part played by subsidy money in the financial business of the Hessian state grew apace. During these years the military treasury received Rt 8.3 million from England alone, and this amount represented 40 percent of all state revenues.[53] The mean annual amount of new subsidy monies (Rt 410,000) flowing into the military treasury totaled more than the mean annual income from the landgravial domains (Rt 350,000).[54]

New monies remained only part of the story, since the Landgrave built up a large reserve fund which he invested in a variety of ways that paid returns. Reserves accumulated because subsidy incomes fluctu-

51. Philippi, *Landgraf Karl I.*, 662–63.
52. Ibid., 663.
53. Vogel and von Both, *Landgraf Wilhelm VIII.*, 111.
54. Ibid., 34.

ated wildly. Lean years yielded half the new money raised in fat years.[55] The reserve fund itself became an important source of state income as treasury officials loaned small amounts of cash from it in each year. Although most of the money went into military expenditures, treasury officials used between 100,000 and 300,000 Reichstaler a year to make up shortfalls in the incomes of the civil treasury (*Kammerkasse*). They did this because estimated incomes to the military treasury during the 1740s amounted to more than Rt 1.2 million — a little less than twice the amount that flowed into the Kammerkasse.

Unfortunately the poor state of accounts allows us only to estimate the distribution of the Rt 1.43 million collected between 1730 and 1736.[56] Military expenditures amounted to Rt 800,000 or 55 percent of the budget. This percentage represents somewhat less than the monetary effort the English made at the same time. This expenditure allowed the maintenance of a subsidy (standing) army of some 14,000 men or one of every nineteen Hessians — a considerably more intensive effort than that which John Brewer has estimated for England (1:36) and Andre Corvisier for Prussia (1:36) over the same period.[57] The remainder of state incomes went to the Swedish royal court of Frederick I (Rt 225,000), the landgravial court of William VIII in Cassel (Rt 75,000), and finally to the Hessian civil administration (Rt 350,000).[58]

The increasing importance of the subsidy business for Hessian state finances encouraged further rationalization of tax assessment and collection procedures. Although Charles I had succeeded in putting collection of Kontribution in the hands of his own officials, they still based assessments on the crude cadastral document created for the purpose in the 1680s. Because the Landgrave and his officials assumed they dealt with a static society, no provision had been made for correcting the documents as village populations grew at the end of the seventeenth and beginning of the eighteenth centuries. With each succeeding generation the cadaster became a more distorted picture of economic and social realities and so diminished both the legitimacy and the efficacy of tax collection procedures.[59] Complaints from rural house-

55. Ibid., 40.
56. Ibid.
57. Ibid., 63; John Brewer, *The Sinews of Power* (London, 1989), 42; Andre Corvisier, *War and Society in Europe, 1494–1789* (Bloomington, Ind., 1979), 113.
58. Vogel and von Both, *Landgraf Wilhelm VIII.*, 40.
59. Karl Strippel, *Die Währschafts- und Hypothekenbücher Kurhessens, zugleich ein Beitrag zur Rechtsgeschichte des Katasters* (Marburg, 1914), 37–49.

holders about the equity of assessments surfaced in the 1720s and 1730s. Also, officials reported defaults by the more heavily burdened peasant households. Moreover, creditors lent peasants money less frequently, because the wildly inaccurate cadaster was the only independent way of verifying who held mortgaged land. With credit drying up, it became even more difficult for peasants to arrange marriages and to pay their taxes since both activities required substantial borrowing.

The prosperity of the Hessian state made it possible for the regent William VIII to intervene in these conditions. After an early failure to regulate credit on the basis of the old cadaster, William empowered a tax assessment commission (*Steuerrektifikationskommission*) to begin work on new cadastral documents in April 1736.[60] The commission began the process of visiting each village in the territory to record each household's income, real wealth, livestock holdings, and tributary obligations. It was carried out too quickly to be accurate, and so officials redid the first attempt, beginning again in 1742. By 1750, the cadastral survey of some 350 villages and eleven cities had been completed when grumblings about the expense of the survey from the Hessian Diet put a temporary stop to the process.[61]

Reform and Crisis under Frederick II (1760–1785)

The Seven Years War was a watershed for the fiscal and military practices of Hesse-Cassel. For the first time in more than a century, Hessians had to defend themselves against hostile armies invading their homeland. The standing army, leased exclusively to England for the duration of the war, swelled to over 24,000 men. Subsidy treaties with Hesse-Cassel obligated England to more than Rt 8 million in payments during the war, and offered both tremendous risks and great opportunities for the Landgrave and his military establishment.[62]

Three principal factors determined Hessian involvement in the war. Deeply concerned by the recent conversion of his son (eventually

60. StaM, HLO, 9.1.1732; Strippel, *Die Währschafts-und Hypothekenbücher*, 182; Klaus Greve and Kersten Krüger, "Steuerstaat und Sozialstruktur: Finanzsoziologische Auswertung der hessischen Katastervorbeschreibungen für Waldkappel 1744 und Herleshausen 1748," *Geschichte und Gesellschaft* 3 (1983): 302.

61. Ingrao, *The Hessian Mercenary State*, 60; Strippel, *Währschafts- und Hypothekenbücher*, 185–86.

62. Ingrao, *The Hessian Mercenary State*, 59.

Frederick II) to Catholicism and under pressure from the Diet, Landgrave William VIII compelled his son to sign an agreement assuring that the territory remained Protestant after his succession.[63] Needing guarantors for an agreement which placed limits on his son's freedom of action and which gave his grandson, the future William IX (1785–1821), direct control of Hanau, the aging Landgrave sought the help of George II. The English king offered help only in the context of the subsidy treaty of 1755 in which the Hessians agreed to provide 12,000 troops should England come under attack. For the first time since the practice of accepting subsidies had begun, the Diet expressed its reservations about a treaty, arguing that it might bring an unwanted confrontation with France, which would have serious military consequences.[64] Nevertheless, the subsidy relationship with England had pushed the Landgrave to use England as guarantor to the Protestant succession. That act, plus continued arrears on past subsidy payments and deep dependence on subsidy incomes, guaranteed continuation of the subsidy policy.[65]

The events feared by the Diet came to pass. After the Hessian subsidy army marched to defend Hanoverian neutrality in and around Bielefeld, the French made a number of attmpts to break the alliance between the Hessians and the English and attempted to ensure that Hessian troops did not interfere with French actions outside of Hanover. When all the attempts failed in 1757, General Richelieu marched into Hesse-Cassel. The militia units left behind to defend the territory proved no match for seasoned French veterans, and the French occupied the territory until 1762.[66]

Occupation and fighting on Hessian soil brought with it considerable hardship. Although eighteenth-century armies maintained stricter discipline and rationalized direct supply so as not to destroy occupied territories, the presence of armies from both sides brought disruption, dearth, inflation, disease, and death.[67] In addition to the exactions of military foraging by armies of both sides, the French command demanded ever-increasing amounts of war taxes from the Hessian Diet.

63. Vogel and von Both, *Landgraf Wilhelm VIII.*, 101–4.
64. Hollenberg, "Landstände und Militär," 104.
65. Vogel and von Both, *Landgraf Wilhelm VIII.*, 122.
66. Ibid., 109.
67. Myron Gutman, *War and Rural Life in the Early Modern Low Countries* (Princeton, 1980), 70; Vogel and von Both, *Landgraf Wilhelm VIII.*, 116–18; Ingrao, *The Hessian Mercenary State*, 57–58.

Beginning with Rt 850,000 in 1757, the requested amounts climbed quickly beyond the normal tax burdens paid into the Landgrave's military treasury. When special extensions of these taxes failed to satisfy the French, the Diet began borrowing heavily, first from the Landgrave's subjects and then from the Landgrave himself, who supplied these funds out of the military treasury reserve fund created by English subsidy payments.[68] Thus, ironically, the subsidies of their own indirect supply helped to fund resistance to English military strategy on the continent.

Despite hard times, the war provided three opportunities for Landgrave Frederick II, who succeeded his father in 1760. First, because the Diet had borrowed Rt 2.5 million from the Landgrave during the war, as a debtor institution, it became more servile to the Landgrave than its predecessors.[69] Second, the anticipated influx of Rt 8 million in subsidies meant the Landgrave relied even less on funds voted to him by the Diet than past Landgraves had. This new financial independence permitted him to embark upon an expensive program of military and administrative reform. Third, Hessian commanders' use of militia and standing army units outside Hesse blurred the legal distinction between the two armies and opened the door to combining the militia with the subsidy army. This ended the double army system, and took a giant step toward establishing a universal conscription policy for the Landgrave's subjects.[70]

The Diet manifested its new servility in the year immediately following the war when it raised the Kontribution obligation of the Landgrave's subjects by more than Rt 55,000 for the next thirty-six years.[71] When the Landgrave embarked upon an extensive reform program during the first fifteen years of his reign, the Diet influenced the course of legislation only by cooperating fully in its drafting.[72] Two of the more intrusive acts among the hundreds promulgated between 1760 and 1773 included an extensive reapportionment of taxes and a detailed revision of inheritance law applied to peasant farms.[73] Finally,

---

68. Joseph Sauer, *Finanzgeschäfte der Landgrafen Hessen-Kassel* (Fulda, 1930), 18; Vogel and von Both, *Landgraf Wilhelm VIII.*, 123.
69. Ingrao, *The Hessian Mercenary State*, 59.
70. Böhme, *Wehrverfassung*, 32.
71. Sauer, *Finanzgeschäfte*, 20. Compare Ingrao, *The Hessian Mercenary State*, 59.
72. Ingrao, *The Hessian Mercenary State*, 38–39.
73. Ibid., 117ff. and 203.

the Diet agreed in 1772 to pay for a new system of local and regional administration based on the system then current in Prussia.[74] The Diet then nominated many of its noble members for the new regional office (*Landräte*) but only those of whom the Landgrave approved ever served.[75] These men donated the use of their own administrative staff and clients in the countryside to oversee tax accounting and military recruitment.

Beside subordinating the Diet as an institution, the Landgrave used the flow of subsidy money from the Seven Years War for individual patronage as well. In 1762, Frederick II began making loans to nobles and bureaucrats, Hessians and other Germans, out of the subsidy reserve fund. Starting with a loan of Rt 279,903, to Baron von Stenglin at 4 percent, more than a half-million had been loaned in large blocks to various German nobles by 1776.[76] Hessian state officials, recipients of smaller amounts from the same source, applied for loans in such numbers that the Landgrave ordered that requests be funneled through the war chancellery (*Kriegskanzlei*), the members of which came from the war office (*Kriegskollegium*). These military bureaucrats not only controlled the flow of patronage but accepted substantial gratuities for processing loan applications.[77] The volume of this business was so brisk that after 1774 the Landgrave permitted officials to process no loans under one thousand Reichstaler. Smaller requests they routed to the managers of the Karlshafen Lazarette, a pension fund and hospital for invalid and retired soldiers.

In addition to patronizing nobles, the managers of the military treasury continued to advance large sums to the civil treasury. Between 1763 and 1765 over Rt 7.5 million flowed through these channels.[78] Some of this money paid war debts, while the rest went to funding the reconstruction process after the war.[79] Financial independence allowed the Landgrave to pay the salaries of the Prussian officials he brought in to help design and manage a program which they based on the legisla-

74. Uhlrich Friedrich Kopp, "Von Landräthen," *Teutsches Staats-Magazin* 1 (1796): 108ff.

75. Peter K. Taylor, "'Patrimonial' Bureaucracy and 'Rational' Policy: The Case of Hessian Recruitment Reform, 1762–1793," *Central European History* 22 (1989): 33–56.

76. Sauer, *Finanzgeschäfte*, 28 and 141–49.

77. Ibid., 35.

78. Ibid., 19–21.

79. Ingrao, *The Hessian Mercenary State*, 57–60.

tive reforms of Frederick the Great.[80] By 1776, the reform program had established the channels of subsidy wealth as they appear in Chart 1.

The reform program included attacks on rural poverty which represented a further articulation between the Hessian state and the peasant producers. The reforms prodded the pace of postwar recovery through a rural emergency credit fund for peasants (*Landassistenzkasse*). Although little of this money ever reached the peasantry, later remissions of the Kontribution may have helped them some. However, the imposition of a system of tax farming for the Kontribution by treasury director Bopp tended to reduce any advantages gained by peasants as the government intensified incentives for efficient tax collection.[81] In 1767, state officials nullified any other tax gains for the rural population when they created a mandatory fire insurance program (*Brandkasse*). It required peasant householders to contribute to yet another treasury and once again to enter their property holdings on another administrative list.[82] The Hessian state came to know more about its subjects and to reach into their pockets in new ways. The Landgrave also contributed money to remedy constant shortages suffered by Hessian charitable institutions for beggars and orphans.[83] Finally he invested Rt 140,000 to revive the linen industry.[84] How subsidy money from the Seven Years War touched productive processes in peasant households is the subject of later chapters.

A third advantage stemming from the war affected peasant households even more deeply than subsidy money. Because so much military activity occurred within and around Hessian borders during war, the legal distinction between militia and standing army regiments became blurred. Militia troops, previously limited to internal defense and police activities, fought outside of Hesse and thus became entwined in subsidy relationships.[85] Though these external campaigns inspired both protest and massive desertion among the militia units, William

---

80. Otto Berge, "Die Innenpolitik Landgraf Friedrichs II." (Ph.D. diss., Mainz, 1952).

81. Sauer, *Finanzgeschäfte,* 36.

82. Ingrao, *The Hessian Mercenary State,* 64: Hans Vogel and Wolfgang von Both, *Landgraf Friedrich II. von Hessen-Kassel* (Munich, 1973).

83. Ingrao, *The Hessian Mercenary State,* 109.

84. Ottfried Dascher, *Das Textilgewerbe in Hessen-Kassel vom 16.-19. Jahrhundert* (Marburg, 1968), 150–51.

85. Vogel and von Both, *Landgraf Wilhelm VIII.* 110–11.

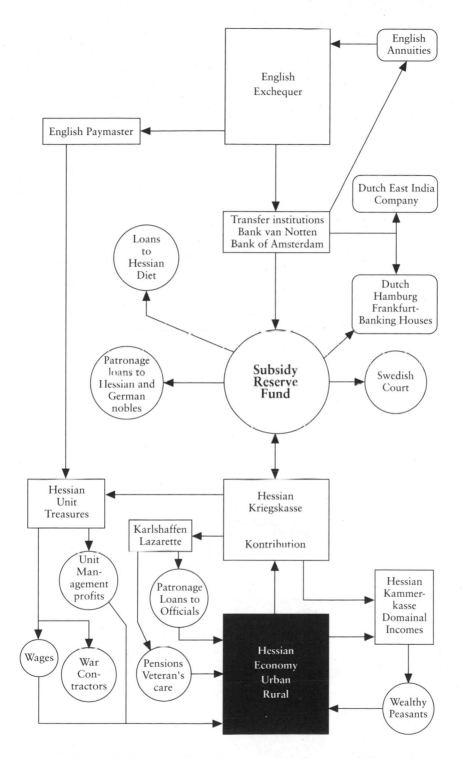

Chart 1. Flows of subsidy wealth in the 1770s. Data from Joseph Sauer, *Finanzgeschäfte der Landgrafen Hessen-Kassel* (Fulda, 1930).

VIII had set an important precedent upon which his successor could base a thoroughgoing reform of military recruitment policy. Immediately after the war, Frederick II instituted a selective service conscription policy modeled on the Prussian system of geographic recruitment districts (*Kantonsystem*).[86] On the one hand, these reforms made recruitment rules more transparent and susceptible to manipulation by the peasants. On the other hand, they exposed far more Hessian rural subjects to possible military service. In making peacetime conscription possible, the subsidy system established in Hesse-Cassel one form of tyranny which the Englishmen who fostered it would not have found easy to tolerate in England.

By 1776, Frederick II appears to have been ready for the biggest financial coup in the entire history of the subsidy business. Over Rt 19 million went into the military treasury as a result of the treaty negotiated by Faucitt and von Schlieffen. During the American campaign over half a million more flowed through the Kriegskasse on its way to soldiers' families.[87] The Landgrave sent nearly 12,400 troops to America in the spring and summer of 1776, of which almost 4,000 were from militia units. Eventually, the Landgrave's military machine provided 18,970 troops to the British war effort, of which more than 4,900 lost their lives and 3,100 could not be accounted for after the war. Another 1,300 received wounds during the war, meaning that nearly half the troops sent were lost or wounded.[88]

The staggering size of an operation that included transfers of wealth and large numbers of men over huge distances seemed to throw the system out of balance. Consistent refusal of the Landgrave to use subsidy income to write off the Diet's debt resulted in the growing disillusionment of its members with the business as a whole. Members of the Diet, who as late as 1764 had requested another treaty with England, were complaining by 1778 that the country could no longer bear the strain of additional recruitment.[89] The wives and children left behind by soldiers sent to America also concerned the regional authorities who reported that many villages no longer wished to bear the welfare burden that soldiers' families represented. Peasants began flee-

86. StaM, HLO 16.12.63, Kantonordnung.
87. Joachim Fischer, "Eiserngespartes aus Amerika 1776–1783," *Aus Geschichte und ihren Hilfswissenschaften: Festschrift für Walter Heinemeyer* (Marburg, 1980), 741ff.
88. Atwood, *The Hessians*, 254ff.
89. Hollenberg, "Landstände und Militär," 107–9.

ing the land to avoid being swept up by recruiters seeking to fill vacancies created in the subsidy army by desertion and death.[90] The remission of half the amount of Kontribution, which Frederick declared for the duration of the war as grace to his subjects, may have increased the discomfiture of some Hessian elites. Tax farmers who had already purchased their farms began requesting returns since the value of their property had been reduced.[91]

Deteriorating relations between Landgrave and Diet continued after the American war. In the first years of William IX's reign, the Diet repeated earlier requests that the Landgrave apply subsidy income to writing off the Diet's debts. Additionally, the Diet requested revision of both the restrictive inheritance legislation passed in 1773 and the conscription law of 1762. In their view, this legislation had combined with heavy recruitment demands to cause chaos in peasant property and credit relations.[92] They argued that parents, heirs, and creditors could no longer be certain who was a legitimate heir or property holder or who could mortgage land. In the context of this rancorous debate, the Diet made the first claims that subsidy money was public money and the Landgrave's discretion over it was limited by the Diet's prerogatives over the purse.

Fueling unhappiness among the elites, the ideological discussions of subsidy treaties in the context of liberty and slavery occasioned by the American war called into question fundamental aspects of proprietary armies. American war propaganda against the English king and his Hessian henchmen drew upon the same long tradition of anti-army sentiment and xenophobia that Alderman Bull invoked in resisting the treaty.[93] An article in a 1778 Philadelphia newspaper encouraging Hessian desertion argued that conscription had rendered private armies public, voiding former military contracts and subjecting them to the limits of formal consent.[94] Criticisms of subsidy practice made their way to Germany associating conscription for subsidy armies with slavery and with family or economic disruption.[95] Perhaps the most famous of these was Schiller's attack in his play *Conspiracies and Love*

90. StaM, B/4h 3700, 4023.

91. StaM, B/5 14737.

92. StaM, B/4h 4072.

93. Lois G. Schworer, *"No Standing Armies!" The English Anti-Army Ideology in Seventeenth-Century England* (Baltimore, 1974), 188–93.

94. Atwood, *The Hessians*, 184.

95. Phillip Losch, *Soldatenhandel* (Marburg, 1976), 43–55.

(Kabale und Liebe). The Landgrave himself had blurred the distinction between militia and standing army, which contributed to the questioning of his right to dispose of that army and its earnings as he saw fit.

The Last Years of Hessian Military-Fiscalism

William IX responded to the Diet's complaints, beginning a pattern that he and his successor repeated with every Diet until 1830. He reasserted his absolute discretion over the subsidy treasury as matter of landgravial prerogative (*Hoheitssachen*), but attempted to assuage further complaints by reducing Kontribution payments. William also revised inheritance legislation and entirely reworked military recruitment procedures. Inheritance reforms eased the restrictions on the portions for elderly retirees and disinherited siblings.[96] Military reforms reinstated the militia and placed recruitment on the basis of selective levies.[97] Several objectively defined categories of economic dispensability replaced the cruder rules previously in place. By law, only the most dispensable members of the rural population would perform subsidy duties.

William also began a concerted attack on the proprietarial army at the company and regimental level. New articles of military justice published in 1794 severely circumscribed the officers' use of unit treasuries and made them liable for any shortfalls in their accounts.[98] These reforms, along with severely increased costs and risks, resulted in the abandonment of regiments as financial interests on a large scale.[99] In 1765, two of twenty-eight lacked proprietors but this number increased to eleven of thirty-nine by 1795. The number of regiments with proprietors who were members of the Hessian nobility (but not of the Landgrave's family) decreased by 25 percent during those two decades. Over the same period, the number of regiments owned by the Landgrave's family more than doubled, from 6 to 14.[100] Thus, military-

---

96. StaM, HLO 21.4.1786.

97. StaM, HLO 30.12.1788, 15.9.1789, 14.1.1794.

98. StaM, HLO 14.1.1794.

99. Redlich, *The German Military Enterpriser*, 2: 67–76; Inge Auerbach, "Marburger im amerikanischen Unabhängigkeitskrieg," *Zeitschrift für hessische Geschichte* 87 (1978/79): 321–37. Compare Fischer, "Eiserngespartes," 742. For England: Fay, *Oeconomy and Discipline*, 33.

100. StaM, HSAK 1765, 1785, 1795.

fiscalism in Hesse-Cassel became more centralized in the latter two decades of the eighteenth century spreading its benefits less widely among the Hessian elites.

William IX's ideological commitments and his diplomatic goals also changed the tenor of the subsidy business. William was a deeply conservative Francophobe. Perhaps more intensely than past Landgraves he desired a promotion to the status of elector within the empire.[101] Many authorities believe that William's ideological commitment to counterrevolution meant military participation against French revolutionary and Napoleonic armies regardless of the opportunity for subsidies. For this reason he received little more than Rt 29,000 per month when his predecessors had come by nearly a quarter of a million.[102] Living with less income was possible because investments of past subsidy monies in Frankfurt banking houses (and elsewhere) had become a more important, and more regular source of income to the subsidy reserve fund as time had passed.[103] Combined with spartan efforts at frugality, these interest payments gave the Landgrave a freer hand with his fiscal manipulations. Participation in the anti-French alliance also became one lever William used finally to acquire an imperial electorship in 1803. His substantial loan to the Habsburg emperor certainly did not hurt his cause in this regard.[104] In any case, after the abolition of the empire by Napoleon in 1806 and after the Congress of Vienna sealed the results of Napoleon's defeat in 1815, subsidy money ceased to be available. England cut back its continental land commitments as the idea of subsidy armies came under increasing fire all over Europe and within Hesse-Cassel as well.

English political and social elites created a strong military state largely on the basis of an indirect supply of arms and men. Elsewhere in Europe, where less wealthy elites applied direct-supply stategies, the institutions of the fiscal-military state shifted the polarities of tribute-taking from local authorities toward the center and absolutist forms of rule. However, England's strong state became a paradigm for "liberty," "modernity," and "rationality" by promoting commercial agriculture through tax breaks and credit policy, by protecting its classes of mer-

101. Demandt, *Geschichte des Landes Hessen,* 212–13.
102. Losch, *Soldatenhandel,* 43–55.
103. Sauer, *Finanzgeschäfte,* 53–56, 141–43.
104. Demandt, *Geschichte des Landes Hessen,* 212–13.

chants in exchange for more intensive taxation, by permitting "un-locked labor" to remain free and exploitable, and, finally, by providing a credit and legal structure open enough to allow new classes of capitalist entrepreneurs to get their start and prosper.

Hessian entanglement with England's indirect-supply strategy shifted the tributary state away from what contemporaries saw as "liberty" by subordinating the Diet, and subjecting ever more of the Hessian population to the fiscal and recruitment apparatus. Even critical commentators, however, pay homage to gains in "modernity" and "rationality" which grew from subsidy wealth. Not only did the Land-graves of Hesse-Cassel use subsidy money to modernize and rational-ize their military, administrative, and fiscal institutions, but they also invested the wealth in a wide range of financial and commercial struc-tures including the English state, the Dutch East India Company, and numerous Frankfurt banking concerns.

Under such narrative conditions the inclination is to write off lost Hessian liberties, such as they were, as one of the costs of bringing to light that English model against which all political economies have come to be measured. Ironically, even these lost liberties can be con-structed as contributions to the model by so clearly highlighting legiti-mate and illegitimate uses of involuntary military servitude and the differences between public and private funds of rulers. It is not the purpose of this work to write anyone off as a necessary victim, but rather, to show that modernity and rationality without liberty in the Hessian environment led to a "new iron cage" of a kind which, at the end of the nineteenth century, rightfully frightened and depressed Max Weber. To show this relationship requires a sharp and unsentimental analysis of the costs of the articulations between the Hessian tributary state and the Landgrave's rural subjects who provided the start-up costs and the human material that funded the subsidy enterprise.

Part II

The Problems of Transforming Social Labor

Creating the military units to supply the subsidy market impelled the Hessian military-fiscal state to reconstruct the way in which it articulated with Hessian peasants who paid tributes from their kin-ordered enterprises. According to Eric Wolf, kin-ordered production can be understood "as a way of committing social labor . . . through appeals to filliation and marriage and to consanguinity and affinity."[1] Hermann Rebel has argued explicitly that we may read much European peasant behavior through Wolf's language.[2] Such a reading allows us to focus attention on the ways in which the Hessian rural subject population "locked" and "unlocked" land, labor, and movable wealth through the connections of blood, alliance, marriage, and inheritance.[3] The same language allows us to speak of the way in which tribute-takers impinged on, worked with, and operated through such kin-ordered enterprises, as they used the wealth and people from them.

The Hessian strategy of direct supply articulated with peasant production in two new ways. First, officials began effectively collecting a new form of tribute to train, equip, and pay the troops of subsidy units. Called the Kontribution, this new form of taxation developed out of

1. Eric R. Wolf, *Europe and the People without History* (Berkeley, 1982), 93–95.
2. Hermann Rebel, "Cultural Hegemony and Class Experience: A Critical Reading of Recent Ethnological-Historical Approaches (Part Two)," *American Ethnologist* 16 (1989): 350.
3. Wolf, *Europe*, 93–95; David Warren Sabean, *Property, Production, and Family in Neckarshausen, 1700–1870* (New York, 1990), 24, 416–22.

the rationalized looting of the Thirty Years War and received official
sanction within the Holy Roman Empire from the Imperial Diet in
1654.[4] Second, the state recruited the vast majority of the troops used
in its subsidy business from the peasant households of the landgravial
domains. This second practice required the state to acquire the "rights
in persons" which were locked up in the symbolic grid of peasant
inheritance and marriage practice.

These intrusive practices involved a number of ideological and practical contradictions which intensified with the increasing use of the
subsidy relationship with England. Intrusive taxation and recruitment
policies seemed to fly in the face of fundamental ideological assumptions of cameralist statecraft held by Hessian rulers and bureaucrats. In
particular, military policy was in tension with a vision of the "whole
house" (*das ganze Haus*) as an independent corporate entity subject to
state authorities only for tribute taking and harmonizing activities.[5]

More practically, the bureaucratic apparatus which performed the
functions of collection and enlistment relied upon what Max Weber
has called "patrimonial authority."[6] Like the princes of other early
modern states, the Landgraves elicited obedience from the officials of
the Landgrave's collegial bureaucracy all the way down to the leaders
of peasant communes through unequal exchanges of service and protection (patronage).[7] The more intrusive taxation and recruitment
became, however, the more necessary it became to render policy and

4. Fritz Redlich, "Contributions in the Thirty Years War," *Economic History Review*
12 (1959–1960): 247–54; Gerhard Oestreich, *Geist und Gestalt des frühmodernen
Staates, Ausgewählte Aufsätze* (Berlin, 1978), 293.

5. Otto Brunner, *Land und Herrschaft: Grundfragen der territorialen Verfassungsgeschichte Österreichs im Mittelalter* (Darmstadt, 1984), 240–48, and "Das ganze Haus
und die alteuropäische 'Oekonomik'," in *Neue Wege der Verfassungs- und Sozialgeschichte* (Göttingen, 1968), 103–23; Hermann Rebel, "Reimagining the *Oikos*: Austrian Cameralism in Its Social Formation," in Jay O'Brien and William Roseberry, eds.,
Golden Ages, Dark Ages: Reimagining the Past (Berkeley, 1991); Mack Walker, *German Hometowns: Community, State, and General Estate, 1648–1871* (Ithaca, 1971),
146–51; Reinhard Kosselleck, "Die Auflösung des Hauses als ständische Herrschafts-
einheit: Anmerkungen zum Rechtswandel von Haus, Familie, und Gesinde in Preussen
zwischen der Französischen Revolution und 1848," in N. Bulst, ed., *Familie zwischen
Tradition und Moderne: Studien zur Geschichte der Familie in Deutschland und Frank-
reich vom 16. bis zum 20. Jahrhundert* (Göttingen, 1981), 109–24.

6. Max Weber, *Economy and Society* (Berkeley, 1978), 2:1088–90.

7. David Warren Sabean, *Power in the Blood: Village Discourse and Popular Culture
in Early Modern Germany* (Cambridge, 1984), 20ff.; Thomas Robisheaux, *Rural Society and the Search for Order in Early Modern Germany* (Cambridge, 1989), 28–36.

practice independent of patron-client relationships but still to use officials who had never ruled in any other way.

Though problematic, these intrusions did not immediately spell failure for the Landgrave's military enterprises. To cope with the ideological tensions between cameralism and the invasive military policy, the Landgrave's officials developed a discourse about "marginal" people in which they defined recruitment targets as "masterless servants and loafers" or later the "household's most expendable people." Within the context of cadastral documents this language invented households where none had existed and treated other single households as two or three. Despite these difficulties, the language of marginality enabled authorities to continue believing in the corporate integrity of the peasant household while they coercively removed some of its members for military service. Pragmatically, the Landgrave had to set bodies of officials and elites with competing interests against one another in a complicated system of checks and balances which circumscribed the operation of patron-client relations.

Although riven with tensions, this military system continued to expand and develop through the terrible depredations of the Seven Years War and into the reign of Frederick II. Under Frederick, the military-fiscal state reached the apogee of its trajectory as the Landgrave refashioned it in a more overtly intrusive and more "rational" mode than ever before. His reforms and the lucrative subsidy treaty of the American campaign finally unbalanced the military-fiscal state ideologically and pragmatically. Crisis revealed itself fully in the communications between the Landgrave and his officials, in the new tensions between Diet and Landgrave, and finally in rural society itself. Although Frederick's successor, William IX, reformed the system, it never fully recovered from a crisis which contributed to the abandonment of the subsidy enterprise.

3 Military Taxation, Recruitment Policy, and the Ideology of "Das Ganze Haus"

The Ideology of Cameralism and the "Whole House"

In the last half century, the discourse of histories about the Hessian subsidy system took on an exculpatory tone which pointed optimistically to the wealth that the system brought in and to the attempts by the Landgrave and his officials to administer the subsidy business in ways consistent with cameralist theories of state management.[1] Other scholars rehabilitated cameralism, finding in it the moral and disciplinary foundations for Germany's subsequent "modernization."[2] Neither view, however, has focused sufficiently on the inconsistencies within this set of ideas or between the ideas and their practical applications. For the beginning of this corrective enterprise we owe Mack Walker a substantial debt.[3]

Walker has called cameralism a "baroque science . . . whose symmetry depended on its being seen for a distance, and whose rationality

1. Otto Berge, "Die Innenpolitik Landgrafs Friedrich II." (Ph.D. diss., Mainz, 1952); Hans Vogel and Wolfgang von Both, *Landgraf Friedrich II. von Hessen-Kassel* (Munich, 1978); Rodney Atwood, *The Hessians: Mercenaries from Hessen-Kassel in the American Revolution* (Cambridge, 1980); Charles W. Ingrao, *The Hessian Mercenary State* (Cambridge, 1987).

2. Oestreich, *Geist und Gestalt des frühmodernen Staates, Ausgewählte Aufsätze* (Berlin, 1978), 196; Mark Raeff, *The Well-Ordered Police State* (New Haven, 1983), 5.

3. Walker, *German Hometowns: Community, State, and General Estate, 1648–1871* (Ithaca, 1971), 145–84; James Van Horn Melton, "Absolutism and 'Modernity' in Early Modern Central Europe," *German Studies Review* 8 (1985): 383–98.

was seen in abstract outline from the top, subject to giddiness when attention moved from that [top] to concrete detail."[4] From the top then, cameralism was the administrative science of taking tribute from the corporate monads of German society, many of which were kin-ordered enterprises of production. Cameralists argued that the state, in filling its fisc for military purposes, performed a superficial skimming operation which left towns, guilds, villages, and peasant households to order their own internal relations. For teachers of cameralist science such as Christian Wolf, who was briefly a professor at Phillip's University in Marburg, development meant enhancing revenues and could be seen only as a process of harmonizing conflicts between and encouraging the interdependence of corporations so that they would form "rational" (read obedient) tax-paying "communities."[5] The state's encouragement of "community" had a strong moral element that saw greed, laziness, and the ritual profligacy of popular culture as corrosive forms of undisciplined behavior, which were within its purview to attack.[6]

Despite its ideology of the independence of social monads, cameralist thinking had elements of interventionism. In addition to making a legal attack on popular culture through sumptuary legislation, cameralist administrators used fiscal administration to form and define the boundaries of the corporations that constituted the fundamental elements of society. Moreover, martial discipline through the militia and through the standing army was highly regarded in the thinking of Hessian princes and others as early as Landgrave Moritz and continued to be a point of pride through the reign of Landgrave Frederick II.[7]

Interventionist thinking became explicit with the late eighteenth-century obsession with police (*Polizei*).[8] The Prussian political theorist Johan Justi came to see the manifold corporations as a medium through which the state could transmit order and harmony to that ultimate monad of modernism, the human individual.[9] Like the En-

---

4. Walker, *German Hometowns*, 145.

5. Rebel, "Reimagining the *Oikos*: Austrian Cameralism in Its Social Formation," in Jay O'Brien and William Roseberry, eds., *Golden Ages, Dark Ages: Reimagining the Past* (Berkeley, 1991), 17.

6. Walker, *German Hometowns*, 149; Karl Pribram, *A History of Economic Reasoning* (Baltimore, 1983), 90–96; Raeff, *The Well-Ordered Police State*, 60–64.

7. Ingrao, *The Hessian Mercenary State*, 134.

8. Raeff, *The Well-Ordered Police State*, 43–56.

9. Walker, *German Hometowns*, 168.

Otto Ubbelohde, *A Hessian Landscape*. Source: Bildarchiv Marburg; by permission of N. G. Elwert Verlag.

glish political culture of "liberty," cameral science permitted officials to talk about the shift of power from locality to center in terms of particularism, privilege, and propriety. Thus, the German idea of freedom was not terribly different in form and function from its English cousin.[10]

A humanist ideology, cameralism used classical methods and spirit to produce the creative tension that linked locality to center. Theorists in this vein developed a "housefather literature" to aid in the management of the economy of the "whole house" (*das ganze Haus*). This genre grew out of a Renaissance prescriptive social psychology for the new noble who was to serve under the new prince.[11] Rather than fight each other in the deadly play of tournaments, the new nobles engaged in the self-conquest of neo-stoicism in order to develop a *virtu* based on work and learning which could be juxtaposed to the *fortuna* of accident, envy, and hatred. Reformers such as Jüstus Lipsius advocated the diffusion of this vision beyond the nobility to subaltern officials and even to peasants in an effort to encourage the just functioning of the state and its many elements. The housefather tracts were one instrument of diffusion, a genre whose roots extended back to the estate management literature of Xenophon and Aristotle.

Hermann Rebel has called the ideology of the whole house an attempt to reimagine and project the Aristotelian *oikos* on to the tribute-producing, kin-ordered enterprises of early-modern central Europe.[12] "Housefather literature" gave the head (housefather) of the reimagined *oikos* the technical knowledge to produce a surplus, and the moral imperative to discipline its members. Thus, the "head" of the household had the same role that was given to the senses, intelligence, and reason of the knight in an earlier literature of noble neo-stoicism. Proper management of the conflicting desires of the household's children and servants would serve the state's purpose by ensuring a more orderly and just production of tribute. State officials and consistorial employees in eighteenth-century Hessian realms promoted this ideology of household "self-discipline" as the task of its *Brotherr* ("loafmaster" or head of the house). These ideas appeared in both law and in catechisms used to teach children.[13] The "good" householder or loaf

---

10. Ibid., 177.

11. Here I follow Rebel, "Reimagining the *Oikos*," 34–35 closely.

12. Ibid., 37–39.

13. StaM, HLO 28.8.1736, 11.6.1739; Johann Jacob Rambach, *Kirchen Gesangbuch* (Darmstadt, 1733). Compare English *hlafweard* in Wolf, *Europe and the People*

master directed the "self" of a monad suspended between the state and the individual, and performed the same harmonizing tasks among the individual members of the household that the state performed for corporations. Cameralists ultimately measured the success of the household by amounts of tribute rendered, thus paralleling the fiscal measure the state held for itself.

The Peasant "Community" and the "Whole House" in Cadastral Discourse

The role of the "whole house" in the scheme of Hessian cameralism revealed itself in the documents that the state constructed to measure those units and to establish their tax liability. Administratively, the most effective of these documents was the cadaster which the state began creating in 1736.[14] Each cadaster provided a transcript of a four-sided but asymmetrical discourse. A representative of the Steuerrektifikationskommission signed the document after it was initially created. Local judicial officials administered oaths to the peasants and probably knew enough as collectors of tribute to verify the information. Village headmen and jury members (*Greben* and *Schöffe*) testified about the community property of the village corporation (*Gemeinde*) and verified the testimony of householders. Householders themselves provided information about their property holdings, the commodities they produced, and the wages members of their household earned in nonagricultural occupations and day labor.

Although the officials entered this initial information in a single set of volumes which remained in the village, other institutions received copies; one for the local court to verify property transactions and one for the regional tax collection agency (*Landrezeptor*) to verify tax

---

without History (Berkeley, 1982), 105, and "destined providers of subsistence" for Bengal in Paul Greenough, "Indian Famines and Peasant Victims: The Case of Bengal in 1943–44," *Asian Studies* 2 (1980). For a critical account that develops the idea of "culturally necessary victims" see Rebel, "Reimagining the *Oikos*," and "Cultural Hegemony and Class Experience," *American Ethnologist* 16 and 17 (1989).

14. Karl Strippel, *Die Währschafts- und Hypothekenbücher Kurhessens* (Marburg, 1914), 173–87; Klaus Greve and Kersten Krüger, "Steuerstaat und Sozialstruktur: Finanzsoziologische Auswertung der hessischen Katastervorbeschreibungen für Waldkappel 1744 und Herleshausen 1748," *Geschichte und Gesellschaft* 3 (1983): 295–329.

burdens. Scribes divided each village document into three separate parts. An introduction (*Vorbeschreibung*) focused on "community" property, resources, obligations, and population. Then came household files, which made up the bulk of the volumes. Each tax-paying household had a file that listed individually every building and strip of land in the village on which the peasant householder held a tenure, as well as the yearly value of any commodity produced in the household. The name of the householder, whether corporate or individual, appeared on the first page of the file. Each strip of land was entered, and the kind of tenure which applied to it (heritable or closed term tenures), the kind of land it was (garden, meadow, or crop land), as well as the kind and amount of tributary obligations owed on it. Of course each strip received an assessed value for tax purposes.[15] The third part of the cadaster contained a summary of these household files arranged in tabular form for the whole village. The cadaster continued to be a living document because when peasants sold property or when they passed estates to their children, court officials verified and recorded these transactions in them.[16] Transactions not recorded in the village copy had no standing in law. The dynamic aspect of the cadaster extended only to household files while the other two segments became gradually more out of date.

Each Hessian cadaster actually attempted to harmonize the greedy selfishness of monads in two distinct "communities" by reifying property rights and establishing a standard measure of value for them.[17] In assigning standard value to some rights, other rights such as gleaning, grazing, or access paths tended to fall out of the picture because they either could not be assigned value or simply were not. Further, certain tribute obligations that might have been deducted from the value of the estate did not acquire arithmetical recognition although their existence was acknowledged.[18] The cadaster used the tax florin (*Steuergulden*) as the fundamental unit on this yardstick. In making this yardstick of tax paying ability and liability, officials attempted to create not only a measure of absolute value but also of potential income. For example, in assigning a Steuergulden value to land, assessors divided land first

15. Greve and Krüger, "Steuerstaat und Sozialstruktur."

16. Strippel, *Die Währschafts- und Hypothekenbücher,* 189–95.

17. E. P. Thompson, "The Grid of Inheritance: A Comment," in Jack Goody et al., eds., *Family and Inheritance: Rural Society in Western Europe, 1200–1800* (Cambridge, 1976), 328–60.

18. StaM, K/I Allna 1746, etc.

into four types, woods, meadow, gardens, and crop land, and then into three categories based on mean yearly productivity in good, moderate, and poor years. This meant that in each village each category of land received a different assessment. According to the work of Klaus Greve and Kersten Krüger, this procedure both rendered the cadaster an administratively neutral instrument and also made it, as far as officials were concerned, a mirror of the society from which they collected taxes.[19]

The "objective" measurement of property values promoted the cameralist version of harmony among a village's households. With such an instrument, officials now could assess the Kontribution roughly on the ability of a household to pay. Peasants and officials could appeal to tax documents to put an end to endless arguments about the just distribution of tax burdens. Using it, the state assessed the peasants' ability to provide local road and bridge repair work, fines levied on villages, state fire insurance premiums, and even eligibility for military service. Not only did the "objective" standards quiet individual householders' complaints (a discourse designed to end discourse) but village corporations, as well, had less opportunity to claim that their burdens weighed upon them inequitably.

The yardstick of the Steuergulden contributed also to the objective measurement of managerial quality. David Sabean has suggested that one of the new elements in the discourse between villagers and state authorities in Würtemburg concerned the success and failure of householders to be "good" managers.[20] Once cadastral documents stood as a record of the ebb and flow of property rights for a particular householder and household, then an objective and quantitative measure of success existed. A "good" householder naturally contributed the most to the fisc and had the highest assessed values. In Hessian regions, such householders acquired the appellation "stark begüterte Bauer" (wellprovided [and providing] peasant) and acquired privileges from the state such as the right to exempt an heir from military service.[21] The cadaster also provided a way of identifying failures by matching assessed household values with numbers of occupants, as one tax official had done as early as 1750. One treasury agent calculated that a house-

19. Greve and Krüger, "Steuerstaat und Sozialstruktur," 303.

20. Sabean, *Power in the Blood: Village Discourse and Popular Culture in Early Modern Germany* (Cambridge, 1989), 149–50.

21. StaM, HLO 16.12.1762.

hold of five (two parents, two children, and a servant) could subsist on the income from an estate valued at Sg 133 after deductions for tributary payments to others who held claim on the estate.[22]

The cadastral discourse also balanced the interests of the tribute collectors as well. Once officials added up the total assessed value of each peasant household, they deducted from that total the value of most other tributary obligations owed by that household to the many tribute takers in Hessian society. For example, the total assessed value of the fifty-five files in the cadaster of the village of Niederweimar amounted to more than Sg 19,840. Householders however, paid taxes on just over Sg 13,340, a total deduction for all villagers of nearly one-third. These deductions represented tribute payments to thirty-seven different corporations and individual members of Hessian noble and official elites. Some of the biggest tribute takers included the various unspecified owners of tithe and service obligations, the landgravial domain, the universities at Gießen and Marburg, the secretariat of the city of Marburg, the Landrat von Schenck zu Schweinsberg, the Teutonic Order, *Konributionrezeptor* (tax receiver) Braumann, and many more. Such deductions could forestall complaints from the "community" of Hessian elites (as represented in the Diet) that the Kontribution reduced their own rights, privileges, and claims to the surpluses of the kin-ordered productive enterprises in the countryside. Not only does the cadaster provide us with a transcript of a form of cameralist discourse, but it provides a basis for analyzing the political economy of tribute taking within the borders of any given village. Complaints about the high costs and corruption within the Hessian Steuerrektifikationskommission ended the work in the early 1750s. Only 350 villages and eleven cities were finished at the time, but work began again in the reign of Frederick II immediately following the Seven Years War. Some concern among the elites about the cadastral project stemmed from the perception on the part of members of the Diet that powers of tax assessment at the local level had now passed out of their hands.[23] As the job neared completion in the 1770s and 1780s, the nobles also recognized that this new efficient tool took more from the peasants than ever before, thus threatening the balance the Landgrave had promised to establish.[24]

22. StaM, B/49d, r 49/9.
23. StaM, B/5 13,446.
24. Ingrao, *The Hessian Mercenary State*, 203–5.

Although the Hessian cadaster stemmed from and reflected impulses of cameralism and its vision of the peasant "community" as a harmonized collection of "whole houses," the imperatives of fiscal efficacy and accuracy required that the cadastral record violate this analytic vision frequently. The problem was the poor fit between the notion of "taxpayer" and "Brotherr" (household head) as well as the disjunction between the village "community" as a geographically bounded entity and as a collection of residences for "whole houses." The difficulties appeared in the discrepancy between the number of household files in a given village cadaster and the number of actual functioning households. For example in the cadaster for the village of Niederweimar, there were fifty-four household files but only thirty-seven houses in the village when the officials first inscribed the cadastral summary in 1747.[25] Thus, the files actually fell into three separate categories, only one of which could be certainly established as consistent with cameralist ideology.

There were people who paid Kontribution on land in one village but lived in another (twelve of fifty-four files in Niederweimar). These householders, sometimes residing in neighboring villages and sometimes living outside the jurisdiction of the Hessian state as far away as Waldeck, shared the tax burden of the "community" but did not share in community decisions.[26] These files not only blurred the distinction between different "communities" of taxpayers but the land transfer activity which occurred in the files, and the similarity of surnames of file holders with those actually resident, suggest a network of kin and marriage connections between households in one village and those in others which blurred the boundaries between households as well.[27] Thus, geographic marginality both disturbed the fiscal borders of the village and the house and conflated outsiders with insiders. Further, it suggests the pitfalls of using a "household economy approach" to peasant productive enterprises too rigidly.

A second difficulty grew from a category of files of people who obviously lived in the village but who held no house.[28] For Nieder-

25. StaM, K/I Niederweimar 1747.

26. StaM, B/17e Niederweimar 16, 17.

27. Compare Savoy in D. J. Siddle, "Inheritance Strategies and Lineage Development in Peasant Society," *Continuity and Change* 1 (1986): 333–61. StaM, K/I Niederweimar 1747.

28. Sabean, *Property, Production, and Family,* 88–101, and literature cited there. David Andersen, *Approaches to the History of the Western Family* (London, 1980), 65–84.

weimar, the number of people with such files was actually relatively small (six of fifty-four). The proportion of people entered under these conditions could become quite large, however, as in the nearby village of Allna with eleven such files out of forty-four. It is unlikely that most of these "taxpayers" represented independent *Brotherrn,* because in the census sections most of them were listed singly and their total assessed value rarely climbed above 50 Steuergulden. There were exceptions. An example is the wife, four children, and one servant of Eyfig Katz, a Jewish cattle dealer and butcher who may have rented space in Allna from a single Jewish male entered only as *Jud* David.[29] It is unclear from the cadaster whether such people were boarders or *Instleute,* or qualified as herrenlose Gesindel and Müßigänger (masterless servants and loafers), or *Böhnhasen* (ground rabbits).[30] *Instleute* (a peculiar mixture of boarder and servant) might have some official status within communities but only under the authority of a Brotherr.[31] Others without such official status suffered constant harassment from local authorities who tried either to expel them as "foreign" indigents or to put them under the authority of a Brotherr.[32] As the eighteenth century passed, Jews became even more marginalized and Frederick II finally expelled them altogether.[33]

People without legal right to residency usually practiced protoindustrial trades such as weaving, sewing, and spinning or did agricultural day labor and sometimes migrated with the seasonal harvests back and forth to the rich agricultural regions of the Wetterau to the south. Many found themselves listed as beggars or handicapped persons. They did not share in communal wealth except occasionally as recipients of village charity. Frequently, village officials accused them of stealing property from the communities. In any case, they represented social and economic margins which seemed to have found no stable existence within a "whole house" but who produced sufficient income to be interesting to collectors of the Kontribution. Their marginal and perhaps mobile life also pointed to the probability that there

29. StaM, K/I Niederweimar 1747.
30. StaM, K/I Allna 1746.
31. Walker, *German Hometowns,* 86–87.
32. Michael Mitterauer, *Grundtypen alteuropäischer Sozialformen* (Göttingen, 1976), and with Reinhard Sieder, *The European Family: From Patriarchy to Partnership, 1400 to the Present* (Chicago, 1982). See StaM, B/23b, ALb Schweinsberg 16 1773.
33. StaM, HLO 28.8.1736.

were others like them whom the officials never counted or assessed. Such a surmise is confirmed by some entries in parish registers and household censuses which list persons heading households who apparently never appeared in cadastral documents.[34] Such difficulties suggest that approaching production as kin-ordered may avoid the ideological traps of cadastral discourse.

The retirement arrangements of prosperous farmers could be a third way in which discourse conflicted with the vision of the "whole house." In most villages in Hesse-Cassel, during most of the eighteenth century, kin-ordered households practiced single-heir inheritance (*Anerbenrecht*). Roughly speaking, when the chosen heir married he received the title and obligations attached to the tenure he inherited. This transfer took the form of a sale (*Anschlagsvertrag*), the proceeds of which provided for the heir's siblings and for the retirement of the previous holder. Many times, the retirement arrangements included either rooms in the house of the heir or a separate cottage which remained part of the estate. In cadastral discourse, these separate houses frequently had their own separate files, with garden and crop lands attached in some instances.

In many cases, the separation of these households was an illusion. In Allna, we find two such cases among forty-four households plus one estate where the house was empty.[35] The census of 1732 explicitly shows that retirees still ate with the heir's family many times.[36] Moreover, marriage contracts suggest that they did not even pay the taxes on the land and buildings in their file, but that this obligation was taken on by the heir.[37] Although these elders had ceased to work, they frequently maintained control of the household. They managed credit arrangements and the more subtle levers which stemmed from their control of marriage and labor markets.[38] Such arrangements were not surprising in the context of kin-ordered modes of production; they too blurred the monadal boundaries of the cameralist ideology of the whole house. Further, they require us to be critical of sources created by eighteenth-century authorities in a way that a "household economy" approach to peasant production might not.

34. Ingrao, *The Hessian Mercenary State,* 203.
35. KaOw, Kp, Br Oberweimar 10.5.1767.
36. StaM, K/I Allna 1746, 2 of 44, plus one estate where one extra house was empty.
37. StaM, B/40d r 29/76 Kaldern und Reizberg 1732.
38. StaM, P/II Reizberg und Kaldern, Ep 1780–1820.

Recruitment, the Ideology of Marginality, and the "Whole House"

If marginality created substantial problems of coherence for the discourse of the Hessian cadaster, it also provided an ideological escape for the interventionist practice of recruitment. Recruitment was never really simply a matter of skimming the surpluses of primary production in the same way as was the collection of the Kontribution, but rather a matter of acquiring "rights to persons" that peasants had bound up in the symbolic language of kinship and inheritance.[39] "Unlocking" such rights required an intervention in peasant production that became ever more direct. The participation by state officials in decisions about inheritance, marriage, and reproduction involved many more people than those who served in the subsidy army of the Landgrave. Initially, officials cloaked this intervention in a discourse of marginality which allowed for the systematic assignment of military service obligations to those defined in official concepts as outside the household monad. Such persons remained in short supply — so much so that by the military reforms of 1762, state policy actually extended the discourse of marginality to members of the whole house. Then, in 1773, when the supply of such persons still did not meet the needs of military recruiters, the state "created" them through the legal manipulation of the symbolic grid of inheritance itself.

In the two-track military system created by Landgrave Charles I, only recruitment for the standing subsidy army presented problems of ideological coherence. Involuntary service in militia units did require extensive time spent training, but involved the defense of "home, hearth, and faith" as Landgrave Moritz had put it.[40] Thus, the defense of the peasant household stood at the center of an obligation that could be read as a reimagining of feudal obligations to defend the territory against attack and help to maintain law and order within it (*Landfolge* and *Gerichtsfolge*).[41] Justifying military service in this way limited it to durations of emergency within territorial boundaries. It also did not amount to a personal obligation of particular individuals. Obligations cast in these terms won approbation from even Jüstus Möser, one of

39. Hermann Rebel, "Peasant Stem Families in Early Modern Austria: Life Plans, Status Tactics, and the Grid of Inheritance," *Social Science History* 2 (1978): 3.

40. Wolf, *Europe*, 95.

41. Thies, *Territorialstaat*, 35.

the most non-interventionist cameralists. He asserted that to put all "corporate members [*Bürger*] in military uniforms . . . would be the first and most important step to reestablishing the common good [*Wohlfahrt*]."[42] Möser wrote here not of an abstract public domain but of the good of actually existing historical communities."

Military service in the standing army caused difficulty because it remained a private-law, contractual relationship between soldier and military commander. Its personal nature showed most clearly in the oaths of soldiers who, as late as 1780, promised to be "true, favorably disposed, and obedient" to their Landgrave and to protect his property from "harm, disruption, and disadvantage."[43] The contract between Landgrave and soldier grew out of the voluntary agreements made between mercenary captains and their men since the fourteenth century. As past mercenaries had, soldiers sealed the agreement to serve by accepting a recruitment bounty called *Handgeld*. In taking the bounty, the recruit had "sold his skin" and could be used for purposes other than common defense.[44]

This subterfuge meant the Landgraves' subsidy business remained within acceptable legal practice. It was a personal, rather than an imperial or territorial army, that he leased to foreign powers. Furthermore, it permitted Hessian Landgraves as early as Moritz to forbid foreign military recruiters in Hessian territory, and as early as Charles I, to forbid using force to recruit men. In theory, a contract made under duress was no contract at all.[45] In practice, this gave Hessian Landgraves a monopoly on the military service of their subjects and rendered subjects vulnerable only to more subtle coercive powers exercised by his state.

The practice of contractual military service could be squared with the ideology of the "whole house" by assuming that soldiers who came to serve in the subsidy army had no obligations to or place in the households of peasants. Indeed, recruitment law bowed deeply in this direction. As late as 1733, the Landgrave instructed recruitment com-

---

42. Hans Georg Böhme, *Die Wehrverfassung in Hessen-Kassel im 18. Jahrhundert bis zum siebenjährigen Krieg* (Kassel, 1954), 34–35. See also Walker, *German Hometowns*, 172–74.

43. StaM, HLO 12.7.1780.

44. Rainer Freiherr von Rosenberg, *Soldatenwerbung und militärisches Durchzugsrecht im Zeitalter des Absolutismus: Eine rechtsgeschichtliche Untersuchung* (Berlin, 1973), 83.

45. Böhme, *Wehrverfassung*, 20.

missioners to take only those men with previous experience in the subsidy army as well as those "masterless loafers [*herrenlose Müßigänger*]
who you can find in the cities and domainal administrative divisions
entrusted to you. . . . see to it with the greatest industry that except for
such loafers that no poor subject necessary for agriculture is taken as a
volunteer."[46] Even the very intrusive legislation of 1762 still required
that recruiters check whether recruits had prior obligations as servants to a peasant Brotherrn or to the household of a noble (*adelige
Hintersaße*).[47]

The phrase "masterless servants and loafers" (*herrenlose Gesindel
und Müßiggänger*) began appearing in Hessian legislation immediately
following the Thirty Years War.[48] Frequently associated with "dismissed soldiers" (*abgedankte Soldaten*), it was used after wars to
justify draconian policing measures against mobile populations. The
free movement of war refugees or migrant workers violated the cameralist assumption that labor should be kept at home and laborers from
outside should be encouraged to settle within.[49] Moreover, any substantial population living outside household authority seemed an in-
tolerable threat to order and to the proper distribution of welfare
payments.

The instructions to target the masterless servants and loafers in
villages implied that the military recruiters swept the land clean of a
dangerous and surplus population. Though recruiting marginals was
consistent with conscriptive recruitment practices of the time, evidence
exists that by 1702, Hessian recruiters could not find sufficient numbers of qualified recruits either within or outside of territorial borders.
In an effort to bring regiments up to strength for the opportunities
presented by the Wars of the Spanish Succession, recruiters received
instructions to inquire about "parents who have different sons on hand
whom they can best do without in their [the parents'] trade or subsistence production [*Nahrung*]."[50] Officials backed off this broader cast-
ing of the recruitment net after the wartime crisis, but the need to cast it
so widely squares better with the pictures that demographers have
given us. In the early eighteenth century, Hesse-Cassel, far from being

46. StaM, B/4h 4053.
47. StaM, HLO 16.12.1762.
48. StaM, HLO 6.1.1698.
49. Raeff, *The Well-Ordered Police State*, 74–78.
50. StaM, HLO 24.4.1702.

overpopulated, was still recovering from the terrible depredations and losses of the Thirty Years War.[51]

Another indication that recruiters could not successfully restrict themselves to theoretically dangerous deadbeats came in early attempts to blur the clear legal distinction between militia service and standing army service. Though militia service was involuntary and subsidy service technically free-will enlistment, much recruiting for the Landgrave's regiments went on from militia units. A commonplace for European armies of the time, such recruiting frequently occurred when militia and subsidy units mustered together for regular yearly exercises.[52] Under these circumstances resistance was suicidal but coercion remained merely an implied threat. Officials mystified the questionable legality of the practice by following militia enrollment procedures which required that every recruit be paid a bounty.[53] Technically this meant even militia soldiers taken involuntarily from households now had "sold their skins" or delivered the rights to their persons to the Landgrave should his recruiters choose to exercise them.

The Landgrave could not afford to allow anyone who qualified for militia service to end up in his subsidy army with its greater risks, longer terms of service, and greater potential disruption of the rural economy. He needed to balance the interests of tribute taken for civil and military treasuries against the income available from subsidy troops. For this reason, as early as 1734 the ever expanding category of marginality was circumscribed when he ordered his muster commissioners to take only those recruits who "in their current place of residence do not have so much to lose and can be used for military service without disadvantage to the public [*Publico*]."[54] A 1741 administrative clarification defined "disadvantage to the public" more precisely as "reduction of military taxes [*Kontribution*] and damage to agricultural production."[55] The discourse of marginality still did not

---

51. Gunther Franz, *Der dreißigjährige Krieg und das deutsche Volk* (Stuttgart, 1979), 41; George Thomas Fox, "Studies in the Rural History of Upper Hesse," (Ph.D. diss., Vanderbilt University, 1976) 268; Ottfried Dascher, *Das Textilgewerbe in Hessen-Kassel vom 16.-19. Jahrhundert* (Marburg, 1968), 160–67.

52. Fred Anderson, *A People's Army: Massachusetts, Soldiers, and Society in the Seven Years War* (Chapel Hill, N.C., 1984), 26–27.

53. StaM, HLO 19.5.1741.

54. StaM, HLO 18.1.1734.

55. StaM, HLO 19.5.1741.

explicitly admit that the Landgrave took his recruits from functioning peasant households.

Intrusions into intrahousehold relationships, however, grew gradually more explicit in the course of the 1730s and 1740s. Officials first formulated a language of direct official intervention into household relations in a nonmilitary connection. Following the theory of the Marburg cameralist Christian Wolf, that the master-servant relationship constituted an "authoritarian society from which advantages on both sides are derived," Hessian officials instituted an ordinance in 1736 which commanded village authorities to regulate contracts between Brotherrn and their employees.[56] Going beyond regulating wages and establishing the master's moral obligation to discipline his servants, the law forbade employers to hire any servant without documentary evidence of good performance in past jobs.[57] Such a system of recommendations established in law the classic double bind of the young job seeker who cannot get a job without experience and cannot gain experience without a job. The law added to the tension by ordering village mayors to "get rid of all foreign and masterless servants who have become a burden to the community tolerating only those who perform their day labor well. Particular attention is to be paid to village inhabitants who would prefer not to serve, that they become accustomed to work."[58] Such double bound legal language worked as much to create a group of masterless (and, I might add, easily recruitable) young men as to assure that all lived under the authority of a housemaster.

During the 1740s, state intrusion into households went further still. A Brotherr lost the capacity to keep his male servants off of village recruitment lists. Officials required heads of households both to prove that a contractual relationship existed between them and their servants and that the servant was indispensable to the local agricultural economy.[59] In practice, this meant that day laborers, their sons, and the apprentices of village artisans became the primary focus of recruiters. One tax official pointed out the contradictions of this policy: "If one needed recruits fast that these [marginal] sorts were the easiest to give up," but recruiting them interrupted their training and reduced their

56. Otto Könnecke, *Rechtsgeschichte des Gesindewesens in West- und Süddeutschland* (Marburg, 1912), 59.
57. StaM, HLO 11.6.1739.
58. Ibid.
59. Könnecke, *Gesindewesens,* 372–75.

capacity to support themselves after military service.[60] Recruitment thus tended to create the very marginals that the army claimed to eliminate from communities. Even worse, according to a 1747 administrative order, "marginals [*Unvermögende*] at the time of a muster, hire themselves outside of the territory or simply flee," leaving military service to the wealthy who had more reason to stay.[61] The problem became so severe that in the years immediately preceding the Seven Years War the Landgrave had to promise that "no one will be taken into military service against their will or with force especially if they cannot go without the decline of their estates or otherwise damaging the subsistence of their household."[62] No longer defined by the needs of village economies, or the abstract needs of the public defined by the fisc, marginality was now put in terms of household relationships. This conception of marginality recalled the abandoned law of 1702 which sought sons which a household could "spare."

The military reforms of Frederick II represented an important watershed and a fruition in the developing language of marginality in recruitment policy. The new army simply eliminated the legal distinctions between the subsidy army and militia units and placed the obligation to serve on a more universal, yet still personal, basis. In the Kanton ordinance of 1762 the Landgrave cautioned his young male subjects "to subject themselves to the obligation and duty which binds them to their prince whom God established."[63] True to the cameralist principal of balance, this conscription law exercised selectively the newly asserted rights to subsidy service.[64] The Landgrave allowed recruits for field (subsidy) regiments to be taken "only if they are the household's most expendable people, or if agriculture and other necessary occupations will not be interrupted."[65] If he limited service in field regiments to "the household's most expendable people" then he reserved service in garrison regiments (former militia units) to those youngsters who "are not entirely expendable to parents who own estates."[66]

60. StaM, B/49d Marburg 556, Niederweimar 1738.
61. StaM, HLO 29.8.1747.
62. StaM, HLO 26.7.1755.
63. StaM, HLO 16.12.1762.
64. Phillip Losch, *Soldatenhandel* (Marburg, 1976), 25; Böhme, *Wehrverfassung*, 27–28.
65. StaM, HLO 16.12.1762.
66. StaM, HLO 10.4.1767.

The law exempted persons who owned a house or an estate requiring a plow-team (*Anspannig*), or sons of well provided peasants or
master craftsmen, apprentices to necessary trades, or journeymen serving widows. Earlier law had defined "well-provided peasant" (*stark
begütherte Bauer*) as paying more than one Reichstaler per month in
Kontribution. The Landgrave instructed his officials to examine carefully the documentary evidence of contractual relationships between
peasants and evaluate the relative necessity of particular laborers.
They were also to "ensure that immature youths and especially those
under twenty years of age neither marry nor inherit estates in order to
escape military service."[67] While at the beginning of the eighteenth
century military recruiters swept villages clean of people perceived to
be superfluous, after 1762 the state reached deeply into the household
and explicitly vetoed the decisions of householders in the most crucial
acts assigning rights to the surpluses of primary accumulation to one
party or another. Officials did so to acquire rights in persons for the
state.

Inheritance Reform and Recruitment

We have come a long way from the language of a household as a Leib-
nitzian monad and approach more closely Justi's vision of householders as intermediate authorities of discipline in a police state (*Polizei-
staat*). This new more transparent language permitted state officials to
think about directly manipulating the rules of marriage, inheritance,
and reproduction in such a way that more persons could be claimed for
military service. They did so in 1773 through an ordinance known as
the Hufen edict which regulated devolutionary practice on all closed
estates listed in the cadaster as held of *Lehn* tenure.

The rural subject population of Hesse-Cassel practiced both partible
and impartible inheritance.[68] Land held of a variety of feudal tenures
(*Lehnland*) was restricted to impartibility in law and for the most part
in practice. Allodial land (*Erbland*) was subject to no restrictions and
passed as the holder saw fit. Whether peasants divided their inheritances or not, an ideology of equal division existed in law and made its
appearance in practice. This meant that peasants practicing impar-

67. StaM, HLO 16.12.1762.
68. Fox, "Studies in the Rural History of Upper Hesse," 368–72 and literature cited
there.

tibility might pass their estates whole to a single heir, but those children who did not receive the land and buildings of the estate still had an equal claim to its resources. These claims took the form of debt or payments in cash and kind spread over several years and sometimes more than one generation. In addition, should former holders still live, they too had claims on the farm for support in their old age. As Hermann Rebel has shown, such claims became golden chains which bound labor and marriage prospects to heirs and their elders who controlled inheritance and marriage networks.[69]

Partible inheritance (*Realteilung*) required actual division of properties and was seldom entirely equal because few people were inclined to divide buildings and moveables equally. This meant that parents usually advantaged one heir over others putting that person in a privileged position for ordering the networks of marriage and labor of which we will hear more below.[70] More frequently, peasants used partible land as part of the settlements of children on impartible estates. That is, such land tended to be marginal parcels which passed from impartible estate to impartible estate as part of marriage settlements of the siblings of heirs.[71] Whether partible or impartible, devolutionary practice occurred in many stages but always revolved around the marriage settlement of the principal heir.[72] The grid of inheritance created through the assignment of heir status and co-heir claims remained the central discourse by which peasants used kinship to organize production. The movable and immovable properties that passed from generation to generation constituted a fund that became increasingly subject to tributary regulation and raids.[73]

Most authorities writing about edicts such as the Hufen edict have discussed how they mandated impartibility and then focused on their fiscal "rationality."[74] For these accounts, the important achievements of such legislation were to prohibit the division (*Zerstücklung*) of

---

69. Rebel, "Peasant Stem Families," and *Peasant Classes* (Princeton, 1983).

70. Sabean, *Power in the Blood*, 154–59.

71. Fox, "Studies in the Rural History of Upper Hesse," 368–72.

72. David Sabean, "Aspects of Kinship Behavior and Property in Rural Western Europe before 1800," *Family and Inheritance: Rural Society in Western Europe 1200–1800* (Cambridge, 1976), 96–111.

73. Rebel, "Cultural Hegemony," 2:356–57.

74. Wilhelm Holtzapfel, "Oberlandsbezirk Kassel," in Max Sering, ed., *Die Vererbung des ländlichen Grundbesitzes* (Berlin, 1899–1910); Teodor Mayer-Edenhauser, *Untersuchen über Anerbenrecht und Güterschluß in Kurhessen* (Prague, 1942); Fox, "Studies in the Rural History of Upper Hesse," 368–72; Ingrao, *The Hessian Mercenary State*, 116–20.

peasant farms, establish a legal framework for impartibility, and harmonize the interests of state, heir, retiring farmer, and dispossessed siblings. Manifestly, state officials wished to keep peasant farms sufficiently large so that they provided both subsistence for those who held them, and taxes and tribute for the state and landed aristocrats. The official line in the Hufen edict of 1773 expressed the belief that "A divided estate [*Erbgut*] only very rarely suffices to support an entire family [*Familie*]" and therefore such families are not able to render "the dues [*Zinsen*], the labor burdens [*Dienste*], taxes, military taxes [*Kontribution*], and all other obligations" which fell upon them as tenure holders.[75]

The edict of 1773 mostly repeated past edicts that stretched as far back as 1545 and came as recently as 1750. But the law went far beyond reasserting the impartibility of closed estates, expressing concern that when dispossessed "co-heirs demand the so-called true value of their portions from the possessor in cash, it frequently comes to pass that the farm is still further divided or so encumbered with debt that the owners do not hold on to large segments of it."[76] Past law, in fact, required that estates passed impartibly still bear the burden of compensating those heirs of the previous holder who did not receive the estate. Moreover, should a tenure pass while any one of the couple who passed it still lived they were entitled to a retirement portion (*Altenteil*).[77]

The new Hufen edict sought to limit co-heirs' portions and the benefits claimable by retiring elders. Using cadastral assessments, it set a limit on the total of all compensatory portions at Rt 80 on estates assessed at a value of Rt 90 or Rt 100 if that estate included a farmstead (*Haus und Hof*).[78] The amount fell or climbed Rt 10 for every Albus per month owed in Kontribution. This meant that the proportion available to take care of co-heirs climbed with value of the estate and diminished as it diminished. If an estate paid twenty Albus in monthly Kontribution, 105 percent of its assessed value would be available for compensation, while an estate which paid five Albus would permit 66 percent of its assessed value to be distributed among the dispossessed co-heirs.

75. StaM, HLO 19.11.1773.
76. Ibid.
77. Ibid.
78. Greve and Krüger, "Steuerstaat und Sozialstruktur," 302–3.

This allotment seems very generous and certainly in line with the principals of equally divided value which lay behind Anerbenrecht. When one recognizes that officials based Kontribution payments on an assessed value after about one-third had been deducted for tribute payments the picture looks less rosy. Beyond this, Klaus Greve and Kersten Krüger have calculated that Steuergulden assessments probably amounted to about a quarter of "real" farm values.[79] Finally, all debts had to be subtracted from the value of the estate as well. What appears as a very generous 89 percent of an estate's value allotted to compensation comes out to be less than 15 percent. This becomes more shocking when we learn that peasants at the time probably valued their estates up to five times the gross assessed tax value and more than twice the market value for the purposes of devolutionary settlements. In 1787, after the law was modified, Magnus Dörr valued an estate at 2500 Frankfurtergulden that he purchased for Rt 810 and valued in the cadaster at Sg 480 (1 Rt = .75 Sg = .64 Fg).[80] Not enough of these contracts survive to provide reliable statistics. Further, the law prohibited land and buildings from being separated from estates for retirement purposes and prohibited retirement funds except in dire need. Thus, the Hufen edict directed a substantial redistribution of surpluses toward heirs within the kin-ordered enterprises of rural Hesse-Cassel.

According to Charles Ingrao, this bold stroke had been intentionally designed "to effect a massive shake-out," particularly among the poorest peasants. Apparently, the hope was to save some households on these tenures by forcing children into more promising careers, the most important of which was the military.[81] In short, the Hufen edict consciously created marginals in both households and in villages to fill the ranks of its subsidy army. Further, it attempted to define exactly who these designated failures and system-necessary victims would be by legally encoding the peasant practice of giving sons precedence over daughters and elder sons over younger, while always making sure the heir was capable.[82] Whether the policy makers had hoped simply to preserve the tax-paying capacity of peasant farms or whether they had also intended initially to create a new pool of conscripts is not clear

79. Ibid.
80. StaM, P/II Hypothekenwesen Allna 3.
81. Ingrao, *The Hessian Mercenary State*, 120, 134.
82. StaM, HLO 19.11.1773.

from the sources. Historically, the latter effect occurred rather more frequently than the former.

A draconian policy of this nature could not but have serious consequences. In fact, difficulties became apparent to the officials of the Agrarian Society who recognized as early as 1776 that the Hufen edict had contributed to a fall of some fifty percent in land values. This was a crisis in both ideology and administrative practice. Combined with the absence of the subsidy army, not just from Hesse-Cassel but from Europe between 1776 and 1784, the Hufen edict created conditions of a general economic and social seizure which unbalanced the military-fiscal state. But before we may begin any account of this ultimate penetration of the household and its consequences, it is necessary to speak of the administrative efforts that turned the discourse of marginality into the actions of officials. Once we explore the practical dimensions of executing recruitment and tax policy, we may provide a deeper account of the subsidy crisis of the years after 1776.

4 Patrimonial Bureaucracy and Rational Policy: Problems in the Administration of Recruitment, 1701–1773

As the recruitment ordinance of 1762 represented a watershed for the discourse of "marginality," so too was it an intensification of the administrative apparatus at the disposal of the subsidy system. Landgrave Frederick II modeled the legislation after the famous Prussian *Kanton* system out of admiration for his mentor and namesake, Frederick II of Prussia.[1] Like much reform legislation of the eighteenth century, the law seemed directed toward both efficient government and more "rational" (that is, productive and harmonious) social relations.[2] Intensive and interventionist administrative practice faced a range of pragmatic difficulties which, even if solved, tended to undermine official effectiveness in the countryside.

Max Weber identified three levels on which reformers could develop bureaucratic "rationality": personnel, policy, and procedure.[3] One ideal-typical approach began with the attempt to change the commitments, preparation, and motivation of personnel. Perhaps, in following this line, Frederick II of Prussia claimed that the prince was the "professional" servant of the state and that his educated and specialized subordinates exercised the levers of authority in the interests of civil society. It is ironic that princes and their servants tended to

1. Compare Eugen von Frauenholtz, *Entwicklungsgeschichte des deutschen Heerwesens* (Munich, 1940), 4:40ff., with Inge Auerbach et al., eds., *Hessische Truppen im amerikanischen Unabhängigkeitskrieg* (Marburg, 1976), 4:36.
2. Mack Walker, *German Hometowns* (Ithaca, 1971), 146–49.
3. Max Weber, *Economy and Society* (Berkeley, 1978), 2:969–73.

identify the interests of civil society with the size of the fisc; as a result an adversarial relationship frequently developed between the many corporate elements of German society and the officials overseeing them. Local officials themselves tended to resist reforms as an attack on their own jurisdictional authority and corporate privilege. Weber argues that such an attitude is characteristic of office holders whose claim to authority remains primarily "patrimonial," based on private law.[4] They could resist attacks on their private rights by a newly defined "public authority" because the central governments had no working alternative but to accept and employ their services. Recognizing this lack of options, princes tended to limit personnel reform to those officials they could directly supervise. Reformed officials produced "rational" policies but rarely had the information or administrative means to put them fully into operation.

To rely exclusively on personnel reform to bring about "rationalization" would have been utopian for small states of the Holy Roman Empire such as Hesse-Cassel. Thus, after professionalizing his top officials, Landgrave Frederick II reformed policy and procedure but then relied on unreformed officials in the provinces, including Hessian landed aristocrats.[5] He used their knowledge of local conditions and the work of their stable of clients and officials who administered private rights to local jurisdiction. Finding any abstract commitment to state or civil society among these subalterns was difficult.

The independence of local officials easily accorded with cameralist theories that the Landgrave's own servants learned at German universities. As we have seen, they learned that state authorities harmonized the diverse interests of the manifold social corporations in German society rather than attempting to dissolve them into a rational "homogeneous" order.[6] But this vision of the relation between state and society assumed that harmony already existed and that officials need only prosecute, adjudicate, and punish "abuses" to preserve it. Such a vision left activist princes and their servants to reconcile genuinely conflicting corporate interests without appearing to upset the other theoretically important balance between corporate autonomy and central authority.[7]

While attempting this double balancing act in the conscription ordi-

4. Ibid., 1088–90.
5. Charles W. Ingrao, *The Hessian Mercenary State* (Cambridge, 1987), 14, 22.
6. Walker, *German Home Towns*, 150–51.
7. Ibid., 164.

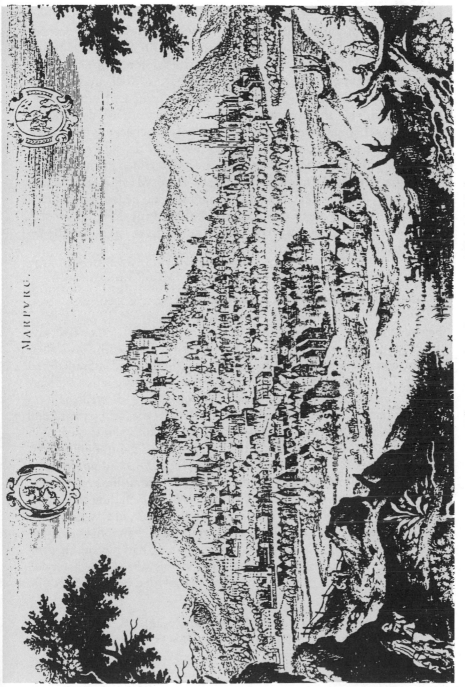

Mattaeus Merian d. Ä., etching of Marburg. Source: Bildarchiv Marburg.

nance of 1762, the Landgrave needed to develop an administrative structure out of patrimonial authorities who would execute recruitment policy on the basis of objective and quantifiable standards and without regard for persons or personal loyalties. His reforms, however, faced fundamental contradictions because the task itself cut across the very patronage systems that they used to elicit obedience from subordinates. It dammed the normal flow of favors that attached clients to patrons. Such an attempt could succeed only by checking and cross-checking the performance of assigned tasks. To do so, Frederick II juxtaposed officials with conflicting interests, provided them with adequate sources of information, and finally imposed enforceable sanctions. Only to the extent that the Landgrave succeeded did military policy develop the potential for rational management. As he succeeded, his efforts corroded the very patrimonial authority so necessary for the performance of the tasks involved.

Administrative Checks and Balances

Before 1762, two bodies of officials whose interests conflicted oversaw a two-stage recruitment procedure. Military officers with special letters of commission selected recruits from villages and administered general loyalty oaths to them. But a diverse group of civilian officials created the muster lists from which commissioners selected their recruits. Village headmen, jurymen, and officials of the local patrimonial court all played some role in making the lists.[8] Militia units created in this manner became a major source of recruits for the standing army.

The administrative processes in effect before 1762 had not worked smoothly, not least because officials had competing interests. Local headmen and jurymen had clients in the village, including their own children, whom they wished to protect. For example, in 1776, officials in the village of Langenstein reported that the headman told colleagues that there were more draft eligible males than he had put on his lists. He was subsequently removed from office for his "disorderly lifestyle" (*unruhige Lebensart*).[9] In nearby Bellnhausen, villagers petitioned the

---

8. Gunther Thies, *Territorialstaat und Landesverteidigung: Das Landesdefensionswerk in Hessen-Kasselunter Landgraf Moritz* (Marburg, 1973), 81.
9. StaM, B/17e Langenstein 67.

regional draft administrator because the village headman he had appointed used the job to protect his son from recruitment.[10] In turn, judicial officials made a living by keeping for themselves a percentage of the various forms of tribute they could extract for their noble employers. They hesitated to allow recruiters to take men needed in rural production because losing them might reduce the total tribute taken.

Conversely, the incomes of selection commissioners and of their commanders depended upon the enrollment of as many healthy young men as possible. Indeed, commissioners received a payment for each recruit. Further, the owners of companies needed as many men as possible on their rosters to maximize income to the company treasuries, which they manipulated as if they were private funds. Frequently repeated warnings to obey the proper procedures testify to the temptations to circumvent the regulations.[11] These temptations became particularly strong during the Wars of the Spanish Succession when the subsidy business of the Landgrave was still relatively young and administrative controls remained weak.[12]

During the 1720s and 1730s, fiscal bureaucrats became interested in the surplus funds as the rental of military units to Europe's major powers became a significant source of income for prince and state. Early attempts to balance these conflicting interests took the form of sending the lists of eligible young men (*junge Mannschaft*) to the war Chancellery (*Kriegskanzlei*). Here, higher authorities who were in a position to take a broader (that is, more fiscal) view completed the selection process.[13] The inability of the central administration to verify the information it received from both military and local officials cast doubt on the effectiveness of this procedure.

The law of 1762 rebalanced the conflicting interests and reduced arbitrariness in the selection process. It assigned to each regiment rights to recruit within a particular geographic area (*Kanton*). In effect, each regiment possessed a number of families from which it filled its recruitment needs because authorities determined canton borders by counting families. This system restricted the freedom of action of

10. StaM, B/17e Bellnhausen 23.
11. StaM, Ms/R. 34, 1688; HLO 30.12.1733.
12. Hans Philippi, *Landgraf Karl I von Hessen-Kassel: Ein deutscher Fürst der Barokzeit* (Marburg, 1976), 647, 655.
13. StaM, HLO 24.12.1702.

military authorities and prevented them from competing with one another for the best recruits. Moreover, because civilian officials now had complete control over recruitment lists in each canton, called the yearly village musters, and certified exemptions and eligibility, it appeared that they determined precisely who would serve.

After the reform, military officers from the regiment assigned to a canton only measured the height and inspected the serviceability of potential recruits at yearly and special musters. Officers who violated these strictures now paid heavy fines and suffered other penalties.[14] In addition, the law forbade officers to do their own recruiting even within their regimental cantons. Should they know of a good recruit, new procedures required that they point him out to civilian officials who would then enroll him only if he was qualified. Finally, the ordinance established punishments for regimental officers who released soldiers unnecessarily to acquire new recruits.[15]

Local officials appeared to gain further strength vis-à-vis their army counterparts in 1772 when the Landgrave, on the suggestion of the Hessian Diet, created the office of Landrat to administer military recruitment and taxation in the countryside. The Landrat audited village Kontribution accounts, created and maintained canton lists, received manpower requests from regiments, and decided (in conjunction with the regimental commanders) how to fill them. Some military officers objected to this new post because it represented a civilian intrusion into affairs they saw as their exclusive domain. As another imitation of Prussian administrative practice, the idea for the Landrat came from members of the Diet apparently worried that military use of their own patrimonial administrators threatened the perogatives of private jurisdictions.[16] Perhaps they also hoped that the office would help intensify their independent domination over the rural subject population as it had in Prussia.[17] The Diet nominated candidates for Landräte from its own membership, usually choosing prominent nobles with private jurisdictional rights over territory they administered for the Landgrave.[18] They received their appointments and instruc-

14. StaM, HLO 16.12.1762.

15. Ibid.

16. StaM, B/4h 3503, 1772.

17. Otto Büsch, *Militärsystem und Sozialleben im Alten Preussen* (Frankfurt, 1981), 67–71.

18. Uhlrich Friederich Kopp, "Von Landräthen," *Teutsches Staats-Magazin* 1 (1796): 108–38.

tions from the Landgrave and reported to him through the General Directory and the privy council.

The Flow of Information

With control of the canton lists and of decisions concerning draft exemptions in the hands of the Landrat, military commanders now negotiated with nobles of substantial stature who had direct financial interests in keeping the army's intrusions to a minimum.[19] Such arrangements could shield local court officials and peasant headmen against the pressures that military commanders could exert. In this way, officials could adjust the recruitment process to minimize disruption to productive processes and thereby protect the tributary incomes of the landed aristocrats and the Landgrave's domains.

Leaning more heavily on civilian officeholders risked both indiscipline and ineffectiveness, as Frederick the Great had already learned.[20] In the years before the reform, clients and clerical servants of Hessian nobles manipulated the recruitment process through their capacity to control the flow of accurate information about draft-eligible men. Early in the eighteenth century, this power over the information in the muster lists must have been a thorn in the side of recruiters and their superiors who, in all likelihood, never knew who had been exempted or why. Indeed, the injunction to local officials in the canton law of 1762 to administer the draft without using "fear or threats" or being swayed "through friendship or other moving causes," was likely to remain ineffective without improvements in the information-gathering process.[21]

Frederick II circumscribed these officials by knitting together several older sources of relevant information. Lists of potential recruits in villages had been part of the recruitment process since the reforms of Moritz the Learned in the early seventeenth century. Throughout the eighteenth century Hessian Landgraves required increasingly complicated and elaborate lists from their local administrators. Just prior to 1762, recruitment lists included the names of all subjects, their age, sex, marital status, names of male children, indications of past military

---

19. StaM, B/23b ALb, Ebsdorf 870, 28.10.1782.
20. Büsch, *Militärsystem*, 134–43.
21. StaM, HLO 16.12.1762.

experience, land held, and military taxes paid.[22] While the detail of this data undoubtedly helped military officials and others find and determine the eligibility of potential recruits, the lists still relied upon the testimony of parties interested in the individual outcomes of the recruitment process.

The canton lists created by the law of 1762 should have solved these administrative difficulties. Communal officers under the supervision of the servants of judicial authority made the lists anew for each yearly muster. They also kept them up to date with quarterly revisions which they sent to the war college (*Kriegskollegium*). The law required additional lists of the names of those already recruited and those who had fled to avoid conscription (*Ausgetretene*). More important, the Landgrave now required parish pastors to cooperate with the process by providing certified extracts of the parish registers which verified information about age, gender, and marital status of persons on the list.[23] This step provided the first independent verification of the information used in the selection process. It was a source likely to remain uncorrupted longer because religious authorities had created it for other purposes which peasants themselves did not wish to compromise.

Adequate cadastral documents, which did exist in some villages, independently verified recruitment information.[24] Officials used cadasters to check the information about wealth and tenurial relationships that appeared on the canton lists. The new canton lists, substantiated by parish registers and the new cadaster, constituted a sharp check to the waywardness of local officials. And, as we shall see, they also helped tie secure land tenure to cooperation in the recruitment process.

Thus, as early as 1762, and certainly by 1772 when Landräte became responsible for recruitment, Frederick II had created a structure of officials, procedures, and information that circumscribed the operation of patronage politics by either military or civilian officials. This new subordination held out the prospect of a rational administration of recruitment despite the patrimonial nature of the officialdom. The Landgrave subordinated officials not by changing the nature of their office but by structuring the relationships into which he placed them.

22. StaM, HLO 18.1.1734.

23. StaM, HLO 16.12.1762.

24. Karl Strippel, *Die Währschafts- und Hypothekenbücher Kurhessens* (Marburg, 1914), 187–95; Klaus Greve and Kersten Krüger, "Steuerstaat und Sozialstruktur: Finanzsoziologische Auswertung der hessischen Katastervorbeschreibungen für Waldkappel 1744 und Herleshausen 1748," *Geschichte und Gesellschaft* 3 (1983): 295–329.

The Sanctions of Authorities

The rational execution of the Landgrave's will also became possible because officials had at their disposal sanctions and procedures that made it more difficult for peasants to avoid compliance. In administering recruitment policy and in attempting to keep regimental rosters filled, Hessian officials faced a variety of forms of resistance to involuntary military servitude. Acting directly, young peasant men deserted after their enrollment or failed to appear at local spring musters. The administrative response to the problem of desertion took a number of different directions. By 1737, the Landgrave ordered civil officials to confiscate the property of deserters.[25] Examples of confiscations appear in the records in the 1730s and extend through 1790.[26] Regimental officers punished deserters by fines and beatings. Though on occasion punishments could be quite barbarous, the Landgrave mitigated their extent by issuing frequent general pardons to encourage deserters to return. Pardons of this type probably attracted mostly those soldiers not intending permanent flight, those who had deserted in response to temporary family pressures, and those who had not left Hesse-Cassel. Though such pardons did not mean complete escape from punishment, pardoned deserters did avert the worst beatings and confiscations.

To forestall flight beyond Hessian borders, officials took preventive action and sought to secure the return of escapees. From 1730 onward, Hesse-Cassel resorted to cartel treaties with neighboring powers for the return of deserters.[27] These contracts provided for the mutual pursuit and exchange of deserters. A later treaty from 1792 put prices on the heads of deserters which were based on how tall they were. Thus, William IX agreed to pay sixty Frankfurtergulden for each deserter over five *Fuß*, eleven *Zollen* that was returned to him. Soldiers who simply met the recruitment minimum (five *Fuß*, four *Zollen*) cost him half that amount.[28]

By way of prevention, the landgrave offered rewards to civilians within Hesse-Cassel for capturing Hessian deserters. For example, a 1778 circular promised a reward of six Reichstaler for information leading to the capture of any person who had violated a military

---

25. StaM, HLO 16.5.1763, reiterates a law of 1737.
26. StaM, B/4h 3553, 1784–1796, 3557, undated, 3558, 1735, 3565, 1770; Ingrao, *The Hessian Mercenary State,* 161.
27. StaM, HLO 23.2.1762.
28. StaM, HLO 8.2.1992.

oath.[29] In addition, informants received half of all wealth confiscated from deserters whom they turned in. To aid the identification of deserters, legislation required all males to carry passports (*Laufpäße*) indicating their military status. The same laws instructed village officials to examine carefully the documents of all young males from their villages as well as of those passing through.[30] This pass system effectively defined deserters as those serviceable young males who did not have believable papers including recommendations from past employers.[31]

Complete avoidance of the recruitment apparatus could take a number of different forms. Once recruitment had been placed on a strictly geographic basis by the canton law, any geographic movement might have the effect of draft-avoidance. Young men could hire themselves as servants outside of the canton. For instance, the Greben of Rodenhausen complained that officials in Oberweimar tried to draft Johann Jakob Schäffer while he was serving Johann Jakob Diefenbach. The Greben, relying on this law, stated that draft status was determined in the village of birth and that soldiers belonged to the canton of their birth rather than the one where they worked. Whether he was protecting Schäffer or simply trying to get credit for his own quotas is unclear.[32] In an attempt to forestall such tactics, the law of 1762 required every young man leaving his native village, for whatever reason, to inform the village headman of his destination. Those who failed to do so were classified as draft-dodgers (*Ausgetretene.*)[33] In spite of this law, draft avoidance remained a matter of moving on once again after leaving one's village of birth. Draft dodging was also possible if one had the protection of village officials who could inhibit the flow of accurate information about the whereabouts of individuals.

Over the course of the eighteenth century the Landgrave's officials increasingly assimilated the legal status of those who left to avoid the draft to that of deserters. This meant that they subjected such escapees not only to confiscations but to the provisions of cartel treaties as well. Moreover, the heads of households or others who connived at or assisted in the escape of either household members or other draft-age young men became liable to heavy fines and similar measures of confiscation.[34] In this way, the Landgrave bound the holding of any prop-

29. StaM, HLO 20.6.1777.
30. StaM, HLO 21.8.1767, 19.3.1773, 18.4.1774, 19.9.1777, 11.6.1739.
31. StaM, HLO 23.2.1764.
32. StaM, B/23b ALb, Rodenhausen 1503, undated (1770s or 1780s).
33. StaM, HLO 16.12.1762.
34. StaM, HLO 19.3.1773.

erty or wealth in Hesse-Cassel to full cooperation with military recruitment procedures — a tie which became increasingly enforceable as tax commissions created reliable cadasters for each village.

Tying cooperation with the recruitment apparatus to the secure holding of land tenures may have had advantages in enforcing the conscription law, but it had difficulties as well. In 1747, a complaint to local officials pointed out that obtaining compliance from better-off people was relatively easy but it was the poorer sort (*Unvermögende*) who were failing to show up for musters. Without property or prospects to hold them, those peasant sons found it easier to relocate than to serve the Landgrave.[35] Thus, the very people who were the primary targets of a selective recruitment policy were the hardest to lay hands on. Both Frederick II of Hesse-Cassel and his mentor, Frederick II of Prussia, eventually recognized how important peasant property was in anchoring peasant families to the territory.[36] Conditions in Hesse-Cassel demonstrated what an important administrative lever landed property could be.

Propertied peasants were left only with the manipulation of established standards and procedures to protect their household members and fellow villagers from the military administration. The Landgrave's officials worked hard to restrict such manipulation. However, there was little anyone could do about the young boys who were willing to maim themselves in order to avoid serving the Landgrave or about those whom parish pastors were willing to protect by altering their registers. After 1766, people claiming occupational exemptions (as miners, salt teamsters, and liveried servants) needed to produce valid written contracts to substantiate their claims.[37] In addition, the law of 1762 required that local officials carefully check documentation of past or present military service to prevent the use of forged papers to avoid service.[38]

Some few lucky peasants escaped conscription through the provisions of the canton law which protected persons directly under the legal jurisdiction of members of the Hessian nobility (*adelige Hinter-saßen*). This exemption stemmed from older provisions in Hessian law and had grown out of long conflict between the Diet and the Landgrave.[39] Moreover, it eventually figured prominently in peasant com-

35. StaM, HLO 29.8.1747.
36. Büsch, *Militärsystem*, 56–61.
37. StaM, HLO 16.1.1766.
38. StaM, HLO 16.12.1762.
39. StaM, B/5 14737, 12.3.1779.

plaints about the unfairness of the recruitment process as a whole.[40] A case from the village of Rockensüß in eastern Hesse-Cassel exemplifies the complications created for the administration of recruitment by the exclusion of *adelige Hintersaßen*. Save for a small hamlet of seven households that lay in the domain of the noble house of von Rotenberg, the Landgrave himself held jurisdiction over the entire village. In September 1778, the Landrat von Baumbach zu Sontra complained that he had not received the full cooperation of parish officials in getting information about these seven households. His concern focused on a very large young man, Martin Schaub, who had attracted the attention of a regimental commander. Schaub's father lived and worked on the von Rotenberg estate but he also held land in the village.

Von Baumbach complained that the younger Schaub worked for his father and not for the von Rotenbergs and thus remained eligible for military service. The Landrat enrolled him despite his failure to show up for the spring muster. At this juncture, the manager of the von Rotenberg domains sent a representative to protest the unilateral action of recruitment officials. The General Directory, in a rescript dated 14 November 1778, ordered von Baumbach to draft the younger Schaub but this order met with another protest from the domain manager (*Vogt*).[41] The manager claimed that the elder Schaub's possession of land in Rockensüß had no bearing on the draft-eligibility of the son, since the father had never worked or lived on the land himself; both father and the son always had been members (*Angehörige*) of the von Rotenberg household.

The final decision in this matter is not clear from the sources, but what we know of the dispute does underscore the problems that were created by the multiple overlapping jurisdictions so common in the patrimonial order of central Europe. Fortunately for the Landgraves of Hesse-Cassel, they held some direct control over most of the tenures in their territory. This substantially reduced the opportunities for conflict that abounded in states such as Prussia, where a much smaller percentage of the land carried obligations to the prince's domainal treasury. Much more of the authority of Prussian kings was mediated through predatory Junker aristocrats and their servants.[42] In addition, we see

---

40. Eihachiro Sakai, *Der kurhessische Bauer im 19. Jahrhundert und die Grundlastenablösung* (Melsungen, 1967), 133.

41. StaM, B/4h 3700, von Baumbach zu Sontra.

42. Hans Rosenberg, *Bureaucracy, Aristocracy, and Autocracy* (Cambridge, 1968), 53, 155.

how nobles could still influence the flow of information through their control over parish officials. Moreover, this story highlights the importance of a noble Landrat's prestige for a functioning recruitment process. It was likely that the von Rotenberg domain manager would have had little trouble protecting the younger Schaub from bureaucrats of lesser social standing than von Baumbach. Finally, it is also clear how closely officials continued to tie the possession of land to the obligation for military service.

Max Weber once argued that the eighteenth-century transition toward a legal-rational bureaucracy came not so much through changing the patrimonial nature of public office, but rather through putting patrimonial officials into structures of offices in which they were compelled to formulate and execute policies rationally.[43] The execution of the Hessian draft law of 1762 seems to be an example of such a process. The officials who participated in selecting and enrolling recruits for the Landgrave's army remained largely patrimonial in nature. Military officers owned their regiments and manipulated regimental funds as if they were private property. Furthermore, most of the civilian officials involved did not serve the Landgrave himself, but members of the Hessian nobility. These educated clerks and managers administered the private rights to civil and petty criminal jurisdiction (*Gerichtsherrschaft*) that belonged to their noble masters. The village officials who made conscription work held their positions because the same influential members of Hessian society patronized them and expected them to use their own patronage networks in the village to enforce recruitment procedures.

Despite the privileged independence of the Landräte, the Landgrave could use them as mere tools because of the effectiveness of the structure of checks and balances which he had created. Proof came as the recruitment apparatus met the manpower demands of the biggest financial coup of Frederick II's reign — the subsidy treaty of 1776. The bureaucracy acted so efficiently for this purpose that one out of every thirteen Hessians served in the army in 1782.[44] For some areas, this

43. Weber, *Economy and Society,* 2:1087.

44. This estimate was arrived at by using the estimate of 22,000 men cited in Hans Vogel and Wolfgang von Both, *Landgraf Frederick II., von Hessen-Kassel* (Munich, 1973), 98, and George Thomas Fox's estimate of Hessian population, 303,000 for 1782 ("Studies in the Rural History of Upper Hesse" [Ph.D. diss., Vanderbilt University, 1976], 20). The figure compares with a ratio of 1:19 for Prussia cited in Vogel and von Both above.

meant one household in two provided at least one soldier.[45] Even some of the aristocratic Landräte who were so deeply implicated in creating these conditions complained bitterly that conscription removed productive farmers from behind the plow.[46]

45. StaM, B/4h 3700, von Baumbach zu Marburg.
46. StaM, B/4h 4023, Von Schenck zu Schweinsberg.

5 Political and Ideological Crisis in the Hessian Subsidy System, 1773–1793

For members of Hessian elites, whose quiet compliance, active encouragement, and participation in the subsidy system had long been a crucial ingredient in its success, the crisis of 1773 grew as a process of revelation. As late as 1764, members of the Diet had encouraged Frederick II to seek more subsidy income, to help pay for recovery from the Seven Years War and provide debt relief for the Diet itself. Discomfiture appeared with the issuance of the Hufen edict, which many nobles almost immediately saw as a mistake. Despite the promise of wealth offered by the subsidy negotiations in 1775 and early 1776, fiscal bureaucrats worried about the deleterious effect of the large (12,000 man) peacetime army on peasant production.[1] After the departure of the subsidy troops for America in May 1776, the need to replace men lost there made further demands and discomfort turned to panic. For the first time, they saw how the military system threatened not only the common good which they had sworn to protect but their own interests as tribute takers as well.

Early reports from the regional administrators of the military system, the Landräte, pointed to three fundamental difficulties which at first they attributed primarily to stresses of sustaining the military operations of the American war. First, Landräte argued that to avoid conscription many young men, and indeed sometimes their entire families, fled the territory.[2] Second, despite all attempts at enforcing

1. LbK, 8° Ms. Hass. 16a, H 34/76, H. C. E. Bopp.
2. StaM, B/4h 3700, von Baumbach zu Marburg.

exemption rules, manpower shortages required that many young men not qualified for military service be put on ships to America, thus "removing peasants from behind the plow."[3] Third, the "indispensable" (*unabkömmliche*) people sent to war left behind wives and children who now had no means of support and thus became a burden on the peasant communities in which they lived.[4] All three conditions threatened not only the level of Kontribution payments but the capacity of peasants to pay other dues (*Abgaben*) owed to Hessian nobles. The Landgrave reduced Kontribution payments by half in June of 1776—perhaps as an attempt to address these growing concerns. He sacrificed this part of the fisc in order to relieve pressure on the producers of other tributary incomes.

Investigating the Hufen Edict

The Hessian nobles' assessments of Frederick's reform grew more sophisticated during the debates in the Diets of 1779 and 1785. On the one hand, they asserted claims to the wealth generated by the subsidy system, while on the other they attacked the fundamental administrative foundations that made the system work.[5] This latter attack came in the form of investigations by two commissions, both of which resulted in fundamental military and social reforms after the death of Frederick II. The first of these commissions focused on the Hufen edict. This act cut so deeply into the sinews of production that it clearly represented a new official attitude toward intervention in peasant households.

The commission's charge to investigate "whether the Hufen edict of 1773 is profitable or damaging to the territory and military" explicitly recognized the intentional connection between inheritance legislation and the military system.[6] Several times during the fourteen different reports issued by Landräte, officials made reference to "the apparently useful policy [*Nuzzen*] that all brothers of heirs [*Anerben*] to an estate [*Hufengut*], who receive their inheritance in cash, are held to be dispensable [to their households] and [thus] qualified for enrollment in

3. StaM, B/4h 4023, von Schenck zu Schweinsberg.
4. Ibid.
5. Günther Hollenberg, "Landstände und Militär in Hessen-Kassel," *Hessische Jahrbuch für Landesgeschichte*, 34 (1984): 107–8.
6. StaM, B/5 3242.

the military."[7] Commissioners perceived that stimulation of tax revenues was a purpose of the edict.

Of the fourteen reports, only two supported the continuance of the legislation and neither one of those believed that either stated purpose had been achieved by that time. All recognized that serious disruptions to peasant social life and production stemmed from the change. Those twelve reports which suggested elimination or modification of the edict implied that this part of the system worked neither for the common good nor even for the military. The law became an important focus for growing criticism of Frederick II's military system from many officials who had in the past supported it.

To criticize a cow as sacred as the Hessian military system, to which the Landgrave was obviously committed, and which was at that very moment proving itself to be more profitable than it ever had been, necessarily required an oblique approach. Official critics needed to show that Frederick's reforms had failed to bolster the system in the ways that he and most other commentators had expected. Indeed, the commission on the Hufen edict tried to show a number of ways in which the edict actually damaged incomes from military taxation. Even more important, they argued that rather than aiding recruitment, the edict reduced the pool of soldiers substantially.

The Diet itself put forward the hypothesis that the new means of assessing estate values on the basis of the Kontribution and the new rules about settling the siblings of heirs had both short- and long-term destructive effects on the size of the rural population. In the short term, those young men already in the military, whose portions gave them "little or nothing to lose, and also, so to say, not a single chance to marry, desert on the principle that they can find in every other territory as much as they lost in their fatherland."[8] Landrat von Baumbach of Sontra argued that this principal applied not only to soldiers themselves but to young men not yet enrolled. Indeed, in another context he had reported the flight of three hundred youths, as well as of whole families for these reasons.[9] This avoidance of military service made it difficult to replace soldiers who had become too old or who had married into estates. In the long term, a larger population would more easily provide the necessary recruits. Once again, commissioners ar-

7. StaM, B/5 3242, von Baumbach zu Sontra.
8. Ibid.
9. StaM, B/4h 3700, von Baumbach zu Sontra.

gued that both sons and daughters, with their reduced inheritance portions, found it difficult to make good marriages and so did not marry at all.[10]

Several commissioners argued that even if the Hufen edict had not resulted in the flight of soldiers and potential recruits, an army made of poor men had undesirable consequences. A man of military experience, Landrat von Dalwick, asserted that poor soldiers had significantly less motivation to fight for the Landgrave and so they functioned little better than foreigners in the ranks. What was more, because of their small portions they could not clothe and feed themselves and had to be supported at the expense of the regiments. This solution remained a risk because such soldiers deserted most frequently, taking much of their equipment with them.[11] In short, he implied that poor soldiers threatened the income from company management, which had been an important element tying members of the elite to the military system. Perhaps even more damaging in the long term, according to Landrat von Stockhausen, the peasant population came to perceive military service as a misfortune fit only for victims of the Hufen edict.[12] Playing a latter-day Tiberius Gracchus, he expressed fear that not having the resources to marry, soldiers might not reproduce themselves culturally or biologically. Von Dalwick may have foreseen an erosion of the myth of happy service by brave Hessian youths long accustomed to military duty by the previous service of their own respected fathers and grandfathers.[13]

Although commissioners almost always tried to speak the language of the common good and represent themselves as defenders of the military system, their concerns always touched on the institutions with which they had entwined their own well-being. In a very revealing passage in his report, von Baumbach of Sontra gives us a brief look into another erosion of the domestic consensus in favor of the subsidy system. According to him, the Hufen edict threatened the solvency of the treasury of the Karlshaffen Lazarette (a military hospital). Since

10. StaM, B/5 3242.
11. StaM, B/5 3242, von Dalwick.
12. StaM, B/5 3242, von Stockhausen.
13. StaM, B/4h 4072, Eigenbrodt; Peter Taylor and Hermann Rebel, "Hessian Peasant Women, Their Families, and the Draft: A Social-Historical Interpretation of Four Tales from the Grimm Collection," *Journal of Family History* 6 (Winter 1981): 371; Rodney Atwood, *The Hessians: Mercenaries from Hessen-Kassel in the American Revolution* (Cambridge, 1980), 19–20.

soldiers were generally disinherited siblings, by reducing their wealth the law reduced the incomes the hospital derived from the confiscated the property of soldiers who deserted or committed other crimes. Moreover, in the practice of the courts, the edict strengthened the hand of heirs by preventing officials of the hospital from acquiring the inheritance portions of deserted soldiers.[14] While the primary function of the hospital was the care and feeding of disabled soldiers, it also played a major role in the patronage and credit relations between the Landgrave, his nobles, and his officials. Through desertion and confiscations, the military system diverted the surpluses of kin-ordered production into the pockets of the Hessian tributary elites. One could imagine desertion being encouraged on the one hand and punished on the other. But the Hufen edict diminished these potential incomes and, implicit in von Baumbach's complaint, threatened the subsidy system by reducing the share of benefits that went to Hessian elites.

The threats to elites' wealth remained a concern as the Diet's commission took up the question of the damages the Hufen edict had caused to the territorial peasantry. The explicit intent of the edict had been to prevent the division of estates and to relieve the burden of debt that the previous system had heaped upon the heirs of estates. No one really challenged that the edict succeeded in the first of these intentions, although several of the reports rejected the notion that partible inheritance reduced tax revenues and hurt agriculture.[15] All but two reports suggested that the Hufen edict failed to relieve the burden of debt upon peasant tenures.

Nevertheless, one supporter, Ernst Martin von Schlieffen, drew a radical distinction between three kinds of debt on peasant estates. One kind stemmed from times of misfortune when the death of draft animals or illness of the farmer or members of his family stopped or slowed household production. In von Schlieffen's view, borrowing at such times was unproductive, but also unavoidable. A second kind of debt was incurred through inheritance arrangements and marriage settlements involving the siblings of the heir to the estate. Called establishment sums (*Abfindungssummen*) or dowries (*Herausgiften*), these debts, in von Schlieffen's view, damaged productive capacity as well, but could be avoided by careful enforcement of the Hufen edict. In his zero-sum reasoning, inheritance-caused debts made it difficult to

14. StaM, B/5 3243, von Baumbach zu Sontra.
15. StaM, B/5 3242.

cover the costs of unavoidable misfortune and also reduced the capacity to borrow for investment. Investment debt, the third kind of debt
and one which von Schlieffen supported, was money borrowed to
improve buildings, increase estate sizes, and improve production. His
fundamental argument favored the Hufen edict because it reduced
funds absorbed by inheritance settlements and rechanneled them into
more fiscally rewarding purposes. He also argued that increasing investment debt eventually allowed peasants to increase the size (but not
the proportion) of settlements for non-heirs. Thus, in an eighteenth-
century version of trickle-down rhetoric, a massive redistribution of
wealth upwards was to have long-term benefits for those siblings of
heirs whose portions the law had confiscated. Admitting that under the
current conditions of general poverty, siblings of heirs received very
little if anything, he wrote off the current generation's losses to the
benefit of the future. He justified the victimization by suggesting that
the dispossessed had actually little to lose in the first place.[16]

The twelve members of the Diet's commission who argued against
von Schlieffen's position were more aware of those whom they ruled
and had a somewhat more sophisticated and complex view of peasant
debt and the dynamics of the rural land market. The domainal administration in Kassel (*Regierung Kassel*) issued a report which made clear
that restricting the portions of those not inheriting peasant estates
actually reduced the capital available to peasants for investment or
misfortune. These members of the commission recognized that dowries of women and portions of men had always been a major source of
incoming capital for peasant tenures and to cut them off or severely
restrict them meant decreases in capital circulation and higher interest
rates.[17] Such restrictions meant that peasants could not handle their
past accumulated debts; this resulted in foreclosures which worked to
the disadvantage not only of peasant property holders, but also of
those who had lent them money.

According to the Hufen edict, a foreclosed estate had to be sold as a
unit. Because of the severe shortage of capital, no one could afford to
buy the whole estate, so that its value was diminished on the land
market. Members of the commission argued that creditors almost
always took a loss when they finally did sell the estates, so they usually

16. StaM, B/5 3242, von Schlieffen.
17. StaM, B/5 3242, Regierung Kassel.

gave up and tried to lease them on a short-term basis (*verpachtet*). Creditors, inexperienced in judging agricultural producers, found their short-term renters managed the resources of these estates so poorly that many farms became wasteland (*verwüstet*). Citing the collapse of the land market, some commissioners argued to allow division of estates. They could show examples in which selling estates in pieces had brought in substantially more wealth than trying to sell the same estates whole.[18]

Besides this argument, commission critics of the Hufen edict also fell back on the cameralist assumptions learned in their university education. Among these, they found the notion that one of the pillars of a strong state was the size of its population. They returned, then, to the argument that emigration by last-born sons and daughters and their failure to marry in Hesse because of their small inheritance portions threatened the size of the population. In addition to the long- and short-term problems that this caused for military recruiters, commissioners considered this effect in light of rural labor shortages. As Landrat von Stockhausen put it, "Estates obviously suffer through reduction in hands which should cultivate and work them."[19] These shortages intensified as more and more troops departed for the American campaign.

The ideological sanctity of the "whole house" appeared in the criticisms made by commissioners as well. Von Stockhausen alluded to the legal inequity between children established by the ordinance as a violation of natural law.[20] To maintain the natural equality among siblings, housefathers contracted secret debts to fund dowries and establishments and thus burdened the heir more than he might have been otherwise. Fighting the "natural" inclinations of parents simply could not succeed.

Landgravial administrators also complained of violating rights of peasant housefathers to dispose estates in a just and dutiful manner. Fathers feared that heirs would fail to care for and educate their siblings adequately. As a result, they asserted, once the estate was turned over to the eldest son, conflicts would break out among siblings and family disharmony would reign. Accordingly, commissioners argued

18. StaM, B/5 3242, von Schenck zu Schweinsberg.
19. StaM, B/5 3242, von Stockhausen.
20. StaM, B/5 3242.

that "the state is not served in any way through institutions which disturb the peace in families and supports strife [*Zwietracht*] and hate between siblings."[21]

Exploding the harmony of the "whole house" had other practical consequences as well. Von Baumbach of Sontra reported that dispossessed sons not only left Hesse to work elsewhere, but among those who stayed "it is their general talk [*allgemeine Rede*], that because they will receive nothing from the estate they also do not want to work upon it, or even less, to serve their brothers as servants."[22] The Hufen edict not only eroded the authority of heirs and parents from above by taking from them decision-making powers, but it meant that they had no leverage with their children either. Conflicts thus impinged directly on the productivity of estates by severing credit relationships, disrupting social reproduction, and destroying parental authority over children and workers.

For any good cameralist, the ultimate issue remained that of productivity as measured by increases or decreases in the amount of revenues generated. The various disruptions of credit, reproduction, and family relations all meant that amounts of Kontribution that could be expected from rural householders diminished. For those noble and official members of the Diet's commission who were also important landlords in the region, whatever impinged upon military taxes also affected their own incomes and so it is no surprise that their reaction was strong and unanimous.

Investigating the Consequences of Conscription

The two reports that defended the Hufen edict admitted the existence of a crisis in the late 1770s.[23] Ernst Martin von Schlieffen, a member of the "Prussian Junta" brought in by Frederick and a coauthor of the Hufen edict, essentially pled for more time. Given the general poverty of the Hessian peasantry, he believed, six years simply did not allow enough time for the beneficial results of the inheritance legislation to appear. Von Malsberg, the other principal supporter of the act, suggested that the difficulties did not result from the edict or from poverty

21. StaM, B/5 3242, Regierung Kassel.
22. StaM, B/5 3242, von Baumbach zu Sontra.
23. StaM, B/5 3242, von Schlieffen.

but from the way military service had been organized. As a military man, he extolled the virtues of less selective conscription, but with service limited to shorter terms. For him, what frightened Hessian peasant youths into flight was not that they had virtually no chance for a good life, but that in this condition they became subject to involuntary military servitude of unlimited duration. Von Stockhausen echoed this concern but said it was a combination of poor prospects and potential military service that caused flight. This line of argument was significant because it encouraged the creation of a second commission charged by the Diet in December of 1785 with the task of investigating whether "the military system and the common welfare would profit eternally, if a specified term of service were gracefully instituted, after which the soldier might receive his release without cost."[24]

This second commission began its task under far better auspices than the first. Though the arguments of the first appeared overwhelming, it resulted in no action while Frederick II remained living. Frederick died six months before the second commission began its work. Because of the temperamental and philosophical differences between Frederick and his successor William IX, as well as the leverage that Diets had at the beginning of landgravial reigns, the prospect for the deconstruction of Frederick's military machine looked good.[25] Indeed, officials even resurrected the work of the first commission, which had gathered dust for several years, and so further work also began on a reformed Hufen edict. This work bore fruit in March 1786.

The Diet suggested that the contradictions between civil and military welfare, which became evident to them through the work of the commission on the Hufen edict, might be eased by setting specific limits to the time draftees could be forced to serve. In 6 December 1785, the privy council requested the local officials (*Landräte* and *Commissarii locorum*) to report how such a reform would change rural society and its ability to meet recruitment quotas.[26]

Although these officials complied with the privy council's request, many took the opportunity to offer wide-ranging criticisms and further proposals for changes which they deemed to be beneficial and consistent with the intentions of the Diet. As members of the Diet, many commissioners had helped to formulate the assignment given to the

24. StaM, B/4h 4072.
25. Karl E. Demandt, *Geschichte des Landes Hessen* (Kassel, 1959), 212–13.
26. StaM, B/4h 4072.

commission. Nineteen reports survive for our use—eleven from Land-räte, who were responsible for rural areas, and eight from the commissioners responsible for towns.[27] These reports represent the most detailed bureaucratic discussion of domestic military policy and its influence on Hessian social life that we have.

When they focused on military institutions, the officials who administered them could not maintain a consensus. Seven of the eleven rural administrators supported the proposal of the Diet, but three of these thought further measures would be necessary to promote both civil and military welfare as the Landgrave intended. Five of the eight city officials supported the proposal as well, but two of these thought more reforms were needed to buttress those already proposed by the Diet. Because there was wide disagreement about how the reforms would affect rural society, however, officials who had criticisms of the system might support the changes or might not. That there was some need for change seemed to be the only point of agreement.

Officials divided most sharply over the issue of the system of deferments and variable eligibility expressed in the bureaucratically-defined categories "expendable people" (*entbehrliche Leute*) and "indispensable personnel" (*unabkömmliche Mannschaft*). As explained earlier, the first were persons deemed sufficiently superfluous to rural production that they could be used in the line regiments which were leased for use in foreign wars by foreign powers. The second category was made up of men who were deemed to be sufficiently useful to keep within Hesse. Supposedly, commanders used such personnel only in garrison regiments and only in dire need. Seventeen out of nineteen reports expressed concern about the size of the pool of usable recruits. Some support for the Diet's proposal came from officials who thought that deferments unnecessarily restricted the size of this pool.

Perhaps the most enthusiastic supporter of defined terms of service, von Baumbach of Marburg, assumed that such limits rendered irrelevant all deferments and other selection criteria except the physical capacity to serve.[28] Von Baumbach believed that economic superfluity and social usefulness were functions of age and that young men who had passed their confirmation but had not married should be drafted because they served no other useful purpose. For him, the proposal

27. Uhlrich Friedrich Kopp, "Von Landräthen," *Teutsches Staats-Magazin* (1796): 108–71.
28. StaM, B/4h 4072, von Baumbach zu Marburg.

meant a large increase in the number of potential recruits. Several other reports supporting definite periods of service did not envision the elimination of deferments as an automatic result of that change. For them, adding such a provision to the proposal remained necessary to keep the pool of potential recruits large enough.[29] Most who argued in favor of removing deferments suggested that it would promote equality among the Landgrave's subjects, and thus keep potential recruits from fleeing because they believed the system was unfair.[30] Von Baumbach, however, captured another aspect of this way of thinking when he suggested that introducing universal short-term military service would reduce the blizzard of petitions for release or special treatment. It appears that he saw reform as a means of bureaucratic rationalization. Some resistance to defined terms of service arose because it promoted the principle of bureaucratic equality. Von Pappenheim argued that establishing equality with respect to military service would dissolve all other social boundaries and reduce the population to an unnatural condition.[31]

The deferments of the Hessian selective service system were an attempt to balance the interests of the social structure and to promote its productivity, while still providing troops for the Landgrave's subsidy adventures. Hessian officials argued about whether deferments: (1) protected both the strong and weak members of society and promoted their moral quality, (2) enhanced administrative efficiency, (3) fed economic productivity, (4) generated population growth. Officials also disagreed as to how proposed changes might affect each of these central concerns.

Protection of those who made the most significant contribution to the coffers of the landgravial state had been a major concern in past recruitment legislation. Surprisingly, this worry seemed somewhat muted in the commission's own deliberations. The issue was still an important one for regional officials because it touched them in their own pocketbooks, as well as the Landgrave's. Usually, officials sought ways of buttressing the social positions of the peasant elite and attempted to enhance or protect peasant productivity.

In order to protect the social and economic roles of the well-tenured,

29. StaM, B/4h 4072.

30. StaM, B/4h 4072, von Baumbach zu Sontra, von Baumbach zu Marburg, Kommisar Eigenbrodt.

31. StaM, B/4h 4072, von Pappenheim.

the Landgrave's local officials concentrated once again on the process of inheritance. Seven of the nineteen reports discussed the issue of deferments for the heirs of "sehr begütherte Bauern." In arguing against the reforms because they meant the end of deferments, von Stockhausen forcefully made the point that deferring the sons of the wealthy resulted in "the unification of the interests of householders and the military," something he felt "must be done."[32] As Hufen edict commissioner, von Schenck zu Schweinsberg had earlier argued, the unification of interests might come without reform if officials enforced the selective service system as it then existed and if the Landgrave reduced military manpower demands.[33]

Local officials also thought that the Landgrave needed to help well-off peasants make good marriages for their children. This concern, raised by nine of the reports finding their way to the Hessian privy council, was used primarily as an argument in favor of defined terms of service. Nevertheless, even those, like von Stockhausen, who had supported this reform in the earlier commission but now opposed it, still felt it was important to support marriage strategies that continued productive tenures. However, the Landräte asserted most frequently that the enhanced predictability of defined terms of service, along with release from the army which occurred between the ages of twenty-five and twenty-seven, would force peasant housefathers to make better marriage matches.[34] Von Baumbach went so far as to argue that defined terms of service could attract more wealth into the land.[35] Even foreign peasants might marry their daughters to Hessian youths if they could then count on getting out of the army in timely fashion.[36] He thought the reform would not only ease peasant marriage negotiations but might also prevent the efflux of dowry money to foreigners since Hessian fathers too could delight in having Hessian sons-in-law. In addition, he believed that changes might promote an influx of dowry wealth by encouraging the marriage of Hessian soldiers to foreign women.

Von Baumbach did not stop with the need to simplify the complexity

32. StaM, B/4h 4072, von Stockhausen.
33. Compare StaM B/5 3242 and LbK, Ms. Hass. 16a, H 34/76, H.C.E. Bopp with StaM, B/4h 4072, von Schenck zu Schweinsberg.
34. StaM, B/4h 4072, von Baumbach zu Sontra, von Keudel, Kommissar Eigenbrodt, von Biedenfeld.
35. StaM, B/4h 4072, von Baumbach zu Marburg.
36. Ibid.

of marriage negotiations. Ending deferments and universalizing service for a set term of years meant that "early marriage would cease finally."[37] Apparently, peasants had combined early marriages with another corrupt practice mentioned by Landrat von Keudel. Those with small tenures avoided military service "by keeping plow teams in disproportion to the size of their estates." The draft law of 1762 and administrative orders surrounding its enforcement made a plow team an important qualification for military deferments.[38] Officials came to believe that any military service arrangement should leave adequate time for marriage, prevent early marriage, ensure that matches were not made to avoid the military service, and increase the likelihood that peasants made good marriages.

The relationship between marriage and recruitment was not simply a matter of protecting the marriage designs of the peasant elite. This consideration, which also appeared in limited forms in earlier recruitment legislation, was expressed by regional officials in their recommendations. For example, those opposing the end to deferments and the release from the army of people who had failed to win exemptions made the argument that should such people be immediately freed, "the land would be seeded with expendable people [*entbehrliche Leute*]."[39] This argument relied on the assumption that the army had become a warehouse for unproductive members of society — an assumption belied by the work of the commission on the Hufen edict. For bureaucrats educated in the theories of cameralism, the productivity of individuals was a moral issue.[40] In this view, the army collected and held immoral people, sequestering them from society. To release people of low moral quality threatened the corrupt society in general.

Those who wished to see the selective service system converted to a universal service system made a different kind of moral argument. Beside the endemic injustices of selective service systems, von Baumbach saw a less selective system as promoting moral behavior. Arguing in a mode reminiscent of the sixteenth-century princes who instituted militias, he asserted that "during their terms of service, youths would become accustomed to order, piety, and thriftiness, and otherwise

37. Ibid.
38. StaM, B/4h 4072, von Keudel; HLO 3.3.1786.
39. StaM, B/4h 4072, von Stockhausen.
40. Karl Pribram, *A History of Economic Reasoning* (Baltimore, 1983), 90ff.; Mack Walker, *German Home Towns* (Ithaca, 1971), 145–61; Mark Raeff, *The Well-Ordered Police State* (New Haven, 1983).

acquire more knowledge."[41] Universal military service helped to generalize such values. This same faith in the moral efficacy of military discipline turned many German armies into reformatories.[42] For example, von Schenck zu Schweinsberg reported the successful rehabilitation of one of two thugs (*Bösewichter*) he recruited to reform.[43]

A second moral argument arose out of the concern that local administrators had for weaker members of society. Von Keudel echoed the intention expressed in the canton ordinance of 1762 that widows not be deprived of sons to work their tenures.[44] Others singled out for protection included older people who were not supporting themselves. Urban commissioners expressed this sentiment most strongly. Protecting these elements had a strong fiscal strain beside the moral one. Tenures left in the hands of widows or weak old people could not produce as much tribute as those that were in the hands of the vigorous and the competent.

Third, the poor also received attention as a group which required some consideration. Von Baumbach of Sontra believed that the elimination of deferments and the strict limitations on the length of service would keep poor men from fleeing Hesse-Cassel. More important, the same changes provided them the opportunity to learn alternative means of earning their upkeep rather than staying in the army until they could do nothing else.[45] Such an argument appealed to military commanders who wished to rid themselves of the obligation to provide for the old and invalid soldiers in their regiments. Also, concealed under this worry for the weak might have been the specter of growing charity rolls in the localities. This consideration emerges explicitly as commissioners fretted about quartering invalids and soldiers' wives in their towns.[46]

As I have suggested, policies designed to protect specific social groups inevitably involved the Hessian fisc. Educated as cameralists, these men recognized the close association between the economic

41. StaM, B/4h 4072, von Baumbach zu Marburg; Gunther Thies, *Territorialstaat und Landesverteidigung: Das Landesdefensionswerk in Hessen-Kassel unter Landgraf Moritz* (Marburg, 1973); Gerhard Oestreich, *Geist und Gestalt des frühmodernen Staates* (Berlin, 1978), 290–310.

42. Eugen von Frauenholtz, *Entwicklungsgeschichte des Deutschen Heerwesens* 4, "Die Heere in der Zeitalter des Absolutismus" (Munich, 1940), 13–14.

43. StaM, B/17e Langenstein 72.

44. StaM, B/4h 4072, von Keudel.

45. StaM, B/4h 4072, von Baumbach zu Sontra.

46. StaM, B/4h 4072, Kommissar von Schotten, Kommissar von Holtzapfel.

welfare of the population and the revenue of the state. Their concern manifested itself in two ways. Some argued that direct fiscal outlays should be reduced and that releasing soldiers after specific and relatively short terms of service would lessen the number of pensions paid out of the treasury of the Karlshaffen Lazarette. The problem with pensions was mentioned in seven of the reports. This concern may have arisen because this treasury was also a source of credit patronage for officials. Two reports suggested that the pensions should have been increased, a proposal that seems strangely out of character.[47]

Though some officials directed their attention toward the reduction of state expenses such as pensions and army size, most worried over the preservation or enhancement of state revenues. The opinions of these officials divided over whether the current system or the system designed to replace it best preserved the productivity of peasant tenures. Eleven of the nineteen statements provided by the Landräte and the local commissioners argued about productivity and recruitment. Many regional administrators argued that both the old system and the proposed one harmed families and the "whole house." Repeating some of the insights gained by the commission on the Hufen edict, von Baumbach zu Sontra described how families had been hurt by what had happened to soldiers in garrison regiments during the crisis years of the American subsidy campaign. When the Landgrave ordered garrison regiments to America in 1776 "they consisted almost entirely of completely indispensable people" and losing them "meant entire families were ruined . . . tenures became wastes . . . and the revenues were completely lost."[48] Both the labor and the management skills of the lost soldier became issues under these circumstances. Commissioner Holtzapfel of Eschweg emphasized "the lost help through which the subsistence of a soldier's parents was injured" when he was caught up in military service indefinitely.[49] Others found the absentee management of tenures for soldiers a problem if deferments for heirs were eliminated.[50]

Six investigators mentioned the difficulties of hiring and keeping servants resulting from military personnel policy. Von Pappenheim bitterly attacked the size of company auxiliaries (*Übercomplette*) be-

47. StaM, B/4h 4072, von Stockhausen, von Pappenheim.
48. StaM, B/4h 4072, von Baumbach zu Sontra.
49. StaM, B/4h 4072, von Holtzapfel.
50. StaM, B/4h 4072, von Schenck zu Schweinsberg, von Stockhausen.

cause they often contained "the poorer and poorest classes, such as those who serve as servants, or otherwise try to make their way." He pointed out that householders refused to hire soldiers because they took "advantage of their outside [military] relationships" or because they were "taken away at the most inopportune times, whereby the employer (needing to hire servants) is quickly put into the position of having no agricultural labor which he can hire inside Hesse, but [must] use either foreigners, or less frequently, otherwise useless people."[51] Extending the 1779 arguments of von Malsberg and von Stockhausen, *Oberst* von Münchausen of Rinteln argued in favor of defined service terms, and (unlike von Pappenheim) suggested that the prospects of lifelong service in the military scared so many people into emigration that it was necessary for employers to hire foreigners at considerably higher cost.[52] The Hessian Landgrave doomed his poorer subjects to military service and then peasants replaced them by hiring outsiders.

Added to labor problems caused by the conscription law of 1762, the financial burden placed upon the family of a conscripted soldier was also noted by officials. Garrison regiments remained a particular problem because they paid so little and expected the soldier to provide for his own personal equipment. Von Keudel pointed out that "there are still different [people] in the garrison regiments who are not able to subsist."[53] He wanted to transfer them to field regiments where the pay was better and where the regiment provided more of the equipment — something which would not have found sympathy among earlier commissioners who had argued against having poor people in the army because of that expense. But even so, having a son enrolled could be a problem, in the view of von Baumbach of Sontra who saw that parents bearing such costs made "continuing tribute payments by having to support their sons in the military estate, because they cannot live on their wages."[54] Addressing this issue, and at the same time proposing an institutional change which would find sympathy among the managers of military units (*Chef*), Landrat von Biedenfeld suggested strengthening the central institutions of *Kompaniewirtschaft*.[55] Though von Biedenfeld advocated the intensified use of *Lohnwacht*, in which com-

---

51. StaM, B/4h 4072, von Pappenheim.
52. StaM, B/4h 4072, von Münchausen.
53. StaM, B/4h 4072, von Keudel.
54. StaM, B/4h 4072, von Baumbach zu Sontra.
55. StaM, B/4h 4072, von Biedenfeld.

manders held soldiers' wages in company treasuries as a surety against desertion and other expenses, he did so in such a way as to imply that the practice would function better with shortened terms of service. Von Pappenheim promoted the same solution as an alternative to defining service terms and ending deferments.[56]

If having a son in the military was an expensive proposition in the eyes of Hessian local officials, getting him out could also be a burden and a threat to family welfare. Both von Pappenheim and von Keudel mention peasants bribing officials to acquire releases for their sons under the current system.[57] Peasants paid bribes in addition to the legal release and marriage permission fees collected by the owners of companies. Even the permitted fees charged became burdensome and disrupted family planning, in the eyes of some Landräte.[58]

A final set of concerns related to conscription and to the productivity of households came directly from the resolution passed by the Diet. Along with desertion, the incapacity of male youth to finish occupational training had been an important issue for the Diet. As a result, it received consideration in twelve of the nineteen reports and seven of the eight from urban officials. Although the Diet had expressed this concern in terms of artisanal apprenticeships, the Landräte raised the issue of training farmers as well. For example, in warning against establishing overly-long careers in the army, Landrat von Meysereberg argued that "farmers and artisans would lose the vital practice time if they were obliged to spend an unbroken string of years in military service."[59] On the other side, von Dalwick argued that short terms of service were acceptable because a youth who learned a trade, spent three years in the army, and received his release when he was 27 or 28 could "still establish himself and worry about his household economy . . . [and] similarly the eldest sons of peasants could serve for some years."[60] For those completely opposed to the proposed reform, deferments rather than the timing of service solved the problem of training.[61]

For some, the perceived disruption of the training schedules of apprentices necessarily affected production and the size of welfare

56. StaM, B/4h 4072, von Pappenheim.
57. StaM, B/4h 4072, von Pappenheim, von Keudel.
58. StaM, B/4h 4072, Burgrath von Köln, von Münchausen.
59. StaM, B/4h 4072, von Meysereberg.
60. StaM, B/4h 4072, von Dalwick.
61. StaM, B/4h 4072, von Pappenheim, von Stockhausen.

rolls. Von Baumbach of Sontra warned that unlimited service meant that soldiers who became grey in the service of their Landgrave's avarice found that they were not "able to feed themselves and their wives with the work of their own hands."[62] Recognizing these conditions, many simply never married and "thus the population of the territory suffer[ed] serious interruption."[63] So, the possibility that old veterans would end up on the welfare rolls, combined with another deep interest typical of eighteenth-century bureaucrats — that of population increase — intensified the interest in reforming the military system.

The issue of conscription and population growth was a central concern for the commission on the Hufen edict and was raised again by the Diet's commission on terms of military service in a number of different contexts. In the earlier investigation, the primary worries were emigration of dispossessed children and disrupted reproduction by those who remained. Members of the later commission singled out the food-producing class (*Hauptnahrungsstand*) as the group most in need of protection from these twin evils. As might be expected, officials who voiced these concerns found the old system overly disruptive and, thus, harmful to the general welfare (*Gemeinenwohl*). Nevertheless, von Stockhausen, who generally opposed the intentions of the Diet, pointed out that limiting the terms of service of the less expendable and less dispensable members of garrison regiments could have beneficial results for food producers. Von Stockhausen went on to qualify his support, however, by questioning whether reduced terms of service would actually promote "the reproduction of the sons of the principal food-producing classes."[64]

Those who focused on emigration as a difficulty were considerably less equivocal. Von Baumbach of Marburg, whose bailiwick had been heavily hit by the flight of draft-eligible males (according to the figures of the census of 1793), criticized the selective service system because of the fear it created. "Many hundreds of people" fled because of the prospects of long-term military service and therefore the population "upon which the state places so much" was reduced.[65] As we shall see, von Baumbach's analysis on this matter did not cut very deeply.

62. StaM, B/4h 4072, von Baumbach zu Sontra.
63. StaM, B/4h 4072.
64. StaM, B/4h 4072, von Stockhausen.
65. StaM, B/5 2107, shows that of 188 draft dodgers from Oberhessen in 1793, 141 came from von Baumbach's area. B/4h 4072, von Baumbach zu Marburg.

The report of Commissioner Eigenbrodt did cut more deeply on most issues raised by the reform proposal. Eigenbrodt opened the door to a somewhat more complicated account of the effects of conscription in the countryside, by combining the insights of the earlier commission on the Hufen edict with those of his own. In the first place, instead of being chained to the analytic categories of the canton ordinance — dispensable or indispensable, or for that matter, wealthy or poor — Eigenbrodt made a real attempt to identify who it was that fled to avoid the draft. In Schaumberg, the very region Ernst Martin von Schlieffen had singled out as an example of how the Hufen edict should have worked for both peasant land holders and the military, Eigenbrodt saw little but disaster. Though he thought his charges "love[ed] their fatherland and their homes," last born sons emigrated "as soon as they are only partially grown-up and hold themselves to be vulnerable to the military" because "they have less to lose here in their homeland."[66] Here, Eigenbrodt identified an important administrative contradiction for a recruitment policy based on family intervention. If such a system concentrated on those who had the least stake in it, then the administration was inviting difficulties by challenging the loyalty of just those people who found it easiest to flee to avoid its clutches. As the first commission had argued, the system needed a way to bind its victims — to create seatedness (*Ansäßigkeit*).[67] The insularity of the peasants and their sentiments of patriotism were simply not enough.

For Eigenbrodt the problem of binding draft-eligible males was created by the Hufen edict. Both because of the fear of military service and because of their small portion, last born sons sought "their future well-being as servants or through some other business outside [Hesse-Cassel] where they could get more income than they risked losing through the confiscation of their inheritance portions."[68] The emigration of the disinherited not only created difficulties in filling regimental rosters, but also forced housefathers to hire servants from the very regions to which their sons fled.

Eigenbrodt proposed the elimination of deferments for heirs, defined terms of service, and a return to unreformed inheritance practices. He wanted tenured heirs designated early and chosen on the basis of skill rather than age. He believed that heirs should serve in the army, along

66. StaM, B/4h 4072, Kommissar Eigenbrodt.
67. StaM, B/5 3242, von Stockhausen.
68. StaM, B/4h 4072, Eigenbrodt.

with their disinherited brothers for terms short enough to assure they could acquire the necessary training to make them useful subjects. Finally, he argued for increased portions for non-heirs so that the threat of confiscation for draft-evasion would have some meaning. In this view, military service would be converted to a stage in the life of most young males rather than an obligation restricted to the dispossessed classes in the rural population over whom administrators had far less control. Despite his greater capacity for empathetic analysis, Eigenbrodt remained bound by the logic and systematically distorted language of the fisc and his solutions were only apparently more humane.

The Reforms

Reform, when it came, took very much the shape which Commissioner Eigenbrodt had hoped that it would. In March 1786, William IX issued a new Hufen edict because, as he put it, "many last born children must leave their paternal estate with no patrimony [*erblos*] which causes very many and manifest complaints."[69] The reform permitted division in the case of necessity (*Notfall*), that is, to relieve debt and only if estates were big enough to begin with. Estates of thirty Ackers (circa twenty acres) could be divided in half, larger ones could be quartered. No estate was to be allowed that was less than a half an Acker. Designating the heir once again became the task of parents. Assessment of the value of the estate which parents divided equally would be based upon "actually valued prices" (*eigentlich wahren Preise*) rather than "true value" (*wahren Werth*) or assessed cadastral values. Market valuation, then, became the standard and one that officials expected would increase the portions of the dispossessed. The law once again established the legality of retirement portions (*Auszug* or *Altenteil*) where previously they had been customary simply on the basis of dire need. Finally, peasants had to confirm their marriage contracts and inheritance arrangements before landgravial courts and the terms of inheritance treaties henceforth would be entered in court records of mortgages and debts (*Hypothekenbücher*).

Reform of military administration began in 1788 with a law that redivided the administrative labor among three divisions, one of which

69. StaM, HLO 21.4.1786.

handled money matters, another handled personnel matters, and a third handled equipment and remounts.[70] More important for the kin-ordered households of the Hessian countryside, William IX authorized a law in November 1789 which limited terms of service to a maximum of twelve years. He ordered company commanders to clear their rosters of "the household's least expendable people."[71] All provisions of the law took effect in 1794, the same year he abolished garrison regiments and reestablished the militia.[72] These reforms instituted a system of graded levies based on "expendability" while at the same time eliminating all deferments. The least expendable people served only in the militia, while the most remained subject to subsidy army service. Military service became a truly universal obligation and an expected stage of life for youths from the countryside.

The Meaning of Crisis and Reform

As the military subsidy system defended the liberties of Englishmen, Frederick's reforms diminished those of Hessian elites and the peasants they ruled. The liberties of Hessian nobles and civilian officials shrank as the landgrave created a system of checks and balances which circumscribed the free play of patrimonial authority in administering military taxation and recruitment. Second, Frederick's reforms centralized the distribution of benefits from the subsidy system in the hands of himself and his family. Additionally, the liberty of house-fathers faded as the Landgrave acquired the rights in persons to the military service of their younger sons by redefining those eligible for military service from "masterless servants" to "the household's most expendable people." The Hufen edict circumscribed the rights of peasant housefathers to distribute their surpluses in the form of inheritance portions and further diminished the interstices of the tributary system in which kin-ordering of production might take place.

The reforms of William IX did not reverse the diminution of liberty in Hesse-Cassel. The new cadasters remained in place and continued to be an important standard of measurement for officials. The free play of the "patrimonial officialdom" did not regain its former strength and,

70. StaM, HLO 30.12.1788.
71. StaM, HLO 15.9.1789.
72. StaM, HLO 14.1.1794.

indeed, as the system of administrative information-gathering and cross-checking gained momentum, the prestige of noble Landräte grew increasingly superfluous. The Landgrave did not replace these patrimonial officials as they died or resigned and some of their private jurisdictional rights came to be administered in trust by the Landgrave's domainal officials.[73] Direct participation in the benefits of the subsidy money also shrank as William IX continued Frederick's direct attack on the exercise of company management (*Kompaniewirtschaft*).[74] Furthermore, limits on peasant authorities also continued as "expendability" and "indispensability" of household members remained crucial categories in determining military service obligations. What is more, the new Hufen edict did not renounce the right to order inheritance legislation, but merely sought to limit damage done by a poor job of it.

Aside from mitigating the worst consequences of direct intervention with aristocrats, officials, and peasant householders, the reforms of William IX did contribute to a peculiarly German idea of freedom. In finessing and frustrating aristocratic criticism of the Hessian subsidy system, William IX ensured that it remained a festering political sore as long as the principality had independent existence. But William also succeeded in defining the terms in which that debate took place. The Hessian aristocracy had to recast its claims to subsidy benefits in terms of the rights of the Hessian state which they now distinguished sharply from the Landgrave's personal wealth. After 1779, members of the Diet made the argument that wealth generated by the service and suffering of subjects belonged not to the Landgrave but to the state. "Liberty" in this context came to mean being a subject of an abstraction rather than of a person. The debate over title to subsidy wealth continued into the 1830s, and it helped to define the quality of Hessian liberalism.[75]

The notion of liberty as subjection to a rational bureaucratic state rather than to a person showed another important aspect in public peasant criticism of military recruitment policy. Peasant gravamens from the Diet of 1815 complained not of the violation of their liberties as parents but rather of the failure to completely universalize military

73. StaM, H/225., Rothamel; B/340, von Schenck zu Schweinsberg A 10 1795–1803.

74. StaM HLO 15.7.1784, 15.4.1787.

75. Hollenberg, "Landstände und Militär," 111–12.

obligations. Complaints thus focused upon the continued exemption of noble household servants (*adelige Hintersaßen*) and amounted to a request that conscription be administered without respect to personal relations.[76]

Such an attitude is even more sharply reflected in the first exhaustive and systematic account of subsidy militarism by Friedrich Kapp.[77] In the second edition to his famous work *The Soldier Trade of German Princes,* Kapp published a letter to a liberal political ally in which he associated the military-fiscalism of territorial princes with what he called a "sovereignty swindle." Here, he referred to the claim of these territorial princes to rights associated with state leadership. The letter, written in 1874, was paean to the "liberation" of Germans from the personal rule of these petty tyrants by the Prussian prince and his bureaucracy. No longer would German resources be dissipated in the treasuries of its princely aristocrats. No longer would long-suffering soldiers and their families sacrifice uselessly to strengthen the other states of Europe. All Germans could devote their resources and sacrifices to a state which would express and extend their power as a culture. This notion of liberty is a far cry from the liberties of Englishmen, but at the same time directly resulted from the defense of them.

Although the last three chapters have offered a critical account of the political theory and administrative practice of eighteenth-century Hessian subsidy militarism, the narrative has been largely an accounting of production and division of spoils for the Hessian tributary elites. As such, it remains a master's narrative to which little critical pressure has been applied. For a more profoundly critical account we need to turn from the receivers of benefits to payers of costs — those rural dwellers practicing kin-ordered production who generated the human beings as well as the animal and vegetable surpluses upon which the entire system was founded.

76. Eihachiro Sakai, *Der kurhessische Bauer im 19. Jahrhundert und die Grundlastenablösung* (Melsungen, 1967), 143.
77. Friedrich Kapp, *Der Soldatenhandel deutscher Fürsten* (Berlin, 1874), i–iv.

Part III

The Military System and the Peasant Elite between Kin and Tribute, 1736–1793

In telling the masters' tale of the Hessian military system and its articulations with the peasant society on which it fed, I used the cameralists' official categories of "community" and "household" to frame the kin-ordered mode of production. To give life to the categories and to rid them of their abstract, false clarity, I must discuss how people ordered their work, created surpluses, and distributed rewards and sanctions. The interests of a "thick description" of text and context require a narrower focus of vision to render the amount of data manageable. While this focus on regional and parish stages inevitably sacrifices some of the certainty in result, the approach has some merit. The perspective from below necessarily had local, segmented aspects while overviews belonged to the directors of tributary systems. Only the gaps in the system provided room for kin-ordered enterprises.

I selected the region of Oberhessen because of the survival of the papers of Landrat von Schenck zu Schweinsberg. This documentation is far richer and more continuous than any other which springs from localities at that time. Von Schenck's family, one of the oldest noble families of the landgraviate, exercised judicial overlordship and landlordship, and operated extensive manorial estates in the region, so that they had a well-developed bureaucracy of their own that had been documenting peasant life long before the military subsidy system came to play a substantial role in the lives of their rural subjects. As a well-integrated part of von Schenck's jurisdiction, the parish of Oberweimar seemed an apt choice because its nine villages offered a broad variety of community and household types unavailable in parishes of only one or two villages. This variety means that work on the parish may make more valid claim to representativeness than might otherwise have been possible.

6 Peasant Production, Tributary Authority, and the Power of the Peasant Elite

In this description of the political economy of peasant life in the Oberhessian countryside, I once again choose to work from the top down. I direct attention to the levers of power and influence which grew out of the kin-ordered mode of production and which some peasant decision makers put to use in the rural households of the region before 1762. These levers grew from three different kinds of process: (1) peasant production, (2) articulations with tributary authority, and (3) social reproduction. I assess the impact of military institutions on these levers and argue that before the reforms of 1762–73 some peasant householders found their own authority and wealth enhanced by the system. Finally, I hope to provide an indication of the structures of rural society which grew from peasant life under systems of kin and tribute.

Peasant Production

Since the Thirty Years War, the region of Oberhessen has impressed most observers with its poverty. This area of 1100 square kilometers, located eighty kilometers north of Frankfurt am Main, did not become a food-exporting region until near the end of the eighteenth century and only during times of dearth elsewhere.[1] In 1782, most of its nearly

1. George Thomas Fox, "Studies in the Rural History of Upper Hesse" (Ph.D. diss., Vanderbilt University, 1976), 11.

50,000 inhabitants wrested a meager existence out of the rough, stony soils of this heavily forested mountain region.[2] The poor natural endowment of most of the region helped to inspire the proverb "Where the Dutch and Hessians are poor, no one can grow anything more," which may indicate a grudging admiration for the ingenuity of Hessian farming under poor conditions.[3] Forests provided the Hessian nobility one of its few sources of big money during the nineteenth century.[4] To protect this resource from overuse and to monopolize it for the region's ruling classes, the Landgrave erected a body of legislation.

A few lucky villages such as Niederweimar, located where the valleys of the Lahn or Eder and their major tributaries broadened out, relieved the overall picture of poor soils on steep inclines. These areas usually contained the rich sandy loams characteristic of bottom lands in the region. The few villages of the Ebsdörfergrund and the Amöneburger-becken (both broad-floored basins with dark soils) experienced the best crop yields for the entire region.

The nine villages of parish Oberweimar lay immediately to the south of the region's major town, market, and administrative center — Marburg an der Lahn. Two villages, Gisselberg and Niederweimar, occupied bottom lands on the west bank of the Lahn. The remaining seven clung to the southern slopes of the Lahnberg — a basaltic uplift that nearly isolated Marburg from the surrounding villages. The soils of the parish ranged from poor to moderately good, according to a 1799 report made by Conrad Friedrich Rothamel.[5]

Rural economic enterprise took varied forms of mixed livestock and grain farming supplemented by rural industry. Peasant farms consisted of strips of land in open fields, part of a three-field rotation system in which farmers plowed and harvested collectively.[6] On poorer soils with steeper inclines, production reverted to the two-field system because manure washed off the slopes and slowed the recovery on fallow fields (*Brachfelder*). Peasants grew, in order of abundance, rye (*Korn*), barley (*Gersten*), oats (*Haffer*), and wheat (*Weizen*). In addition to working

2. StaM, B/5 2107, 1793, shows 70 percent living in villages rather than cities.

3. Karl E. Demandt, *Geschichte des Landes Hessen* (Kassel, 1959), 12.

4. Gregory Wick Pedlow, "The Nobility of Hessen-Kassel: Family, Land, and Office 1770–1870" (Ph.D. diss., Johns Hopkins University, 1980).

5. StaM, H/118, Rothamel 1799.

6. Uhlrich Möker, *Nordhessen im Zeitalter der Industriellen Revolution* (Vienna, 1977), 70–78; Hans Lerch, *Hessische Agrargeschichte des 17. und 18. Jahrhunderts* (Hersfeld, 1926), 94–102.

The parish of Oberweimar. Based on Hessisches Landesvermessungsamt, "Kreiskarte 1:100000:Marburg—Biedenkopf—Lahn/Dill Kreis" (Frankfurt, 1981).

cropland (*Ackerland*), peasants also grew hay (*Heu*) on meadows (*Wiesen*), and cabbages (*Kohl*), beets (*Ruben*) and other greens in smaller garden plots. Garden produce appeared to be the most marketable crops for peasants. From orchards and hop fields came the raw materials for beer, brandy, and cider which could be marketed locally or more broadly. Innkeepers, the wealthiest members of rural society, did most of the brewing and distilling.[7]

The prices of grains, though controlled by the landgravial state, rose throughout the century, punctuated by sharp rises and falls surrounding harvest failures. (See Graph 1.) The biggest price surges of the century occurred during the Seven Years War and the general European economic crisis and harvest failures of 1771–73.[8] Prices also peaked in 1713, 1740, and 1792–93. Except during the Seven Years War, Hessian price spikes seemed somewhat less sharp than those in Berlin. With price trends generally upward, peasant producers might have gotten more wealthy but there is little evidence that they did so — a fact probably explained by the increasingly extractive state.[9] Moreover, peasants probably did not market the bulk of their own grain crops. Rather, tributary overlords who collected tithes and groundrents in kind brought a large portion of the grain to market. Much of the harvest remained at home in household and village economies still dominated by subsistence imperatives.

Precise information on new techniques and crops actually in use is difficult to come by before the 1790s. Potatoes were probably introduced as a major crop sometime in mid-century. Kurt Scharlau dates the introduction of the potato for human consumption in Hesse to 1747.[10] Administrators during the Seven Years War ordered the stockpiling of potatoes and winter vegetables as a hedge against shortages of food (*Mangel des Lebensmittels*).[11] The importance of potatoes along with dairy products for the subsistence of peasant households — particularly marginal ones — cannot be overemphasized.[12] Other changes, such as planting fallows with nitrogen-fixing crops or more extensive

7. StaM, K/I 1746ff.

8. Fox, "Studies in the Rural History of Upper Hesse," 429–33.

9. Charles W. Ingrao, *The Hessian Mercenary State* (Cambridge, 1987), 203–4.

10. Kurt Scharlau, "Landeskulturgesetzgebung und Landeskulturentwicklung im ehemaligen Kurhessen seit dem 16. Jahrhundert," *Zeitschrift für Agrargeschichte und Agrarsoziologie* 2 (1954): 139.

11. StaM, HLO 28.11.1757.

12. Compare the Swiss in Robert Netting, *Balancing on an Alp* (Cambridge, 1981), 159–60.

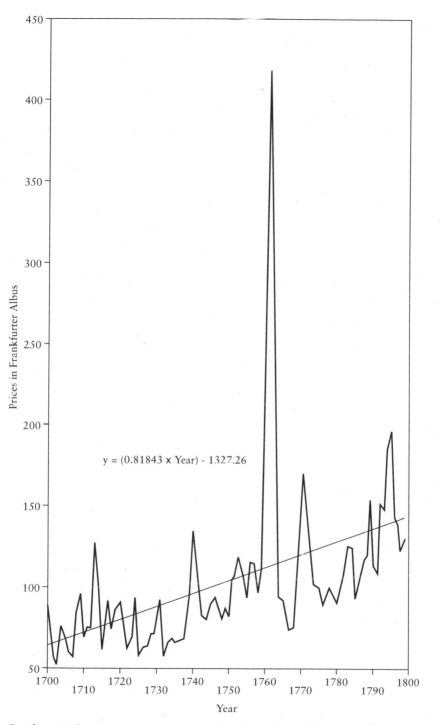

450

400

350

300

Prices in Frankfurter Albus

250

200

$y = (0.81843 \times \text{Year}) - 1327.26$

150

100

50

1700   1710   1720   1730   1740   1750   1760   1770   1780   1790   1800

Year

Graph 1. Marburg rye prices, 1700–1799. Data from George Thomas Fox, "Studies in the Rural History of Upper Hesse" (Ph.D. diss., Vanderbilt University, 1976), pp. 429–33.

manuring developed from stall feeding, appeared later in the century but apparently spread only at a snail's pace.[13] The slow rate of agricultural intensification suggests the inflexibility of the agricultural tribute-taking system, militarily-caused labor shortages, and an endemic shortage of investment capital.

Oberhessen's poor integration into the growing system of transregional markets in central Germany also provided little stimulus toward the sort of agricultural intensification that took hold in other parts of Europe and Germany at the same time. To the south lay the rich agricultural region of the Wetterau, which supplied Frankfurt grain dealers with enough grain so that they rarely appeared in Oberhessen except in times of dearth. The area around Marburg depended on Frankfurt as a market for produce and manufactured goods. Consequently, its currency remained bound to the Frankfurter gulden rather than to the currencies of other parts of the Landgrave's domains.[14] The city of Frankenberg in the northern part of Oberhessen had more ties to the Rhine valley. The two cities provided the largest regional markets while peasants also used village markets at Ebsdorf, Lohra, and Fronhausen. The latter two played some role for the peasants of Oberweimar even though Marburg was as close. Commodities found in city and village trading centers included grain, livestock, pottery, linen and wool in various stages of completion, and leather. Rural dwellers often produced manufactured goods in certain villages which specialized in pottery or leather or other particular products.[15] Jews provided a network of trans-local and itinerant livestock traders that tied the region to producers and consumers on the outside. Parishes such as Oberweimar might have one or two resident Jewish households that traded in cattle and processed meat as well as linking the parish to wider markets.[16]

To argue that Oberhessen remained an isolated backwater would be incorrect. The available transportation network did link this area with the Main valley to the south, the Rhineland to the west, and Leipzig and Saxony to the east. These roads provided the basis for both imperial and local postal systems; traders frequenting the fairs in Frankfurt and Leipzig used them as well. One of the main crossroads

---

13. Möker, *Nordhessen im Zeitalter der Industriellen Revolution*, 70–78.

14. Otto Berge, "Die hessische Währungsreform nach dem Siebenjährigen Krieg," *Hessische Heimat* 4 (1964): 10–12.

15. Fox, "Studies in the Rural History of Upper Hesse," 26.

16. StaM, K/I Allna 1746.

of the region lay in the parish of Oberweimar, and road traffic provided customers for eight inns in the villages of Gisselberg, Niederweimar, Oberweimar, and Allna. Allna had a postal station as well.[17]

Some households of Oberweimar raised livestock primarily for subsistence and others engaged in commodity production. The changing patterns of livestock usage after 1725 indicated that by 1775 more households than in the past kept small numbers of livestock, particularly cows, in order to supplement incomes earned through artisanal or day labor. During the middle years of the century, the number of cow herds with more than three animals (a size that appears to indicate a marketable surplus of dairy products) dropped from 88 in 1725 to 85 in 1773. Over the same period, the number of small herds with three animals or fewer increased from 35 to 47. The higher number of small herds on parish common meadows accompanied a slight growth in the number of animals from 755 in 1725 to 773 in 1773.[18] The importance of one or two cows for poor families must be seen in connection with the introduction of the potato as a foodstuff. A potato and milk gruel provided marginal households with an alternative protein source to bread grains whose cultivation in sufficient amounts required extensive arable land. Thus, a cow or two grazing on common lands combined with potatoes grown on their small parcels of land now made possible a meager existence for such cottagers.

We need not rely solely on the evidence of changes in the holding of cows to show that more poor households lived in villages at mid-century. Though there were clearly households in the parish that were raising swine for the market, with their herds of fifteen or more animals, swine production also had a subsistence sector. The number of pigs in the parish increased from 606 in 1725 to 945 in 1773, while the number of herds of eight or more animals increased from 29 to 49. Nevertheless, pig herds with fewer than three also increased from 38 to 52, which was consistent with a swelling subsistence sector in the villages. Larger herds, particularly those with eight or more adult animals, indicated production for a meat market. Despite growing numbers of small herds, people raising swine for their own use took up less of the mastage of common woodlands after 1747.[19]

17. StaM, K/I Allna 1746, Gisselberg 1747, Niederweimar 1747, Oberweimar 1747.
18. StaM, B/23b ALb, Reizberg 61, 1725, Hadamshausen 1773, Hermershausen 1773, Oberweimar 1773, Niederweimar 1773, and Weiershausen; B/17e Allna 1773, Kehna 9, Gisselberg 3, Cyriaxweimar 10.
19. Ibid., and K/I Allna 1746; etc.

In eighteenth-century Oberweimar, swine competed with the one animal that peasants nearly always raised as a marketable commodity — sheep. For some reason, as Oberweimar's peasant householders approached mid-century, larger sheep producers first got out of the business to some extent, returned to it, left it, and apparently returned to it once again. In 1725, peasants kept 26 herds of 30 or more sheep, in 1733 only 19, in 1747 up to 25, and back down to 16 in 1773. In 1793, the total number of sheep exceeded the figure for 1725 by 28.[20] This pattern of fluctuation suggests a response to the variations of the wool or mutton markets. It occurred despite nearly constant pressure by Hessian Landgraves to increase wool production. Ottfried Dascher has suggested that the military's demand for uniforms had beneficial effects on the wool market. Despite military orders, however, the wool industry went into a state of endemic crisis in the 1740s from which it began to recover only after 1785.[21] Erratic military demand certainly explained the surges in sheep populations in 1747 and 1793 when subsidy treaties came into effect, but it fails to account for the sharp drop that occurred in 1733. More significant is a negative correlation between the numbers of swine and of sheep, which suggested that these two animals competed for space on common grounds. If this was the case, then the positive response of better-off villagers to high wool prices threatened the space available for the pigs of the poor — particularly in the latter part of the century as the population grew.

During the eighteenth century economic pressure also increased on those middling types who had sufficient land or skills to support themselves without working for others, but who could not count themselves among the village's richer members. We find this trend reflected in the shifting usage of oxen and horses as draft animals. As David Sabean has noted, such shifts may signal new forms of cropping and new ties of dependence and cooperation.[22] The peasants of Oberweimar preferred horses to oxen as draft animals. Cadastral and census records show that wealthier families owned two and sometimes even three teams of horses, while families with modestly-sized holdings had to be satisfied with teams of oxen (Table 2). Among the poorer of these, we even find some who hitched their cows to plows.

20. Ibid., H/118 Rothamel, 1799.
21. Ottfried Dascher, *Das Textilgewerbe in Hessen-Kassel vom 16.-19. Jahrhundert* (Marburg, 1968), 110–19.
22. David Warren Sabean, *Property, Production, and Family in Neckarshausen, 1700–1870* (New York, 1990), and *Power in the Blood* (Cambridge, 1987), 11.

Table 2. The distribution of draft animals and the mean gross value of tenures in Oberweimar, 1747

Tenures with:	Number of tenures	Mean value (Sg)
2 or more horseteams	16	1228.1
2–3 horses	34	794.4
3 or more oxen[a]	7	527.0
1 oxteam	25	376.4
1 draft animal	2	278.0
Total animals	84	770.1

SOURCE: StaM, K/I Allna 1746, etc.

[a]Includes two estates that owned both oxen and horses.

Graph 2 shows that an increasing number of Oberweimar's farmers worked with ox-teams as the century progressed. Despite the relatively constant number of farmers owning plow-teams over the years 1725 to 1773, by the end of that period a majority of those with draft teams made do with oxen. Before that time, a majority had enjoyed the use of horses. This shift, to some extent, appears to be the result of an increasing difficulty in securing horses. A farmer explaining a loan request to the Landassistenzkasse in Kassel reported that it had been necessary to travel as far as Frankfurt to find horses in the years following the Seven Years War.[23] Yet foals were common enough to suggest that peasants could breed their own horses.[24] Hence, we may infer that the decline in the use of horse power resulted from the high costs in grain needed to feed horses—a sign of generally increased poverty or perhaps important changes in cropping.[25]

An apparent decline in rural artisan trades also affected middling families in the parish of Oberweimar. Many of the less wealthy families in the parish had combined a trade such as blacksmithing, barrelmaking, whitewashing, thatching, carpentry, or cabinetmaking with marginal farming and gardening activities. Most of these artisans joined the rural guilds of their respective trades. Indeed, law required such membership in order to practice many of these occupations. The number of parish families who had members belonging to guilds declined from 65 in 1747 to 43 in 1793.[26] The decline in the number of

23. StaM, B/23b ALb, Niederweimar 19.
24. StaM, B/23b ALb, Niederweimar 1773.
25. Sabean, *Property,* 54, 437–52.
26. StaM, K/I Allna 1746, etc., B/5 2107, 1793.

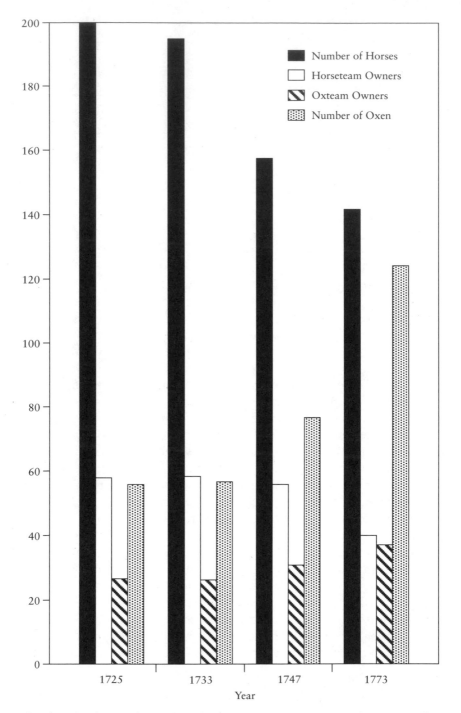

Graph 2. Draft animal usage in Oberweimar, 1725–73. Sources: StaM, K/I Allna 1746, etc., B/17e Allna 1773, etc. (Menschen- und Viehbestände), Reizberg 61, B/23b ALb Allna 1773, etc. (Menschen- und Viehbestände), B/40d, r29 n76.

guild members and in the number of people legally practicing skilled trades suggests that skilled workers may have been suffering a gradual slide into an economy of makeshift like the one described by Olwen Hufton.[27] In such an economy, poor persons practiced multiple semi-skilled and unskilled jobs along with seasonal begging rather than a single, more secure, skilled craft.[28]

The directors of kin-ordered production amassed wealth through rural proto-industrial production as well. Though glass, pottery, and wool all played some role in Oberhessian rural industry, the manufacture of linen was the largest rural industry. Indeed, aside from the marketing of soldiers, linen remained one of the few ways in which Hessian peasants became involved in international markets. Merchants assiduously sought Hessian linen, which brought high prices at fairs in Frankfurt and Leipzig.[29] As demand quickened in the eighteenth century, Bremen became the center of a brisk trade in the finest of Hessian products, a bleached white cloth that found its way to the British Isles, Spain, and the European colonies in the New World.

Spinning and weaving flax had long been part of the winter activity of peasant households and spinning bees. Most of the linen was used in the household, or to pay the servants, or to provide dowries for daughters. Cruder yarns and cloth had wider circulation in the sixteenth and seventeenth centuries. The standards of a rural guild had regulated quality. The state's active intervention to ensure quality and to establish the freedom of all to spin and weave led to shifts in the structure of production. Previously, wealthy households dominated linen manufacture, a trade in which they controlled every phase even though they practiced it only as a sideline (*Kaufsystem*). These enterprises made the fine cloths which reached distant markets through a network of merchants who traveled the countryside and purchased wares on the spot. As the market opened up, merchants took advantage of the situation by calling into existence weaving specialists who purchased their yarn instead of spinning it themselves. As trade quickened, merchants set up putting-out systems (*Verlagsystem*) and the poorest weavers who

27. Olwen Hufton, *The Poor in Eighteenth Century France 1750–1789* (Oxford, 1974).

28. Heinz Reif, "Vagierende Unterschichten, Vagabunden, und Bandenkriminalität im Ancièn Règiem," *Beiträge zur historischen Sozialkunde* 11 (1981): 27–35; StaM, B/49d, Marburg 12, 13, 14, 128, 186, 250, 316, 470, 490, 576.

29. Lerch, *Hessische Agrargeschichte,* 146.

rented equipment and bought their materials on credit became the largest group of producers.[30]

Oberhessen was not the most important Hessian linen region. In 1747, the region's farmers planted just over 7400 Ackers of flax, compared with 19,000 in Niederhessen or 9100 in Fulda.[31] None of the villages of parish Oberweimar had a large sector of linen producers at mid-century.[32] Only 10 families wove among more than 174. But, to the southeast of the parish, where von Schenck zu Schweinsberg had cultivated rural industry, the village of Wenckbach could brag of 12 weaving households among 38.[33] These households showed the typical tripartite division, five having more than twenty Ackers of land, three more than ten, and the remainder less than ten. The numbers of the latter increased as the century progressed even though they were special targets for military recruiters.

The means of generating wealth available to the directors of kin-ordered enterprises in Oberhessen varied widely. Although a wide range of income-producing activities existed, no single one appeared sufficient or dominant. Thus, families cobbled together many different sources of income. Even so, success appeared a relative matter for the most part, and less successful enterprises grew in numbers as the century progressed and markets became more complex and important for rural dwellers.[34] (See Table 3.) This development did not mean, however, that the large, multi-faceted productive enterprises of big peasants shrank in number (there were a few more of them) but only that the less well-off households increased in number more sharply than the better-off.

Articulations between Kin and Tribute

It may seem strange to see the exercise of tributary authority, which removed anywhere from one-third to two-thirds of the value of peasant production from their hands, as a resource for some members of kin-ordered enterprises. However, as David Sabean has pointed out, the exercise of authority (*Herrschaft*) was not a simple process of

30. Ibid., 135.
31. Ibid., 145.
32. StaM, K/I 1747.
33. StaM, B/49d Marburg 37; Wenckbach 1750.
34. Sabean, *Power in the Blood,* 7–9.

Table 3. Success and failure among the kin-
ordered households of Oberweimar, 1726–1747

Percent of families:	1725	1747
Wealthy (> 75 Ar)	27.6	29.2
Independent (> 17 Ar)	24.7	19.0
Poor (> o Ar)	35.6	33.9
No land or buildings	12.1	17.9

SOURCE: StaM, K/I Allna 1746, etc. 17e Reizberg
61.

extracting resources by force. Rather, tributary authorities needed to "evoke obedience" through a series of exchanges of protection (*Schutz und Schirm*) for service.[35] Peasant villages and their officials played a crucial role in mediating these exchanges. Those who acted as mediators became privileged in relation to other members of their communities. As Werner Troßbach has shown for the Vogelsberg southeast of Hesse-Cassel, peasant mediators parlayed their positions as brokers of authority into political and economic advantage.[36]

Rural communities in Oberhessen consisted of two overlapping social groupings: the incorporated village (*Gemeinde*) and the community of village residents. On the one hand, the Gemeinde represented the legal personality of the village. It had a distinct geographic territory with carefully defined borders and consisted of a group of householders who held seats on the village council. Ideally, the council protected community interests and supervised such common resources as buildings, woodlands, meadows, cropland, and fishing rights. In addition, they controlled at least two different treasuries.[37] Enfranchised villagers (*Gemeindemänner*) also oversaw village morals — a

35. Ibid. 21ff.; Otto Brunner, *Land und Herrschaft: Grundfragen der territorialen Verfassungsgeschichte Österreichs im Mittelalter* (Darmstadt, 1984), 394–98.

36. Werner Troßbach, *Soziale Bewegung und politische Erfahrung: Bäuerlicher Protest in hessischen Territorien, 1648–1806* (Weingarten, 1987), 228–40.

37. Karl Siegfried Bader, *Dorfgenossenschaft und Dorfgemeinde; Studien zur Rechtsgeschichte des mittelalterlichen Dorfes* 2 (Cologne, 1958), and "Dorf und Dorfgemeinde im Zeitalter von Naturrecht und Aufklärung," in *Festschrift für Karl Gottfried Hügelmann* (Aalen, 1959), 1–35; Heide Wunder, *Die bäuerliche Gemeinde in Deutschland* (Göttingen, 1986); Herbert Reyer, *Die Dorfgemeinde im nördlichen Hessen, Untersuchung zur hessischen Dorfverfassung im Spätmittelalter und in der frühen Neuzeit* (Marburg, 1983); John Theibault, "Coping with the Thirty Years War: Villages and Villagers in Hesse-Kassel 1600–1680" (Ph.D. diss., Johns Hopkins University, 1986).

role which some reinforced by also becoming part of the parish consistory as church elders (*Kirchenältester*). For the purposes of moral supervision, village councils appointed officials who answered to the landgravial administration and other institutions in the Hessian system of Herrschaft.[38] Their accountability to both the state and other instituted forms of domination made village councils an important instrument in extracting surpluses as tribute.

On the other hand, in nearly all villages a minority of householders lacked seats on the council although they worked and held rights to land and other resources in the village. In 1747, disenfranchised households in Oberweimar were 37 percent of all households. This climbed to 42 percent or more by 1799.[39] These villagers and their families paid taxes and tribute and contributed to the village's wider social identity. This more extensive community of householders became the focus of census takers and tax collectors concerned with gathering information for the state.[40]

The disenfranchised householders generally occupied subordinate economic and social positions as well as legal ones. Some received legal recognition of their status and were called *Beisitzer*. Such persons paid fees and acquired certain commons use rights.[41] Normally, these were rights to use small sites for cottages and to graze livestock on the common meadows. Most Beisitzer became permanent residents; many were related by ties of kinship and dependence to other villagers. The better-off villagers employed them or patronized their skilled or semi-skilled trades.

Others who received legal recognition as village residents were the more-or-less itinerant shepherds, swineherds, and cowherds found frequently on the lists of inhabitants and in the tax records.[42] The village council hired them to manage the herds that grazed on common grounds. They included shepherds who owned substantial flocks of their own and who paid the village council for the privilege of grazing within the community boundaries.[43] Although some of the better-off shepherds acquired both land and the more settled Beisitzer status,

38. StaM, HLO 11.6.1739, Reyer, *Die Dorfgemeinde*, 113–24.
39. StaM, K/I Allna 1746, etc.
40. Ibid., B/23b ALb, Schweinsberg, 1773.
41. StaM, B/23b ALb, Oberwalgern, 1783.
42. StaM, K/I Allna 1746, etc.; B/17e Allna 9.
43. Wolfgang Jacobeit, *Schafhaltung und Schäfer in Zentraleuropa bis zum 20. Jahrhundert* (Berlin, 1961), 353–66.

most remained in the condition of Johann Friedrich Mahr who moved from Hesse-Darmstadt to serve as herdsman (*Viehhirt*) in Oberweimar for five years before moving on somewhere else.[44] Those persons living in the village illegally and without permission obviously had even more itinerant and marginal lives. Often, soldiers and their wives or lovers found themselves in this position after returning home from a campaign.[45]

In mid-eighteenth century Oberhessen, enfranchised villagers dominated the disenfranchised because the latter could make ends meet only through their ties of dependence with the better-off. The system of authority and domination in village corporations rested on three legs. (1) As part of the system of tributary Herrschaft, the village corporation and its officials acquired the power to use sanctions against other villagers. The same position established ties of patronage to tributary lords who protected the village from a variety of possible intrusions. (2) The capacity of enfranchised villagers to act in concert thwarted undesirables from taking up residence in villages and protected common resources from the village poor. (3) Finally, control over common resources gave the dominant group in any village a way of selecting who might survive as an independent household in the village and under what conditions.

Before the reforms of Frederick II, both military recruitment and taxation could be used to reinforce each of these legs. As yet another aspect of tributary authority from which peasants needed protection, the threat of military service was used as a sanction against certain community members. Kontribution was another source of cash flow into village treasuries, and peasants willing to collect it could use it as a risky way to alleviate temporary monetary needs.

Three other structures for evoking obedience that were common to Europe's tributary societies also enhanced the authority of the enfranchised members of Oberhessian villages. These were landlordship (*Grundherrschaft*), labor lordship (*Dienstherrschaft*), and jurisdictional lordship (*Gerichtsherrschaft*).[46] Each requires a separate discussion. The importance of a fourth form of domination, personal heredi-

---

44. StaM, K/I Allna 1746; B/17e Allna 18.

45. Otto Könnecke, *Rechtsgeschichte des Gesindewesens in West- und Süddeutschland* (Marburg, 1912), 68–69.

46. Lerch, *Hessische Agrargeschichte*, 13–84; Eihachiro Sakai, *Der kurhessische Bauer im 19. Jahrhundert und die Grundlastenablösung* (Melsungen, 1967).

tary servitude (*Leibeigenschaft*), is difficult to assess and will be left out of the discussion.[47]

The Hessian landed aristocracy also practiced direct domain management (*Gutsherrschaft*), but it tended to undermine the control exercised by peasant big men.[48] In Oberweimar, the Gutsherr von Heydwolf used his two shares in the commons to control how many sheep were grazed on village meadows. The villagers of Hadamshausen protested the size of the von Heydwolf herd and cited it as the reason for the small size of their own herds. In addition, the need of the self-administered von Heydwolf estates for day labor and artisanal support seems also to have altered the social structure of both Oberweimar and Hadamshausen, where those estates lay. Overall, these villages had far more marginal households than did similar-sized villages in the parish where the presence of the local Gutsherr was less palpable. Village councils generally tried to limit the number of such marginal households because of the drain on the common resources that they represented. These cases illustrate the threat posed to village authority from above. This threat also extended to the practitioners of other kinds of Herrschaft who had a strong interest in limiting the independence of village officials. Because the lords needed to use hirelings and they were dependent on village officials to administer the process of tribute-taking, however, other forms of Herrschaft tended to enhance village authority rather than erode it.

Grundherrschaft was a complicated set of tributary obligations taken in money and in kind.[49] Generally, obligations of this sort grew out of the conditions of land tenure and most originated in the middle ages or later. More recent obligations often had their roots in credit and credit-like transactions between lord and peasant, patron and client and rested as liens against the peasants' land. One of the most long-standing of all tributes, the tithe, yearly took from 1 to 8 percent of the gross value of different tenures in the parish of Oberweimar.[50] Originally collected by the church, the tithe became a prerogative of the Landgrave during the Reformation. Subsequently, some of these rights were dispensed to members of the Hessian *Ritterschaft* or high

47. StaM, B/23b ALb, Hadamshausen, 1778.
48. Bader, "Dorf und Dorfgemeinde," 1–35; StaM, B/340, von Schenck zu Schweinsberg A 10, 1760–1806; P/II, Kaldern und Reizberg, Ep 1780–1820.
49. Lerch, *Hessische Agrargeschichte;* Jerome Blum, *The End of the Old Order in Europe* (Princeton, 1978), 50–55.
50. StaM, K/I Niederweimar 1747.

state officials through pawns or sales. Villagers from Niederweimar paid tithes to six different Grundherrn including the Landgrave, the von Schenck family, the von Heydwolf family, and the village of Rohnhausen.[51]

Extractions other than the tithe also tended to flow to the Landgrave's regional treasuries in Marburg and Cassel. Twenty-seven of the thirty major peasant householders from Niederweimar held tenures from the Landgrave.[52] Although the prince was the dominant Grundherr for the region and in Hesse-Cassel in general, a large number of other members of the Hessian tribute-taking classes held rights to such dues. The peasants in the village of Oberweimar owed obligations in kind to nineteen different external lords beyond the Landgrave.[53] Among these we find the heirs of landgravial officials, the Marburg chapter of the Teutonic Knights, the Universities of Gießen and Marburg, and the Gerichtherr von Schenck zu Schweinsberg.[54] These lords had been making some effort to convert obligations from payments in kind to payments in cash as other seigneurs did in the rest of Europe during the eighteenth century.[55]

Dienstherrschaft, or the right to claim the labor service of the peasant population, primarily belonged to the Landgrave by the eighteenth century. These burdens included work on the estates of the Dienstherr: plowing, weeding, and harvesting. They could also entail carting services to destinations specified by the lord. In Oberhessen, some villagers burdened with military baggage train service (*Heerwagendienst*) helped to move the troops and equipment of the Hessian army inside the borders of the territory. In Prussia, the expropriation of carts and draft animals at the most inopportune times had serious consequences for peasant producers.[56] This onerous burden did not fall upon the peasants of Oberweimar but they were often required to work on parish roads. The Landgrave imposed road and bridgework over and above the established normal service duties.[57] Such arbitrary service burdens (*ungemessene Dienst*), including work on fortresses, seemed

51. Ibid.
52. Ibid.; Fox, "Studies in the Rural History of Upper Hesse," 26.
53. Stam, K/I Niederweimar 1747.
54. Ibid.
55. Blum, *The End of the Old Order*, 50–55, 241–51.
56. Otto Büsch, *Militärsystem und Sozialleben im Alten Preussen* (Frankfurt, 1981), 21–27.
57. StaM, K/I Allna 1746, etc.

to arouse the peasants' resistance more frequently than others. In the 1760s, Hessian peasants successfully struck against such service burdens in *Amt* Bauna.[58]

The better-off peasants rarely performed service obligations themselves. Often they sent carts and wagons driven by one of their children or servants. The number of human and animal hours each tenure provided had been established earlier by local custom and the terms of land tenure. With the introduction of effective cadastral documents in mid-century, however, service burdens were assessed on the basis of the value of a tenure and entered into the service register (*Dienstbuch*) of each village. Officials then deducted the value of the extracted labor power from the taxable value of tenures. But some villages claimed that this change increased the amount of service they were obligated to perform.[59] Service could amount to as much as 25 percent of the value of the estate.[60] As they had with other tributary burdens in this eighteenth-century society, lords began to convert the obligation from work to cash payments.

The administrative apparatus that developed under the patrimonial jurisdiction of the Gerichtherr held the entire system of tributary domination together at the village level. Village officials who collected tithes and other tributes taken by Grundherrn came under the supervision of officials appointed by the particular member of the Hessian Ritterschaft who held jurisdiction over the village courts (*Gerichte*) in the area.[61] For Oberweimar during the last quarter of the eighteenth century, the Gerichtherr von Schenck zu Schweinsberg's man, *Amtschultheiß* Karl Kroeschel, performed this task.[62] He was assisted in his duties by other clients of the Gerichtherr von Schenck who had won appointments to the village offices of headman (*Greben*) or juror (*Gerichtschöpf*). Both Kroeschel and the village Greben also supervised the performance of service obligations and kept the records of who owed what service. In addition, the officials of the Gerichtherr applied sanctions to those who disrupted the productive process in the villages, disturbed the peace, disobeyed other authorities, and violated the moral order established by the church. The village misdemeanor

58. Hans Vogel and Wolfgang von Both, *Landgraf Friedrich II. von Hessen-Kassel* (Munich, 1973), 42.
59. StaM, B/17e Nanz-Willershausen 8, 1782.
60. StaM, K/I Niederweimar 1747.
61. StaM, K/I Allna 1746, etc.; H 225, Rothamel, 1801.
62. StaM, B/340, Adelsarchiv, von Schenck zu Schweinsberg A 10, 1760b–1806b.

court (*Rügegericht*) usually applied these sanctions on the basis of information supplied by village officials themselves. Villagers held quarterly sessions of the Rügegericht in parish Oberweimar.[63] The same officials also kept the records of tenure transfers, mortgages, and credit transactions.[64] Another court official recorded marriage contracts.[65] Finally, as mentioned before, the officials of the Gerichtherr mediated the domination of the Hessian state at the village level by overseeing military recruitment and tax collection.

The rewards of Gerichtsherrschaft were not limited to the lord's ability to administer other forms of domination and to establish dense patron-client relationships in Hessian villages. Direct fines assessed in the Rügegericht and fees extracted for entering marriage contracts, land transfers, and mortgages in the court records helped to maintain the tribute-taking classes' interest in these positions. For example, sixty-five infractions in 1769 resulted in fines worth almost 41 Gulden from parish Oberweimar alone — the net worth of the small tenures in the parish.[66] Ten percent of this amount went to pay the salary of the *Amtschultheiß*.

The Landgrave and the Hessian Ritterschaft divided the rewards of patrimonial jurisdiction between them. The Landgrave claimed exclusive rights to jurisdiction over all serious crimes in his domains. Jurisdiction over lesser crimes remained the prerogative of nobles (mainly the von Schencks zu Schweinsberg) in many of the southern jurisdictions of Oberhessen. In the north, the Landgrave and his officials also exercised the right of low justice.[67] Whether the Landgrave held direct jurisdiction or not, decisions from the local courts could be appealed to higher courts controlled exclusively by the Landgrave's officials.

Until 1762, the military system enhanced this system of domination. The added threat of conscription intensified the need for protection and the ties of dependence which made tribute-taking possible. The effective administration of patrimonial jurisdiction still depended heavily upon the lord's clients, who performed their duties as village

63. Reyer, *Die Dorfgemeinde im nördlichen Hessen*, 52–70; StaM, B/340, von Schenck zu Schweinsberg A 10, 1786b, 437ff.
64. StaM, P/II, Alter Währschaftsbuch, Allna, 1768–99.
65. StaM, P/II Caldern and Reizberg, Ep 1781–1820.
66. StaM, B/340, von Schenck zu Schweinsberg A 10, 1769b.
67. Kurt Dülfer, "Fürst und Verwaltung, Grundzüge der hessischen Verwaltungsgeschichte 16.-19. Jahrhundert," *Hessische Jahrbuch Landesgeschichte* 3 (1953): 150ff.; StaM, K/I Allna 1746, etc.

officials. These brokers could conceal information about land transfers, conspire to defraud tithe collectors, protect potential draftees
from recruitment, and embezzle funds that passed through their hands
on the way to the powers of domination.[68] It was important for a
Gerichtherr to grease the wheels of his administrative machine with
favors. Patronage enhanced the servility of officials who also needed to
maintain their position within the village corporation. Favors could
take the form of the remission of fines or service burdens, or the
vigorous pursuit of shady characters in the village.[69] When Greben Jost
Bender of Allna reported a dispute between the Domainsrat Preuss and
the village about unpaid Kontribution, von Schenck zu Schweinsberg
ordered Preuss to pay up even though as an absentee noble landlord,
not a peasant, he was not normally subject to such taxation.[70] The
capacity to win boons of this kind enhanced the effectiveness of the
officials because they could, in turn, distribute patronage.

The lack of village solidarity was evident when, in June 1781, the
village council of Hermershausen met to consider the attempt by
two disenfranchised young men — George Koch and Johannes Weyersheuser — to build a new house on a small plot of ground given them by
Koch's father-in-law.[71] Some of the enfranchised members of the council were angry enough to forward a petition to the Landrat to get him
to help block the construction of this house. They perceived that the
addition of yet another poor household to the village rolls threatened
a number of resources including common meadows, village welfare
treasuries, and the satisfactory apportionment of service burdens.[72]
Despite the threat to the commons represented by this new house, the
twenty enfranchised members of this community could not reach an
agreement. Only twelve signed the petition opposing it, and this lack of
unanimity may have accounted for the Landrat's willingness to grant
permission for the cottage to be built. At the very least, when unanimity occurred it made sufficient harassment possible to render tenure in
the village very difficult for the new householders.

68. Strippel, *Die Währschafts- und Hypothekenbücher,* 189ff.; StaM, K/I Allna
1746, etc.; B/340, von Schenck zu Schweinsberg A 10, 1760b–1806b; B/23b ALb,
Niederweimar 17, 1774, Oberweimar, 1788.

69. StaM, B/340, von Schenck zu Schweinsberg A 10, 1760b–1806b; B/23b ALb,
Hermershausen 1788; B/17e Cyriaxweimar 9, 1780.

70. StaM, B/17e Allna 17, 1780.

71. StaM, B/23b ALb, Hermershausen, 1781.

72. StaM, B/17e Kehna 6, 1785; B/23b ALb, Ebsdorf 433, 1781ff.; Möln 175, 1775;
and Chapter 8 of this book.

The capacity of enfranchised community members to act in concert was a source of their authority and also provided protection for their property. Even for the productive processes to function smoothly, action in concert was required, for it was the council who assigned the days for plowing and harvest under the three-field system. The village itself, in conjunction with its officers, protected the fruits of the fields and commons from the trespasses of humans and animals. The council's capacity for conspiracy affected the weight with which tributary burdens fell upon its individual members and the quality of information given into the hands of state officials seeking to tax them and recruit their sons. Solidarity affected the collective lawsuits brought by the village against authorities or other villages. Because unity seemed so important, villagers developed both formal and informal sanctions against those who did not cooperate with the dominant factions in collective projects.[73] These "quiet ones" (*Ruhigen*), as villagers called them, could find themselves shunned — not only cut off from village discourse but from critical resources as well. Such shunning could become violent and end with barn-burnings, beatings, and other forms of petty terrorism.

Collective actions requiring solidarity frequently seemed to be projects of one faction or another. Political factions expressed such projects in terms of a variety of issues but the factions themselves were constructed by peasants in the discourse about friends and foes (*Freundschaft und Feindschaft*). As David Sabean has convincingly demonstrated for villages in Wurttemberg, and Werner Troßbach for villages just south of Oberhessen, division into factions placed village power and politics squarely on the footing of kin-based alliances.

The threat of military service could easily become a weapon in kin-based village politics. When, in September 1780, Jost Becker of Cyriaxweimar continued to court a woman whose parents had betrothed her to another man, he became the focus of such a faction fight. The parents of the woman complained to *Kommissions Rath* Uhlrich and enlisted the help of the village headman and his servants to produce testimony that Becker had been a generally disreputable and stubborn subject since his youth.[74] Even the parish pastor put in his criticism of the young man's behavior. As a result of this dispute Uhlrich recommended Becker as a candidate for military service. That Becker was not

73. Troßbach, *Soziale Bewegung*, 82.
74. StaM, B/17e Cyriaxweimar 9.

without his own political resources in the village became clear when it took three days for the detachment of four soldiers, the woman's parents, and the village authorities to find him, even though he had only gone as far as the village's herder cottage. As it turned out, Becker was too much even for the army and ended up in prison before they could send him to America.

Official members of villages used their exclusive rights to use commonly held property to dominate marginal householders and to limit their numbers. Most of these common resources were carefully specified in the cadastral documents prepared (in the case of Oberweimar's villages) during the late 1740s.[75] By controlling access to these rights, village councils frequently determined whether a new household survived within the village boundaries. In addition to monopolies over some of the everyday means of production, councils also might make loans from two important treasuries to tide households over the inevitable rough patches of life. Such assistance was sometimes crucial for the survival of poorer residents.

In the parish of Oberweimar, the value of common property varied from only 12 Steuergulden in Weiershausen to over 1700 Steuergulden in Allna. The low total for Weiershausen seems to indicate that common property had been distributed to individual householders.[76] Allna had over 1000 Ackers of land divided between 18.5 Ackers of cropland, 35.75 Ackers of meadow and garden, 499 of woods, and 481 of wastes and hedges.[77] Woods, meadows, and wastes were the most important of these because they provided grazing and hay necessary to keep livestock. When grazing, villagers kept animals in common herds watched over by herdsmen hired by the village council. Usually, they separated herds of cattle, sheep, and pigs. In Allna, an enfranchised villager with four persons in his household was entitled to graze two pigs in the common woodlands but could not leave them overnight there because the village did not have a common corral. Other than the limitation on pigs, villagers in Allna could keep as many other livestock as they felt the commons would bear and that they could afford to keep. In 1747, villagers owned 27 horses, 17 oxen, 79 cows, and 352 sheep.[78]

75. StaM, K/I Allna 1746, etc.
76. Ibid.
77. StaM, K/I Allna 1746.
78. Ibid.

In addition to providing mastage for pigs, the woodlands were also an important source of wood used to build houses, to heat them, and to bake bread. Collectively, the villagers of Allna had rights to cut 4 *Schwellen* of 6.174 foot (English) beams for building purposes. For firewood, they were entitled to cut 1.5 *Klafter* of oak and .5 *Klafter* of birchwood.[79] Finally, they could collect up to three wagonloads of windfall wood out of the common forests. If these amounts did not suffice, then authorities specifically enjoined them to purchase their wood from the local Gutsherr, the von Heydwolf family. Thus enfranchised villagers had the advantage of first use of the commonly owned resources and were less likely to be at mercy of the von Heydwolf wood monopoly.

In addition to lands, the council in Allna also controlled a church, a bake-house, and a small cottage. The church entitled the village to a once-monthly service by the parish pastor who sat in Oberweimar. The bake-house became an increasingly important property as the eighteenth century progressed because the Landgrave tried to eliminate private bake-ovens to protect his rights to the wood from village woodlands.[80] This policy forced those without the right to bake bread in the village to buy it from their better-off neighbors. Living in the herder cottage was one of the compensations for those whom the council hired to look after the village herds.[81] Some villages, such as Niederweimar, had independent brewing rights which the village council usually allocated to members.[82]

Beyond the taxable rights owned by the corporation, each village had a community treasury (*Gemeindekasten*) and a church treasury (*Kirchenkasten*). The use of this money by the village council is illustrated by the loan made by the Allna church treasury in November 1771. Probably because of the short harvests and economic crisis of that year, two destitute and indebted widows were in jeopardy of losing their meager properties. These women borrowed 100 Gulden from the administrator of the Treysa convent widow's fund and another 100 Gulden from the Allna church treasury to refinance an earlier mort-

---

79. Ibid. Christian and Friedrich Nosbeck, *Münz-, Mass-, und Gewichtsbuch* (Leipzig, 1858), tell us that a *Schwellen* is a pile of wood 6.178 English feet in circumference and just as high. A *Klafter* was the Hessian equivalent of a cord and contained 154.353 English feet cubed.

80. StaM, K/I Allna 1746; Scharlau, "Landeskulturgesetzgebung," 139–43.

81. StaM, B/17e Allna 9, 1775.

82. StaM, K/I Niederweimar 1747.

gage.[83] The loans carried 5 percent interest. The community account books from other villages in the parish contain smaller loans, often in times of dearth, that attest to the welfare functions to which this treasury was put.[84] Without such village-based charity, some marginal households (enfranchised or not) might not have survived.

In 1784, the Allna council made another kind of transaction. Johannes Scheld from Allna transferred 20 Ackers of land to acquire a loan of 600 *Gulden* from the Gemeinde by using a guaranteed repurchase (*Wiederkauf*) contract.[85] The purpose of this loan is difficult to determine since Scheld took the loan in cash and never repurchased the land. Scheld had acquired the property in early 1776, perhaps to render himself a more substantial farmer in the eyes of officials assigning draft exemptions. He disappears from the records after 1784. Did the council simply buy out another of the marginal households as it did when it bought the small cottage owned by a Jewish family in 1786?[86] They subsequently transferred this latter property into the hands of one of the village's influential men, Jost Mathei, in a contract that each member of the council signed. Thus, village funds were sometimes used to transfer land from poorer villagers to a wealthier one.

The influx of Kontribution money paid quarterly by each villager also became a temporary common resource before it found its way into the hands of higher fiscal officials. The Landrat von Schenck zu Schweinsberg actually received official recognition when he reported the practice to the war department in 1790.[87] Bureaucrats cautioned him that village officials be required to request permission to borrow from Kontribution funds and that they not be permitted to mix the funds with regular village treasury accounts. This latter practice resulted in such a terrifying accounting mess in the 1770s that the Landrat threw up his hands in despair.[88] The village tax collectors (*Gelderheber*), of all people, were in the best position to benefit from these cash flows, and some succumbed to the temptation to peculation. In the village of Abterode in Niederhessen, one such official bought

83. StaM, P/II, Altes Währschaftsbuch, Allna 3, 1768–99.

84. StaM, R/II Allna 1, Cyriaxweimar 1, Hermershausen 1, 3.

85. StaM, P/II, Altes Währschaftsbuch, Allna 3, 1768–99. Ralph Giesey, "Rules of Inheritance and Strategies of Mobility in Prerevolutionary France," *American Historical Review* 82 (1977): 2.

86. StaM, P/II, Altes Währschaftsbuch, Allna 3, 1768–99.

87. StaM, HLO 15.5. 1790.

88. StaM, R/II Reizberg 1776–80.

his son out of the army in 1768 using Kontribution funds to find a replacement.[89]

The articulations of tributary overlordship with the institutions of rural villages provided some peasant producers with a wide variety of levers which they could pull to their advantage. Though mediating authority did not come without heavy costs, peasants who had access to noble patronage, village office, common resources, and seats on village councils gained tremendous advantages over those who did not. Less fortunate villagers continually faced the choice between dependence on these clients of nobles or various forms of ruin. The strong authority of village elites made it possible to capture and hold villages in a state of dynamic equilibrium for the middle years of the eighteenth century and enhanced the position of those who operated the levers of production well. Control of social reproduction was yet another important resource for this peasant elite.

89. StaM, B/23b ALb, Abterode 11, 1768.

7 Labor, Social Reproduction, and the Peasant Elite to 1762

We may call Hessian peasant production kin-ordered because peasant decision-makers distributed the material surpluses and the rights to the labor of persons through a grid of symbols which defined the members, potential members, and nonmembers in given networks of blood (consanguinal) and maritally defined (affinal) relations.[1] Inheritance and marriage constituted the central acts in the reproduction of these social networks.[2] Although substantially hemmed in by the conditions of land tenure, the directors of peasant enterprises could still use marriage, servitude, and inheritance to enhance their positions as they competed for status, success, and the realization of their individual life plans.[3] Even before the brutal interventions of the Hufen edict in 1773, the peasant household was no haven from the heartless world of articulations between kin and tribute. Rather, it was an arena in which privileged persons used the labor and resources of the underprivileged to promote their own security and success. Before 1773, the harshness and the consequences of this class division of the peasant family were

1. Eric R. Wolf, *Europe and the People without History* (Berkeley, 1982), 93–95; David Warren Sabean, *Property, Production, and Family in Neckarshausen, 1700–1870* (New York, 1990), 24, 416–26.

2. Hermann Rebel, "Cultural Hegemony and Class Experience: A Critical Reading of Recent Ethnological-Historical Approaches," *American Ethnologist* 16 (1989), 1:117–36, 2:350–65.

3. Hermann Rebel, "Peasant Stem Families in Early Modern Austria: Life Plans, Status Tactics, and the Grid of Inheritance," *Social Science History* 2 (1978).

determined by the conditions of tenure and authority that made success difficult.[4] With the institution of the Hufen edict, the state attempted to define many more of the terms of underprivilege as well.

The particular roles that individuals played in the productive process may well have determined the realization of a hoped-for course of
life. On this view, productive roles were embedded in a network of
obligations and rights which determined who performed given tasks at
given times. Some roles in the peasant society of Oberhessen provided
easy and substantial access to the surpluses of production and the
advantages of mediation. These privileges stemmed from the working
out of life chances and resulted from the privileged influence some
individuals had over the life chances of others. Thus, housefathers had
the right to the labor of children, and husbands the rights to labor of
their wives; children were employed by parents or other kin. At the
same time, household managers used kinship as a way of ordering
property devolution. Thus, kinship helped to determine those who
acquired advantaged roles (those roles to which rights primarily ad-
hered) and those who acquired disadvantaged roles (those roles for
which obligations predominated). Without wealth generated by labor
and without the property with which to use that labor, few other
opportunities were available.

The Directors of Oberhessian Kin-ordered Production

Until now I have been satisfied with the vague and reified category
"directors of kin-ordered enterprises." To speak precisely of the ways
in which such authority was exercised among Oberhessian peasant
producers, it is necessary to become more specific about who occupied
these directing roles and how the authority was divided among different roles. For the cameralist bureaucrats who made policy for the
Landgrave, the ideology of the "whole house" provided a simple an-
swer. They named the directors of production as the heads of households (*Hausväter*) and the providers of subsistence (*Brotherr*) — essentially those whose names had been entered in the cadaster and on the
tenurial contracts as the holders of peasant farms. There is obvious
truth in this designation, for those who feed and those who hold the

4. Hermann Rebel, *Peasant Classes: The Bureaucratization of Property and Family
Relations under Early Habsburg Absolutism, 1511–1636* (Princeton, 1983), 194ff.

means of production certainly have a privileged position and can, within limits, sustain their authority to decide the fates of others. They hold in their hands ultimate sanctions of life and death, and, at the very least, the possibilities of social connectedness.

But Hermann Rebel has taught us to treat with skepticism the ideological designations of tributary authorities about authority relationships within kin-groups.[5] The focus of Rebel's skepticism is what past authorities and current social historians have called "retirement arrangements," in Austria, *Auszüge,* in Oberhessen, *Altenteil.* Rebel found through the analysis of estate inventories and other sources that such "retirements" did not necessarily mean the beginning of a period of ease and decline after a hard life, but the entry into changed and rather directive activity.[6] Retired elders used their portions to render themselves independent of tribute production and began loaning money, functioning as matchmakers, as guardians and tutors of legal minors, and as church elders. Elders manipulated inheritance portions and debt related to wages and devolutionary settlements. Using these means, elders maintained an exalted position similar to that enjoyed by a chief in a tribal society or a mafia Don in more recent times.[7]

A second complicating factor that arises when trying to identify the "directors of kin-ordered enterprises" with the heads of households was that although legal title might have passed between generations at a single instant in time, property transfers occurred as a long and drawn out process — sometimes taking more than a single generation to accomplish.[8] For example, a piece of property might be given a woman as part of a marriage portion but only appear as a debt owed to her by her parents. That debt might be passed to a child of hers who then redeemed it on the death of the grandparent. Examples of this practice frequently occur in the cadaster of parish Oberweimar.[9] Add the ambiguities of the wide variety of feudal tenures which separated use right (*dominum utile*) and proprietarial authority (*dominum direc-*

5. Rebel, "Peasant Stem Families."

6. Compare Michael Mitterauer and Reinhard Sieder, *The European Family: From Patriarchy to Partnership, 1400 to the Present* (Chicago, 1982), 162–68.

7. Rebel, "Peasant Stem Families;" Wolf, *Europe,* 99; compare Anton Blok, *The Mafia of a Sicilian Village, 1860–1960: A Study of Violent Peasant Entrepreneurs* (New York, 1974), 7–8.

8. David Sabean, "Aspects of Kinship Behavior and Property in Rural Western Europe before 1800," in Jack Goody et al., eds., *Family and Inheritance: Rural Society in Western Europe, 1200–1800* (Cambridge, 1976), 96–111.

9. StaM, K/I Hadamshausen 1806, F 29, 136.

tum) and it is easy to see why a Hessian peasant from the Schwalm could carve on the external beams of his house a verse of quiet desperation:

> This house is mine
> and yet not mine
> For who comes after me
> so too will it be[10]

No clearer critique of the reifications of the cameralism in the Hessian cadaster could be made. In neither space nor time could kin-ordered enterprises simply be sharply bounded monads. Lines of authority remained ambiguous and confused throughout various family life cycles.

Ambiguities appear in the census of 1732, which begin to reveal the full complexity of household authority in the parish. The census recognized the autonomy of some married couples while they still belonged, in some way, to another household. For example, officials listed Christ and Eliesabetha Schmidt of Niederweimar separately from their son Hans and the rest of his household. However, next to Christ's entry came the notation "maintains a separate house, but goes to eat with the above-mentioned Hans Schmidt."[11] Twenty such entries appeared with these marginal notations in the census of the parish. For the most part, they indicated older married couples who shared roofs and/or tables with their married children, having given up at least some of the authority over the farm. Another three entries involved young married couples, with or without children, who still lived under the authority of one set of parents. The remainder involved siblings living together.

Such complex households characterized the three-generation (*Ausgedinge*) families found in areas in central Europe where impartible property devolution predominated and where demographic conditions permitted people to survive long enough to become family elders.[12]

10. Compare Arthur A. Imhof, "Von der unsicheren zur sicheren Lebenzeit: Ein folgenschwerer Wandel im Verlaufe der Neuzeit," *Vierteljahrschrift für Sozial und Wirtschafts Geschichte* 71 (1984): 185, who interprets this as belief in continuity. Hermann Rebel suggested the debt interpretation which I extended to cover splits between use and ownership.

11. StaM, B/40d r 29 n 76, 1732.

12. Compare Peter Laslett, *Household and Family in Past Time* (Cambridge, 1972), 623, to Lutz K. Berkner, "Inheritance, Land Tenure and Peasant Family Structure: A German Regional Comparison" in Goody, *Family and Inheritance*, 71–95; Rebel, *Peasant Classes;* and Michael Mitterauer, *Grundtypen alteuropäischer Sozialformen* (Göttingen, 1976), 42–96. Also see Wolf, *Europe*, 3–4.

Oberhessian peasants established the authority relationships in their households through marriage contracts. Their nature varied widely. For example, Hans Henrich Meyer and his wife Eliesabetha were designated "Auszügler" on the estate of their son-in-law Johann George Laucht. This ordering of household relationships usually meant that the old couple had separate quarters, either in the main farmhouse or in an associated cottage, but that they would nonetheless share the table of the couple managing the farm. The terms of the heir's marriage contract usually gave the old couple incomes from the tenure and some of its best fruits for marketing purposes.[13] In addition, the older couple, while maintaining some authority in the management of the farm, paid no taxes, debts, or tribute. In a sense, they too became tribute-taking overlords of the farm and its inhabitants while giving over the day-to-day management decisions to someone else.

Another disposition indicated in the 1732 census was that of the widow Barbara Heuser of Niederweimar who had given over the management of her tenure to her son Johannes in whose household she ate. She also held an independent household on the basis of a pawn relationship ("hat ihr Haushaltung an pfant gemeldet").[14] This probably meant she was receiving an annuity paid on loaned capital. Other examples simply mention the fact that the authority of the household had been transferred from the older couple to the younger one and that the elders shared at least the table with their children.

In cases in which authority still rested with the elder couple, the pair with children received the marginal notice. These were the clearest cases where marriage had been used to recruit and bind labor. Albrecht Minck of Gisselberg had four children who worked as part of their grandfather's household until their father received the family tenure. Minck's marriage provided up to five laborers for his father. As long as the children remained under five years in age they represented mouths to feed rather than labor resources. However, assuming normal two-year birth intervals and that none of the children were twins, the oldest child would have been at least eight and probably already helped the women with the poultry and livestock. Albrecht's family, when combined with his father Gothard, his two brothers, and three servants, resulted in a total labor force of 12 people — one of the largest peasant households in the parish at any time during the century.

13. Compare Rebel, "Peasant Stem Families," 255–80; StaM, P/II Kaldern and Reizberg 1780–1820, Ep.
14. StaM, B/40d r 29 n 76, 1732.

In 1732, one complex household not fitting the German model of a three-generation family was that of Johannes and Barbara Naumann, a brother and sister who lived together on an estate with three male and three female servants. Officials listed these siblings as children, rather than as a housefather or housemother, and thereby suggested that an appointed guardian managed the tenure at that time. Managing the estates of orphans was a frequent task performed by tutors or guardians (*Vormünder*). Those performing this role had often been the child's sponsor at baptism or could be a retired peasant (*Altenteiler*) of importance in the community.[15] Guardianship (*Vormundschaft*) became an increasingly central concern of state regulation as the eighteenth century passed. Such arrangements show how kin-ordered enterprises extended beyond the corporate boundaries of the "whole house." Unlike potatoes in a sack or sharply-bounded, incessantly-moving molecules in a solution, rural society showed itself as a tapestry of strands weaving and reweaving themselves in space and time.

The Relations of Rural Servitude

It is possible to identify four different sources of labor available to the managers of peasant tenures. Eighteenth-century cameralist legislation attempted to regulate labor relationships in the countryside and changed hitherto roughly made distinctions into relatively sharply defined legal categories. These laws distinguished among family members, servants (*Gesinde, Knechte,* and *Mägde*), apprentices, and more or less free day laborers (*Tagelöhner*).[16] Of the four, day laborers approached most closely the position of today's wage laborers whose stimulus to work is based primarily on market conditions.

Distinctions among household workers were a matter of contract and authority as far as the police bureaucrats of Hesse-Cassel were concerned. Short-term contracts that bound day laborers did not subject workers fully to the authority of their employers because they lived in separate households.[17] Conversely, servants and apprentices came directly under the administrative authority of their employer in his role

---

15. Rebel, "Peasant Stem Families," 275.

16. StaM, HLO 11.6.1739.

17. Rolf Engelsing, "Der Arbeitsmarkt der Dienstboten im 17. 18. und 19. Jahrhundert," in Hermann Kellenbenz, ed., *Wirtschaftspolitik und Arbeitsmarkt* (Munich, 1974), 159–237.

as the head of the household which workers joined as full, if temporary, members. Contracts bound servants at least one year and often tied apprentices for more than four years, but both shared the status of the householder's children — living with them and usually eating at the same table.[18] The law held employers responsible for their misdemeanors, moral and spiritual supervision, and technical training.[19] Children and other subordinate members of the family fell under the authority of the household head, even though bound by no contract except perhaps that of "natural law."

Servitude seems to have been viewed as a stage in life for many rural children in Hesse-Cassel. It began with confirmation — at age fifteen or so — and ended at marriage which, under normal circumstances, occurred sometime before age thirty-five.[20] Apparently, parents employed servitude as an alternative when they could not afford or were unwilling to keep children at home. Thus, children of poor parents frequently found themselves subject to surrogate fathers for whom they worked.[21] The performance of menial tasks such as the care of livestock and poultry may have prepared children for a better future. This hope, however, was often an illusion. Even if the servant succeeded in finding a spouse, a sufficient endowment for independence was unlikely to be forthcoming from poor parents. Servitude for some, moreover, extended to life's end, while in other cases, widows and widowers reentered servitude in later years by reason of misfortune or failed retirement arrangements. In Oberweimar, their burial entries indicated that they died as servants but also said they had returned to the parish to die among friends.[22] It seems particularly true of women who lived with their married daughters that provisions for their widowhood had not been at the expense of their husbands' tenures.

Although censuses distinguished sharply among children of the family, servants, and apprentices, the practices of peasants and authorities did not. Indeed, those older children confined to celibate life in the household of their birth because of some physical or social handicap were sometimes called servants. Moreover, some marriage contracts

18. Ibid., 160, Rolf Engelsing, "Das häusliche Personal in der Epoche der Industrialisierung," in Rolf Engelsing, ed., *Zur Sozialgeschichte deutscher Mittel- und Unterschichten* (Göttingen, 1973), 225–35.
19. StaM, B/340, von Schenck zu Schweinsberg 10 A, 1762b–1805b.
20. KaOw, Kp, Kr, 1665–1774, StaM, B/4h 4072. KaOw, Kp, Br 1665–1774.
21. StaM, HLO 28.8.1736.
22. KaOw, Kp, Br, 1665–1774.

specified that married life for certain new couples would begin in this status.[23] In Austria, older children not only shared the same work also but the same less desirable living quarters as servants.[24] Legislation regulating servitude specifically enjoined employers to treat live-in workers as their own children and that, too, blurred the distinction between family members and servants.[25]

In keeping with the principles of cameralism and good police policy, states after the Thirty Years War concentrated on maintaining the supply of people entering the service of housefathers.[26] They found servitude beneficial because it guaranteed a source of closely disciplined labor under conditions that minimized the advantages of free laborers in the years of labor shortage of the later seventeenth century. Bureaucrats argued that servitude acclimated children to hard work and other forms of morally upright behavior. Furthermore, they saw free laborers largely as loafers.[27] Paul Kollmann believed that eighteenth-century day laborers (*Tagelöhner*) in German lands earned enough during yearly peaks of employment at harvest time to survive the rest of the year providing they saved.[28] It is more likely that officials interested in maximizing fiscal returns blamed laborers for their inactivity when it was dictated by seasonal labor markets. Peasant householders also may have preferred the more reliable bound labor to that of the free, even though using workers under these contracts meant responsibility for their discipline, religious instruction, and moral behavior. They too feared the "idle" elements in the village as much as the Landgrave did.

The importance of servant labor for the peasants of parish Oberweimar was also established in the 1732 census.[29] Over 20 percent of

23. StaM, P/II Reizberg and Kaldern, Ep, 1780–1820; KaOw, Kp, Br, 1665–1774; George Thomas Fox, "Studies in the Rural History of Upper Hesse" (Ph.D. diss., Vanderbilt University, 1976), 312–13.

24. Roland Sandgruber, "Gesindestuben, Kleinhäuser, und Arbeitskasernen: Ländliche Wohnverhältnisse im 18. und 19. Jahrhundert in Österreich," in Lutz Niethammer, ed., *Wohnen im Wandel: Beiträge zur Geschichte des Alltags in der bürgerlichen Gesellschaft* (Wuppertal, 1979), 118.

25. StaM, HLO 28.8.1736.

26. Engelsing, "Der Arbeitsmarkt," 162–73; and Paul Kollmann, "Geschichte und Statistik des Gesindewesens in Deutschland," *Jahrbücher für Nationalökonomie und Statistik* 10 (1868): 246–48.

27. StaM, HLO 11.6.1739.

28. Kollmann, "Geschichte," 259.

29. StaM, B/40d r 29 n 76, 1732.

the parish population was in service at that time. Moreover, during 1732, 81 of the 151 households used servant labor. It seems clear that most who needed labor and could afford the obligations attendant to keeping bound servants made an effort to do so. Of ninety-one households with sufficient land to produce an agricultural surplus, nearly 80 percent kept servants.[30]

Military servitude probably began to compete with household servitude in peasant households only after the 1740s. Landgravial recruitment policy remained consonant with the aims of police bureaucrats and holders of tenures who sought to maintain the supply of bound labor until masters (*Brotherrn*) lost their rights to protect servants.[31] As long as the military concentrated on "masterless servants and loafers," the threat of possible military service remained an incentive for parents to bind their children into servitude or for young men to find an employer. Thus, before it became more intrusive, the military system tended to enhance the authority of peasant employers as well as village officials. Some peasants even used phony contracts of servitude as a means of avoiding military service.[32] Day laborers eked out a marginal existence, but the military system made this a less secure alternative and the protection afforded by signing on as servant became a necessity.

Marriage, Labor, and Property Devolution

Of all events likely to occur during the lifetime of an individual, the history of a household, and the yearly round of village and parish life, marriage remained unquestionably the most important. It was through this complex set of negotiations, rituals, exchanges, and celebrations that directors of kin-ordered production wove and rewove the social tapestry of peasant life. More specifically, it was these events which began the process of reproducing units in a kin-ordered mode of production.[33] Participants in the process tried to provide not only for

30. StaM, B/23b ALb, Reizberg 61, 1725.
31. Otto Könnecke, *Rechtsgeschichte des Gesindewesens in West- und Süddeutschland* (Marburg, 1912), 379–82.
32. StaM, HLO 16.12.1762.
33. Pierre Bourdieu, "Marriage Strategies as Strategies of Social Reproduction," in Robert Forster and Orest Ranum, eds., *Family and Society: Selections from Annales* (Baltimore, 1975), 117–37; Wolf, *Europe*, 88, Eric R. Wolf, *Peasants* (New Jersey, 1966), 60.

biological reproduction but for immediate and future labor needs and other factors such as skill, land, tools, and buildings. Marriage also provided the capital resources for reinvestment in the productive processes, insurance for the retirement of elders, and care for siblings of heirs. Marriage asserted the value of a particular household within local society, and established the paths of kinship through which material aid, credit, information, and other economic goods could flow.[34]

Our window on the complex matrix of calculation and feeling, competition, and care that went into matching couples is provided by officials whose attempts to intervene in and regulate certain aspects of peasant marriage were increasingly successful. Landgravial legislation required recording peasant marriage contracts by the 1720s.[35] The survivals of such early documents suggest that rural dwellers recorded only those contracts likely to be challenged in the landgravial courts.[36] By the 1780s, more complete collections indicate that full compliance had begun.[37]

Documents recording marriage contracts suggest both the complexity of the process of making a match and the difficulty of bringing it to a satisfactory conclusion. It appears that the entire wedding party appeared before an official of the patrimonial courts who committed oral contracts to writing in the presence of all principals and witnesses.[38] All parties attested to the truth of information recorded in the document. Attestations included the names of bride, groom, and guardians (parents of the couple or others). There followed a formal request that the marriage vows be given official validity (*Bestätigung*).

Following the request for validity came a report of any possible legal obstacles to the match. Of the two hundred or so contracts I examined, only five different obstacles appear to have been matters of concern. Foremost were violations of the degrees of consanguinity (*Blutfreundschaft*). Where any such suspicion arose, parents provided genealogies and the required exemptions were provided by the Marburg consistory. If the age of one or both members of the couple was an issue, then it was resolved by sealed copies of birth entries from parish registers. If either marrying partner was less than twenty years of age, the couple needed a signed and sealed judicial dispensation. Required in all cases

---

34. Sabean, "Aspects."
35. StaM, HLO 18.2.1724.
36. StaM, P/II Reizberg, Gp, 1751.
37. StaM, P/II Reizberg and Caldern, Ep, 1780–1820.
38. Ibid.

where the groom was a subject of the Landgrave of Hesse-Cassel was certification by the keeper of the recruitment lists from his home village that he had no legal obligation to the military. If he did, the groom was required to provide written proof from his company proprietor (*Chef*) that he had permission to marry. For second marriages, permission from guardians of the children of the first marriage, along with a death entry for the previous spouses, was necessary for final approval.[39] If either the bride or the groom was a bondsman (*Leibeigene*) to anyone other than the Landgrave, official release from this status had to accompany the contract.

The second part of the marriage protocol—the actual marriage contract—was called a "marital address" (*Eheberedung*). The document recorded a series of promises made to many people, and represented the tying of various social knots. The couple promised to have and hold each other in life-long love, faithfulness (*Treue*), and friendship (*Freundschaft*). The groom promised to take the bride into his household and accept her as a co-owner (*Mitbesitzerin*). Usually, the bride's side promised a dowry which often included a cash sum representing an inheritance portion (*Herausgift* or *Abfindungssumme*). Exchanges might include livestock and grain which, together with the cash, came from the estate of her father or brother. If the groom happened to enter the house of the bride's family, his family made the payments.[40] The household of the bride always seemed to be responsible for bedding, clothing, and household utensils.

Finally, participants defined the status of community property. Often, parents postponed the formation of the marital community of property until the couple produced children. If bride or groom died before offspring, then all obligations were canceled and a specified part of the dowry was returned. Not infrequently, however, the marriage itself was held to create community property.[41] Since this procedure risked parental control over the couple, it was used most often when the couple was not immediately receiving an estate or when the estate was of no great value.[42] These provisions attempted to ensure biolog-

39. StaM, P/II Reizberg and Caldern, Ep, 1780–1820, Adam Wolf and Margretha Bürauth of Cappel, 12.2.1781.

40. StaM, P/II Reizberg and Caldern, Ep, 1780–1820, Jost Grosch and Margretha Kentner of Nesselbrun, 23.4.1781.

41. Wilhelm Holtzapfel, "Oberlandsbezirk Kassel," in Max Sering, ed., *Die Vererbung des ländlichen Grundbesitzes* (Berlin, 1899–1910), 16.

42. StaM, P/II Reizberg and Caldern, Ep, 1780–1820, Ernst and Cathrein Löwer of Hadamshausen, 10.1.1784.

ical reproduction and also to provide tenures with new land, tools, livestock, and produce — all of which may have been depleted by dowries for earlier-departed siblings of the heir.[43] They also established a fund from which any future settlements for the issue of the marriage might come.

Other promises, while diverse, fell into two basic categories: (1) commitments that established labor and authority relationships within the altered household; and (2) the obligations that channeled movable and immovable property to different persons. The most straightforward case of labor provisions in marriage arrangements occurred when parents took the couple into one of the parental homes as servants (*Knecht und Magd*) to await title to the farm.[44] This happened for Johann Henrich Thomas of Bellnhausen who married Eliesabetha Schneider of Dilschausen in April 1782.[45] In taking the couple in, the bride's mother promised yearly wages and the income from one Acker of land. Couples could also be saddled with the taxes of the tenure before they came to possess it. Johannes Naumann of Weitershausen extracted this promise from Werner Koch before he completed the contract leading to his daughter's marriage.[46] Whether this promise had its quid pro quo is unclear from the document. Newlyweds could become servants even when the tenure went to someone else, as happened to Conrad Mertin and his bride Anna Caletsch.[47]

Explicit as these commitments were, they actually concealed the most important type of labor recruitment involved in marriage. If the couple acquired the tenure of the bride's parents, the woman's parents had recruited male managerial skills for the future and his labor for the present.[48] If the groom inherited his parent's tenure (the most frequent situation), the household acquired a new member presumably skilled in women's work.[49] Evidence suggests that this included many tasks beyond the household chores and child care.[50] Authorities fined the women of parish Oberweimar for thefts and violations of various rules

43. Holtzapfel, "Oberlandsbezirk Kassel," 34–40.

44. Ibid.; Sabean, "Aspects," 105.

45. StaM, P/II Reizberg and Caldern, Ep, 1780–1820, Johann Henrich Thomas, 18.4.82.

46. StaM, P/II Reizberg and Caldern, Ep, 1780–1820, Werner Koch and Eliesabetha Naumann, Weitershausen, 4.5.1782.

47. StaM, P/II Reizberg and Caldern, Ep, 1780–1820, Conrad Mertin, 8.4.1783.

48. Bourdieu, "Marriage Strategies," 117–37.

49. Compare ibid., 131 n. 22.

50. StaM, B/340, von Schenck zu Schweinsberg 10 A, 1762b–1805b.

as they engaged in tasks (gardening, root-farming, dairying, and caring for poultry) expected of them. Further, women's involvement in many of the activities associated with agricultural intensification may have enhanced the value of daughters in the marriage market as the eighteenth century wore on.[51] A poor or middling farm family might also try to diversify the tenure's sources of income by marrying a daughter to a boy skilled at a trade. In this way, Anna Lozen's parents became involved in the tailor trade. The marriage contract directed her new spouse, Jost Niederhöffer, to continue making clothing.[52] Similarly, Werner Koch's contract contained provisions aimed at the continuation of his linen weaving when he moved into the house with his bride's father, Johannes Naumann.[53]

Labor relationships might appear in the marriage contract even when both sets of parents were gaining nothing obvious as a result. When Ernst and Cathrein Löwer married, their contract specified that they would be servants on the estate of *Rentmeister* Duntzen in Dagobertshausen.[54] The meaning of such a contract is unclear, but it might have been a way of repaying a debt to an official of the landgravial domains who was having difficulty acquiring labor during the shortage caused by the military system. But it may also have been the only way to get official permission for the marriage. The oddest case encountered was that of Johannes Mertin of Nesselbrun and his wife Eliesabetha of Niederourfa — both children of millers — who were married in 1783. The nuptial agreement specified that each would continue to live with their respective parents for three years after the marriage — he as Knecht and she as Magd.[55] Was this one more sign of a strained labor market when parents could not agree to forgo the labor of their respective children? Had things come to such a pass that the security of the agreement and the reproduction of a household was sacrificed to more immediate labor needs? The contract itself remains silent on these issues, yet such possibilities cannot be dismissed out of hand.

51. David Warren Sabean, "Small Peasant Agriculture in Germany at the Beginning of the 19th Century: Changing Work Patterns," *Peasant Studies Newsletter* 7 (1978): 218–24.

52. StaM, P/II Reizberg and Caldern, Ep, 1780–1820, Jost Niederhöffer and Anna Lozen, 6.5.1783.

53. StaM, P/II Reizberg and Caldern, Ep, 1780–1820, Werner Koch, 6.5.1783.

54. StaM, P/II Reizberg and Caldern, Ep, 1780–1820, Ernst Löwer, 4.5.1782.

55. StaM, P/II Reizberg and Caldern, Ep, 1780–1820, Johannes Mertin and Eliesabetha Becker, 24.12.1783.

Marriage also helped redistribute the means of production across generations. As children married into and out of Oberhessian peasant households, they participated in a long-term process of property devolution that had many intentions and values behind it. Moreover, the way peasants carried out these acts changed the "life courses" of the couple, both sets of parents, and both sets of siblings and established, at least temporarily, whose life plans were going to take precedence in the future.[56]

As we have seen in the discussion of the Hufen edict, two broad categories of inheritance practice existed for the peasants of Oberhessen and the parish of Oberweimar. The dominant system, Anerbenrecht, peasants practiced primarily on tenures that were technically not inheritable. Called *Lehnland,* farmers held such tenures under the *Landsiedelrecht, Meierecht,* or other short term tenure (three to seven years).[57] On the one hand, they separated ownership from usefruct so that peasants passed short-term leases of land use to their heirs through fictive purchases. Leases were not heritable and the land covered by them was not legally divisible.

On the other hand, the right of Hessian landlords to recall leases for redisposition eroded over the course of the eighteenth century. The Landgrave's judicial officials invoked a variety of principles from Roman law to achieve this result.[58] The Landgrave came under fire on this score from the Ritterschaft in the Hessian Diet, but peasants gained more secure possession over their land.[59] Karl Strippel argued convincingly that the hold of landlords over closed estates weakened sufficiently so that the institution of separate cadastral documents for peasant land and noble holdings rendered peasant tenures essentially private property on which they owed some dues.[60] The loss of control by landlords over these tenures meant that the Landgrave had to step in to prevent the fragmentation of closed estates through inheritance legislation which forbade the division of such land.[61] Closed tenures

56. Rebel, "Peasant Stem Families," 260; and Sabean, "Aspects," 96–111.

57. Holtzapfel, "Öberlandsbezirk Kassel": Teodor Mayer-Edenhauser, *Untersuchen über Anerbenrecht und Güterschluß in Kurhessen* (Prague, 1942); Fox, "Studies in the Rural History of Upper Hesse," 368–71.

58. George Lenneps, *Abhandlung von der Leye zu Landsiedelrecht* 2 (Marburg, 1768–9), xxiv ff.

59. StaM, B/5 14725, 40, 1764.

60. Karl Strippel, *Die Währschafts- und Hypothekenbücher Kurhessens* (Marburg, 1914), 150–72, 180–87.

61. StaM, HLO 19.11.1773.

passed to the next generation through a fictional sale by the current holder to the selected heir.[62] The heir remained responsible, both for compensating his parents through some retirement arrangement and for providing his siblings with a share of the value of the community property created by their parents' marriage.

The alternative practice of real division of the community property (*Realteilung*) was commonly used on tenures that were specifically designated heritable leases, or in some cases, peasant-owned (*Erbland*). Here parents divided immovables but designated an heir who they advantaged with the buildings and the draft animals.[63] Some divisions were fictional because siblings would sell the heir their portions in order to keep the tenure whole. Others were not, which necessitated the reconstitution of farms in each generation through judicious marriages.[64]

Differing forms of devolution in the parish of Oberweimar may have been linked to class differences. According to the cadastral surveys of the 1740s, less than half of the tenured residents (71 of 150) of the parish held any land by Lehn tenures. Nevertheless, these tenures accounted for just over two-thirds (3,600 Ackers) of all land. Still, all but twenty-one tenures had some Erbland, though holdings of Erbland averaged less than twelve Ackers. Although there were only four tenures that were all Lehnland, twenty-nine were exclusively Erbland. Of seventy-one tenures containing indivisible property, only nine held less than twenty total Ackers.[65] This figure is significant in light of G. T. Fox's calculation that seventeen Ackers was the minimum amount of tillable land capable of yielding an agricultural surplus for a normal household.[66]

Given the distribution of Lehn and Erbland in Oberweimar, it is not surprising to find that there was a strong and significantly positive correlation between the total size of a tenure and the percentage of Lehnland in the tenure.[67] A somewhat weaker negative correlation

62. StaM, P/II Allna 3, Hypothekenwesen 1768–1799.

63. Ibid., and compare Goody, *Family and Inheritance*.

64. Holtzapfel, "Oberlandsbezirk Kassel," 41 ff.

65. StaM, K/I Allna 1746, etc., compare Berkner, "Inheritance," 71–95. The practice of unofficial division was certainly not nearly as widespread in this area of Hesse-Cassel because the cadaster denied its existence. On the other hand, the proliferation of small dwellings on the same property, which Berkner took as substantial evidence of unofficial division of tenures, did not occur frequently.

66. Fox, "Studies in the Rural History of Upper Hesse," 372–73.

67. Pearson's r = .79; two-tailed significance (T sig.) shows less than a .001 chance

existed between large estates and high percentages of Erbland.[68] These findings confirm Fox's belief that larger farmers used fragments of divisible land to settle children not inheriting the major indivisible portion of their estates. For this purpose, it would appear that even the largest farmers had some such land on hand.[69] Only nine tenures holding indivisible property were tenures that contained less than half of that kind of land. Furthermore, over half (69 of 129) of the householders holding divisible property were found to have estates in which the total holding in the parish contained more than half Erbland. Because three-quarters of all holdings of Erbland were less than twelve Ackers in size, it seems safe to assume that a class of large farmers practiced both Anerbenrecht and Realteilung, while a class of smaller farmers used the complexities of real division. This latter impoverished class grew in numbers after 1762.

It would be tempting to conclude that Anerbenrecht predominated over the land, while most people had at least some experience with Realteilung — either full or partial. This conclusion is weakened, however, because in more than two hundred marriage and devolutionary contracts for the years 1780–1820, I have found only four cases in which a property was divided relatively equally among several heirs.[70] Moreover, the cadastral material of the parish Oberweimar does not reveal the complexity that would result from reconstitution of viable productive units in each generation. Finally, the frequency with which land appears as part of dowry arrangements was also fairly low. This evidence suggests that many peasant tenure holders probably practiced Anerbenrecht even when it was not a legal requirement.[71]

The marriage contracts available to us reveal a number of different patterns regarding the timing of property devolution. In some cases, contracts constituted the actual act by which managerial authority and legal title changed hands. Alternatively, we find the title handed over, but not the managerial authority whose transfer occurred at some later time. Under a third set of circumstances, the document represented only a promise that both title and managerial authority

---

that this is the result of random variation. Michael Lewis-Beck, *Applied Regression: An Introduction* (Beverly Hills, 1980).

68. $r = -.60$; T sig. $\langle .001$.
69. Fox, "Studies in the Rural History of Upper Hesse," 371.
70. StaM, P/II Reizberg and Caldern, Ep 1780–1820.
71. Bourdieu, "Marriage Strategies," 127.

would eventually pass to the couple. Despite this variety of circumstances, some conclusions may be drawn about the values embedded in
these agreements.

The contracts of rural people from southwest Oberhessen manifested four principal intentions: (1) continuity of the lineage in the
male line; (2) economic viability of the tenure; (3) just disposition of
household resources among siblings; and (4) provisions for old age and
retirement. Although all concerns found expression in most contracts,
the relative weight given to a particular concern depended upon the
varying strength of the interested parties and the strength of interest of
the strong parties.

Those residents of parish Oberweimar who made devolutionary
arrangements showed interests clearly consistent with the value of
lineage continuity. Legislative intervention by the state also supported
continuity in the male line.[72] Devolutionary practice in the village of
Allna was a clear example of the results of the pursuit of this value. For
the twenty-five tenures owned by peasants during the 1740s, there
were fifty-nine devolutionary transfers over the next eighty years.[73] Of
the fifty-nine, forty ultimately maintained the ownership of the tenure
in the male line despite the high mortality rates of the times. Jack
Goody suggests that the attempt to preserve male-line continuity must
come to grips with the demographic fact that 20 percent of all couples
will have no children and another 20 percent will have no male children. Oberweimar's parents with more than 60 percent success rate did
about as well as they could if not a little better.[74] For eleven tenures in
the village, continuity in the male line was maintained for three or
more generations while another eleven showed the same pattern for
two at least.[75] Preservation of the male line was more likely for large
tenures than for small ones. The eleven estates that fathers passed to
their sons two or three times in the eighty-year period under consideration averaged seventy-five Ackers, while those which were passed
only once averaged forty Ackers. Tenures that showed no continuity in
the male line (four) had a mean size of only two Ackers. Thus, not only
were wealthy farmers less likely to divide estates, but they were more
likely to give them to sons.

72. StaM, HLO 19.11.1773, 21.4.1786.
73. StaM, K/I Allna 1746.
74. Jack Goody, *The Development of Family and Marriage in Europe* (Cambridge,
1983), 44.
75. Two acts of devolution are required for three generations of continuity and one
for two generations.

By contrast, this value was under direct attack in the Hessian Diet and in the landgravial courts by tributary lords who wished to re-establish their right of recall on Lehn tenures.[76] This appears to be part of a European-wide inclination on the part of landlords to find ways of raising rents. The Landgrave's judicial officials had used the Roman law principles of bona empheteusis to defend the *de facto* heritability of these tenures. Others interested in the weakening of lineage continuity were men who found themselves marrying widows and the children of these second marriages. Inheritance law and practice meant that children of first marriages whose mothers had remarried frequently were given priority over those of the second and also over the retirement plans of their stepfather.[77]

The interest outsiders supported most frequently was that of economic viability for the tenure. Bureaucrats wanted the tax flow to remain uninterrupted, and landlords wanted their tributary rents placed on a secure footing. The larger and more unified the holding, the better were the prospects for the heir and for the couple retiring on the tenure. The concern for viability resulted in widespread support for the indivisibility of tenures — a practice which seemed to harm only those children who never became heirs. These dispossessed had to be satisfied with some portion of the calculated value of the estate.

That siblings of the heir got anything at all indicated that at least the appearance of a just division of community property was still valued. While siblings of heirs had a clear interest in support of this value, the state was ambivalent. After 1773, Frederick II made a concerted effort to reduce the portions of non-heirs by rigidly circumscribing the official value of tenures and by limiting the size of the portions themselves.[78] However, one of the first acts of his successor, William IX, softened this policy somewhat in light of complaints raised about children forced onto the roads with little or no portion at all.[79] Reduced portions for such children meant greater burdens on communal and other welfare institutions — a concern we have seen voiced in other contexts. It was not in the perceived interests of the Landgrave to create paupers on a massive scale.

Undoubtedly, some heirs welcomed Frederick's legislation as a way of unburdening themselves of the long-term debt on their estates repre-

76. Lenneps, *Abhandlung.*
77. StaM, HLO 19.11.1773; K/I Allna 1746.
78. StaM, HLO 19.11.1773.
79. StaM, HLO 21.4.1786.

sented by these portions.[80] One clear instance of this burden of debt comes to us in a loan application to the Landassistenzkasse made by the widow of Johann Dietrich Hermann. Attached to the application were accounts that show dowry debts dating from the 1760s which were not resolved until the late 1790s. Officials used debt encumbrance on peasant tenures as a rationalization for the restrictions on the size of dowry payments imposed by the inheritance legislation of 1773.[81] Landlords saw the harsher legislation as a boost for their incomes. Yet some of them also recognized that reducing portions for non-heirs meant reduced dowries and, hence, reduced chances for heirs to attract new resources into tenures.[82]

Closest to the heart of any rural parent negotiating a marriage contract must have been the prospects for a comfortable and influential retirement. Such arrangements seemed quite generous, often including full room and board with regular cash and produce subsidies.[83] Altenteil dispositions could be very extensive — as in the case of Johann Phillip Mathai of Niederweimar and his bride Anna Eliesabetha Fenner.[84] This couple was required to support the retirement of the bride's grandmother, her father, and the groom's father. Though this was quite a large estate (114 Ackers), the support of three non-working adults represented a substantial burden.

Burdens of this kind inspired attempts at limitation from several quarters. The law of 1773 directly prohibited retirement portions except in cases of pressing need (*dringende Noth*).[85] The Hufen edict seemed to represent an attempt by the Landgrave to diminish the wealth and authority of independent peasant elders. As we have seen, he failed in the end. The prohibition against early retirement was also reversed in the inheritance legislation of 1786. Such a capitulation was almost as significant for marriage settlements as the loosened restrictions on portions for non-heirs.[86] As with the removal of those latter restrictions, Landgrave William IX and his officials may have been worried about the stresses they caused on the structure of kin-ordered and patrimonial authority in the countryside.

80. StaM, B/23b ALb, Niederweimar 18, 1781.
81. StaM, HLO 19.11.1773.
82. StaM, B/4h 4072, Eigenbrodt.
83. StaM, P/II Reizberg and Kaldern, Ep, 1780–1820.
84. StaM, P/II Reizberg and Kaldern, Ep, 1780–1820, Johann Phillip Mathai and Anna Eliesabetha Fenner, 17.7.1783.
85. StaM, HLO 19.11.1773.
86. StaM, HLO 21.4.1786.

Weddings signified more than the joining of two persons. They also intertwined two wider networks of kin and of friends. In reinforcing old relationships and in creating new ones, a marriage often enhanced the productive capacity of both households through patronage ties, political alliance, credit, employment, and marketing. In-laws could be called upon for a wide range of favors. For example, when the Greben of Allna, Jost Bender, wished to hide a servant from military recruiters in 1780, he sent the young boy to live with his wife's brother in another village.[87] Marriage also helped to blur the hard lines of insider and outsider amongst the rural elite. When Magnus Dörr of Allna matched his daughter Cathrein to Johannes Mathai's son, Jost, sometime during the spring of 1783, he more than ensured his daughter's well-being.[88] Dörr had married the widow of one of Allna's most substantial farmers some twenty-one years before and had become one of the most expansionist peasants in the parish. Despite this economic success, he had not completed his social and political integration into the village.[89] Johannes Mathai, the father of the groom, was from an old family that had dominated parish politics since before the Thirty Years War.[90] Unlike Dörr, who had not even held rotational offices in the village, Mathai was an officer of the village court. The acceptance of Dörr's daughter into Mathai's family probably represented an important step in Dörr's integration into the parish elite, providing him with new connections.

Marketing relationships between households may have been another tie created by marriage in the Oberhessian countryside. Three market towns in the southwestern part of the region supplied in-marrying spouses more frequently than any others outside of the parish of Oberweimar. Among the 434 marriages I studied between 1722 and 1808 in the parish of Oberweimar, 266 spouses came from outside the parish. Of these, Marburg applied two brides and nine grooms, Lohra provided nine brides and nine grooms, while Fronhausen furnished seventeen brides and fourteen grooms. Together the three market towns supplied 21 percent of all outside spouses.[91] Though markets might be excellent places to meet future spouses and discuss

87. StaM, B/17e Allna 18.
88. StaM, P/II Reizberg and Kaldern, Ep, 1780–1820, Jost Dörr, Spring 1783.
89. KaOw, Kp, Hr, Allna 1665–1773; K/I Allna 1746, B/23b ALb, Reizberg.
90. Herbert Kossog, "Aus Vergangenheit und Gegenwart unserer Gemeinde," *Heimatswelt* 10 (1981): 19; StaM, B/23b ALb, Allna and Niederweimar.
91. Numeric data, unless otherwise cited, comes from the nominally linked data files; see the Appendix for descriptions.

potential matches, connections in market towns offered another valuable commodity — that of marketing information. Moreover, Fronhausen was also the seat of Amtschultheiß Kroeschel, who administered patrimonial jurisdiction over eight of the nine villages in parish
Oberweimar. Here we may see the influence of broader and more
political patronage networks at work.

Love, too, found a place in the process of matchmaking although
whether it played a creative or destructive role appeared, to some
extent, to be a matter of luck. Jost Becker's experience with unrequited
love, cited earlier, landed him first in the army and later in prison.[92] We
don't know what the woman whom he continued to court felt about
him, but her parents certainly strongly objected to his feelings. In 1801,
the *Landrat* von Schenck zu Schweinsberg also received a petition
which suggested how love might disrupt various kinds of plans. The
petitioning couple claimed that they had "loved one another in honor
for many years . . . with the hope that the future would finally fulfill
our wish that we could bind ourselves together and marry."[93] The
couple had fled Hesse-Darmstadt, where parents had frustrated their
desire to marry, and come to live in Schweinsberg. They had slept
together in a moment of weakness and soon expected "the pawn of
love [a child]." They hoped the Landrat would release them from the
fornication fine and permit them to marry. Whether or not the hearts of
most German peasants easily followed the dictates of economics as
Pierre Bourdieu claimed was the case for French peasants is not easy to
determine.[94] On some occasions the pastors of Oberweimar noted an
abiding love when one member of aging couple passed on.[95] Whether
this love presided over weddings or whether it developed over long
years of common life cannot be said.

Affection and love were important. Conflict inevitably arose over
decisions about material and disciplinary considerations and so families needed some strong counterweight to keep things working. Perhaps because love developed more easily among people likely to know
one another, almost 78 percent of all marriages celebrated in parish
Oberweimar were endogamous within the small group of parishes
bordering one another in southwest Oberhessen. This pattern could be

92. StaM, B/17e Cyriaxweimar 9.
93. StaM, B/340, von Schenck zu Schweinsberg A 10, 1810b.
94. Bourdieu, "Marriage Strategies," 117–27.
95. KaOw, Kp, Br, Oberweimar 1760–1774.

a matter of information as well. A peasant negotiating a marriage arrangement would naturally prefer to know more about the people he was dealing with (and for), and since information about reputations, property relationships, and other important topics traveled mostly by word of mouth, it was likely to be of higher quality from near by.

While peasants appeared to be very careful about crossing geographic distances to make their marriage matches, they appeared less concerned about crossing chasms of wealth. Of 173 marriages from the Oberweimar sample that peasants celebrated between spouses of Oberhessian origin before 1756, only one third (58) connected social equals. (See Tables 4 and 5.) Equal marriages seemed overrepresented among the poorest couples in relation to the number of such families which existed in the parish in 1725. However, they were less so compared to 1747 figures and were underrepresented considering the numbers of spouses who came from the poorest sectors and the number of

Table 4. Wealth and marriage matches I, 1722–1808

Wealth	None (0 Ar)	Poor (<17 Ar)	Independent (<75 Ar)	Wealthy (>75 Ar)	Totals	Missing
N =	104	89	76	105	414	40
% Total	36.2	13.8	20.7	29.3		
% Bride's families	26.6	19.3	17.3	28.5	207	17
% Groom's families	23.7	23.7	19.3	22.2	207	23
% couples	29.5	17.9	17.9	25.1	207	8
% equal couples	20.7	34.5	15.5	29.3	58	0

SOURCE: Marriage database described in Appendix.

Table 5. Wealth and marriage matches II, 1722–1748

Wealth	None (0 Ar)	Poor (<17 Ar)	Independent (<75 Ar)	Wealthy (>75 Ar)	Totals	Missing
% children in equal matches	29.3	20.7	13.8	36.2	116	0
% grooms going down/up	—	13.9	17.6	22.0	46	0
	(29.5)	(29.1)	(24.3)	(—)	69	0
% brides going down/up	—	15.2	28.4	36.0	69	0
	(32.6)	(11.4)	(8.1)	(—)	46	0
missing	3	9	10	2	5	—

SOURCE: Marriage database described in Appendix.

couples who ended up there. Independent couples were also under-represented among equal marriages perhaps because they both needed and were able to make marriages which connected them with folks below them and above them. Their insecure position might make them more willing to risk the welfare of their children in order to secure themselves.

When we turn to unequal marriages we find some interesting discrepancies. Given Oberhessian preference for male heirs, it is not surprising that regression analysis shows that the wealth of the groom's family was a better predictor of the couple's wealth than that of the bride's family. (See Table 6.) If we return to Table 4, we see that these conditions produced substantial asymmetry. It was obviously more likely that wealthy and independent parents would match their daughters more frequently with men from poorer families than they would match their sons with women from lower strata. It would appear, then, that the social direction of daughters was primarily equal or downward. Pierre Bourdieu suggested that French peasants made upward matches for women to insure the subordination of wives to their husbands.[96] In Oberhessen, the conservation of dowry resources seemed more important. To marry a daughter to a lesser family probably cost less than to marry one to a family of equal or higher status.

The predominance of the complementary strategy, that of upward matches for men, did not mean that peasants necessarily transferred resources from dowering women to providing portions for men. According to Table 4, when couples received their portions many more of them ended up with nothing than the percentage of such propertyless families would indicate in the cadaster. Although only 12 percent of parents whose children married in 1725 and 18 percent of the same group in 1747 held no taxable wealth, nearly 30 percent of all couples ended up in this condition. When combined with the indication that wealthier families provided substantially fewer grooms (42) than brides (57), we receive the strong impression that rather than allow men to marry down, wealthy parents preferred not to marry them at all. Those not marrying were not heirs, but dispossessed brothers, particularly among the wealthier segments of the population. With little prospect for marriage, these young men saw few alternatives to military service or emigration.

Another, but opposite, asymmetry appears in the behavior of poor

96. Bourdieu, "Marriage Strategies," 117–27.

Table 6. Regression analysis: wealth of bride's family, groom's family, and couple (one-tailed test of significance)

	Bride's family	Groom's family	Couple
Bride's family	—	.161	.302
	—	(.017)	(<.001)
Groom's family	.161	—	.602
	(.017)	—	(<.001)

SOURCE: Marriage database described in Appendix.

but propertied peasants. Grooms from this group outnumber brides (46 to 33). Most grooms in this case married women from wealthier families. What could justify such an expense and a shift of resources from female dowries to male portions? Were parents trying to shield sons from military service through marriage exemptions in place since the late seventeenth century? Or did independent families recruit among the village's artisans in an attempt to diversify household sources of income? Descriptive sources remain silent about such marriages during this period, and so little may be said with certainty except that upward matches for males declined with rising wealth of the groom's family while downward matches for women became more likely.

In conclusion, the marriages in Oberweimar represented one way in which a predominantly impartible system of inheritance worked. Usually, male heirs received estates and their sisters married equal or less wealthy heirs. This arrangement was more true for the wealthy than for the poorer and middling types whose need for connections made them less selective in this manner. The wealthier the family the less likely the dispossessed sons were to marry. As Claude Lévi-Strauss and others have suggested, exchanges of women between families — in this case, wealthy women to poorer families — were used to extend networks of kin-related dependency.[97] Although the system of social reproduction helped produce substantial differences in wealth between the families of the parish, marriage and servitude also cut vertically across these differences. In doing so, peasants established a tendency for the number of propertyless persons to increase. (Compare 1725 with 1747 in Table 3.) At the same time, conjunctural considera-

97. Claude Lévi-Strauss, cited in Goody, *The Development of Family,* 240–41.

tions and careful husbanding of resources meant that the numbers of wealthy also increased. In short, the gap between rich and poor widened. The lines between possessed and dispossessed within families were quite clear and were only sharpened by recruiters sweeping the countryside of "masterless servants and loafers."

Before 1762, the increasing penetration of regional, European, and worldwide markets, the intensification of agriculture, the operation of impartible inheritance, and the articulations between kin and tribute all tended to divide the peasant society of Oberhessen into haves and have-nots. At the same time, their world was not riven by open class conflict. Rather, conflict was repressed and diffused by ties of authority that cut across boundaries of wealth and privilege. The directors of the kin-ordered productive enterprises blurred those boundaries by manipulating the relations of servitude, marriage, and inheritance to create networks of dependency and exchange which kept the system from exploding. In general, the military system tended to reinforce existing authorities by providing mandatory military service for the dispossessed, by making protection by village authorities more important, and by providing a threatening and unfortunate alternative to becoming contractually bound in civilian service. But this was all to change with the military reforms of Frederick II after 1762.

8 Military Reform, Social Change, and System Crisis, 1762–1793

Studies of social change in rural eighteenth-century Europe have focused on demographic growth, the formation of classes of rural wage workers, and the modification of authority in households, communes, and states. In this chapter I draw connections between these dimensions of social change in Hesse-Cassel and the reforms of military recruitment and property devolution carried out by Landgrave Frederick II after 1762. Thus, the reforms discussed in earlier chapters "rationalized" and rendered transparent the rules of recruitment and thereby contributed substantially to typical patterns of eighteenth-century social change in the parish of Oberweimar. As the peasants attempted to protect their sons by changing marriage behaviors and inheritance practices, the Landgrave attempted to control peasant inheritance and to further rationalize authority in the countryside. Both official responses and peasant adjustments accelerated an erosion of intimate and patrimonial authority. The accelerated pace of social change also contributed to the end of the longstanding consensus among Hessian elites about the benefits of the Hessian mercenary military system. More important, it helped sharpen social differences within villages and kin-ordered productive enterprises. As Hesse-Cassel embarked upon the road to capitalism, these sharpened social differences meant that each generation produced a dispossessed underclass whose members left to seek their fortune elsewhere.

Population Growth, Parental Authority, and Social Change

The demographic movements in Europe's kin-ordered societies are a major focus of social historians — particularly those who write about the eighteenth century. Population fluctuations have been compared to the "immense respiration of a social structure."[1] Many scholars give precedence to the study of population because they believe the number of people represents in some very crude summary form the relative performance of systems of production organized around biological reproduction. However, as I will show, the growth that came under the influence of the Hessian subsidy system was not a happy circumstance for many Hessian subjects.

E. A. Wrigley and Roger S. Schofield's *Population History of England* made two significant contributions to our understanding of the demographic sea change in eighteenth-century kin-ordered societies which we may apply to Hessian conditions.[2] First, their equilibrium model of preindustrial demographic patterns represents substantial progress over earlier models which stressed growth as the "natural order" of human populations — a growth held in check in early modern Europe only by the stalking horsemen of the apocalypse — fire, disease, famine, and war.[3] In the new model, increased fertility and nuptiality explain more of England's demographic surge beginning in the mid-eighteenth century than does reduced mortality. According to this view, new opportunities for subsistence-sustaining wage work enabled more poor English men and women to marry, and also encouraged them to wed at younger ages than before. This new "proletarian" mode of family formation destroyed a preindustrial homeostasis and resulted in more than a century of sustained, if irregular, growth in the numbers of people.[4] Second, this new perspective opened doors to various local

1. Emanuel LeRoy Ladurie, *The Peasants of Languedoc*, trans. John Day (Chicago, 1974), 4.

2. Edward Anthony Wrigley and Roger S. Schofield, *The Population History of England: A Reconstruction* (Cambridge, 1981); Roger S. Schofield, "Through a Glass Darkly: *The Population History of England* as an Experiment in History," in Schofield and Wrigley, *Population and Economy: Population and History from the Traditional to the Modern World* (Cambridge, 1986), 11–34.

3. E. A. Wrigley, "The Growth of Population in Eighteenth-Century England: A Conundrum Resolved," in E. A. Wrigley, *People, Cities, and Wealth: The Transformation of Traditional Society* (Oxford, 1987), 215–41.

4. Myron Gutman, *Toward the Modern Economy: Early Industry in Europe, 1500–1800* (Philadelphia, 1988), 155–93.

explanations of demographic change which focused upon the central decisions made by directors of kin-ordered productive enterprises.

Of the triad of demographic events — birth, marriage, and death — marriage was the central act in ordering labor, distributing surpluses, and continuing social reproduction. Cultural limits to marriage in European kin-ordered societies almost certainly contributed to any preindustrial population equilibrium. These restraints, including inheritance practices, strict governance of village common rights, and moral supervision of marriage by a variety of authorities and methods, varied widely according to custom and locality.[5] One way or another, these restraints firmly attached reproductive license to the possession of land and communal enfranchisement.

Some historians offer protoindustrialization as one explanation for the erosion of traditional restraints on marriage.[6] Rudolf Braun's original analysis of the putting-out system in Switzerland demonstrated that new opportunities for wage work gave children the chance to avoid the sexual discipline stemming from parental control of family and village property.[7] A pattern of early marriage and sustained population growth followed the separation of the right to marry from rights to land. While such studies do not ignore the social and economic costs of such developments, they remain inclined to picture population growth as a sign of liberation from familial authority.[8]

While explanations based on a wide variety of forms of rural industrialization remain instructive, they focus too narrowly upon processes growing out of commodity exchange. The central characters in commodity exchange, merchants, redirected flows of wealth to supply consumer markets and so stimulated the development of rural indus-

---

5. Jack Goody et al., eds., *Family and Inheritance: Rural Society in Western Europe, 1200–1800* (Cambridge, 1976); Thomas Robisheaux, *Rural Society and the Search for Order in Early Modern Germany* (Cambridge, 1989), 105–16.

6. David Levine, *Reproducing Families: The Political Economy of English Population History* (Cambridge, 1987); Peter Kreidte, *Peasants, Landlords and Merchant Capitalists: Europe and the World Economy, 1500–1800* (Cambridge, 1980); Franklin Mendels, "Proto-Industrialization, the First Phase of Industrialization," *Journal of Economic History* 32 (1972): 241–61. Compare L. A. Clarkson, *Proto-Industrialization: The First Phase of Industrialization?* (London, 1985).

7. Rudolf Braun, *Industrialisierung und Volksleben: Die Veränderung der Lebensformen unter Einwirkung der verlagsindustriellen Heimarbeit im ländlichen Industrialgebiet vor 1800* 2 (Göttingen, 1979).

8. Hans Medick, "The Proto-industrial Family Economy," in Hans Medick et al., eds., *Industrialization before Industrialization* (Cambridge, 1981), 56.

tries.[9] The fiscal-military states of Europe, however, redirected even larger sums in search of power, security, and glory.[10] Under these circumstances, the social and demographic effects of consumer markets seem less exclusively interesting than potential changes stemming from vast outlays for war-making activities. To begin with, the need to supply armies and navies with men, material, and weapons contributed to the development of rural industry in more than one region.[11] What is more, war itself was a crucial — if negative — influence on the numbers of people.

To date, Myron Gutman's study of the Basse-Meuse, *War and Rural Life in the Early Modern Low Countries,* is the most systematic examination of the effects of military activity on economic and demographic trends in pre-industrial Europe. Gutman's findings support the common view that military and fiscal reforms between 1650 and 1750 increased the total burdens of war but spread them over wider geographic areas and larger segments of the European population. For the Basse-Meuse itself, the negative impact of almost constant military activity during the seventeenth century became part of a self-equilibrating demographic system. Although seventeenth-century warfare had its most terrible demographic effects in tandem with bad harvests, contact alone — the mere presence of armies — caused lower rates of marriage and higher rates of mortality, as well as destruction of rural industry and reduction of agricultural investment.[12] At no time did this region suffer the serious demographic losses which laid waste to many areas of Germany during the Thirty Years War.[13] If German people "failed" to adapt successfully to the locally intense effects of seventeenth-century warfare, how then did they cope with the more

9. Kreidte, *Peasants,* 136.

10. Joseph Schumpeter, "The Crisis of the Tax State," in Alan T. Peacock et al., eds., *International Economic Papers: Translations Prepared for the International Economic Association* (New York, 1954); Geoffrey Parker, *The Military Revolution: Military Innovation and the Rise of the West 1500–1800* (Cambridge, 1989); Fritz Redlich, *The German Military Enterpriser and His Workforce* 2 (Wiesbaden, 1964–65); Charles Tilly, ed., *The Formation of National States in Western Europe* (Princeton, 1975); John Brewer, *The Sinews of Power* (London, 1989).

11. Ottfried Dascher, *Das Textilgewerbe in Hessen-Kassel vom 16.-19. Jahrhundert* (Marburg, 1968), 127–42.

12. Myron Gutman, *War and Rural Life in the Early Modern Low Countries* (Princeton, 1980), 198–99.

13. Gunther Franz, *Der dreißigjährige Krieg und das deutsche Volk* (Stuttgart, 1979).

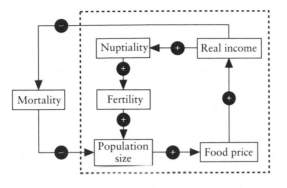

Chart 2. E. A. Wrigley's model of demographic equilibrium. Adapted from E. A. Wrigley and Roger Schofield, *The Population History of England: A Reconstruction* (Cambridge, 1981), reprinted with permission of Cambridge University Press.

diffuse, and extractive military institutions of the eighteenth century?[14] As this chapter will show, the new institutions of the Hessian fiscal-military state articulating with kin-ordered peasant enterprises contributed to population growth, the erosion of intimate authority, social differentiation, and a crisis of "legitimation" for tributary authorities. These changes reversed seventeenth-century demographic and social relationships with grimly paradoxical consequences for peasant households. Leviathan's military practices helped to produce the very people it sacrificed on the altar of modern war.

Constructing a model of the influences of the Hessian subsidy system on demographic behaviors is a difficult task because several variables exerted contradictory pressures. Wrigley and Schofield's equilibrium model in Chart 2 gives an idea of the complexity of the problem. The subsidy system impinged directly on demographic events by taking young males from the population and replacing them with older ones. A 1793 census shows for that year 343 men of every 1000 between the ages of fifteen and twenty-five served in the Hessian army.[15] Earlier, in 1773, the Hessian army had a total of 18,600 troops under arms — a ratio of 1 soldier for every 14 Hessian subjects (males and females of all ages).[16] This is considerably higher than the ratios of 1:19 reported

14. Gutman, *War and Rural Life*, 196–208; Otto Büsch, *Militärsystem und Sozialleben im alten Preussen* (Frankfurt, 1981).

15. StaM, B/5 2107.

16. Army size from Hans Vogel and Wolfgang von Both, *Landgraf Friedrich II. von Hessen-Kassel* (Munich, 1973), 98; Hessian from George Thomas Fox, "Studies in the Rural History of Upper Hesse" (Ph.D. diss., Vanderbilt University, 1976), 20.

before the Seven Years War and also the 1:23 ratio reported for Prussia (often cited as the most militarized eighteenth-century state).[17] In 1787, the soldiers from a typical conscripted regiment averaged seven and one half years of service and had an average age at recruitment of 19.2 years. Forty-six percent had served more than a decade and 13 percent more than fifteen years.[18]

Presumably, such a service profile had prominent negative effects on the crucial variables of fertility and nuptuality. Moreover, the payment of military taxes tended to reduce real incomes. On the other side of the ledger, the absence of young men for long periods of time might have contributed to a reduction in food prices and resulted in rises in real income. Furthermore, protoindustrial income earned in supplying military uniforms and weapons along with military wages may have contributed yet more to rural wealth.[19] Complicating any of the above assessments is the probability of human adjustments and attempts to manipulate the rules of recruitment and taxation in ways which affected population size.

During the eighteenth-century, the negative demographic effects of the subsidy system appear to have been overwhelmed by positive factors. Graph 3 shows that Oberhessen experienced two long periods of population growth on either side of a period of stagnation between 1730 and 1763. The first period of growth extended well back into the seventeenth century and lasted until 1730. It is usually explained as a recovery from the destruction of the Thirty Years War, which hit the region particularly hard.[20] The second period of growth, beginning after the Seven Years War, has been attributed to reductions in mortality over the course of the entire century — reductions whose effects were delayed by the terrible demographic crisis of the Seven Years War.[21] But no study of these movements would be complete without taking a more intimate look at the details of the demographic system at the parish level. The register of parish Oberweimar shows population trends in the parish which roughly paralleled those of the wider Oberhessian region (Graph 3) and varied only slightly from a second parish

17. Hans Vogel and Wolfgang von Both, *Landgraf Wilhelm VIII. von Hessen-Kassel: Ein Fürst der Rokokozeit* (Munich, 1964), 68; Andre Corvisier, *War and Society in Europe, 1494–1789* (Bloomington, Ind., 1979), 113.
18. StaM, B/11 MRb, vacantes Bataillon 783.
19. Dascher, *Das Textilgewerbe,* 127–42.
20. Franz, *Der dreißigjährige Krieg,* 41–45; Dascher, *Das Textilgewerbe,* 160–67.
21. Fox, "Studies in the Rural History of Upper Hesse," 316 and 348–51.

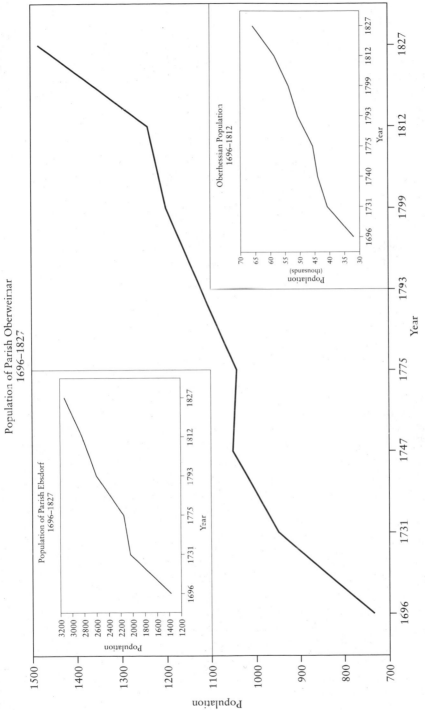

Graph 3. Hessian population movements in the eighteenth century. Sources: StaM, H/118 1799; George Thomas Fox, "Studies in the Rural History of Upper Hesse" (PhD. diss., Vanderbilt University, 1976), 2c.

fifteen kilometers to the east.[22] Arthur Imhof's results show vital rates which are also roughly comparable for parishes outside Hesse-Cassel and in the area 30 km to the south.[23]

The history of population movements in parish Oberweimar allows us to make two statements with confidence. First, in rural parishes not heavily affected by protoindustrial development, the connection between the subsidy system and population size was primarily negative. Second, the parish of Oberweimar maintained a surplus of births over deaths because peasants changed marriage behavior, had more children in wedlock, and experienced increased numbers of illegitimate births. The important demographic story for this parish lies in the intricate unfolding of the changes in patterns of social reproduction.

The demographic history of Oberweimar and its five villages and four hamlets was more complicated than the rough curves in Graph 3 indicate. Periods of growth and recovery punctuated periods of crisis and stagnation. (See Table 7.)[24] Four times during the century the parish suffered from multiple consecutive years in which deaths outnumbered births; 1717–1718, 1731–33, 1757–61, and 1772–73. Epidemics caused the first two declines and a European-wide subsistence crises with harvest failures and food prices triple what one might expect given eighteenth-century trends contributed to the fourth.[25] The Landgrave had not ordered his troops to serve outside the territory during any of these three crises and so we cannot with confidence assert any direct relationship between them and the subsidy system.

The third crisis — by far the worst — came during the war years 1757–61, along with the absence of troops on subsidy duty, military occupation, and fighting around Oberweimar. Military activity, combined with high prices and outbreaks of disease, yielded 109 more

22. Ibid.

23. Arthur A. Imhof, "Die nicht-namentliche Auswertung der Kirchenbücher von Giessen und Umgebung. Die Resultate," in his *Historische Demographie als Sozialgeschichte: Giessen und Umgebung vom 17. zum 19. Jahrhundert* (Marburg, 1975), 1:243.

24. KaOw, Kp, Tr, Kr, Hr, Br, 1660–1830, 1–8. All aggregate demographic figures were provided by G. T. Fox. They differ from those found in Taylor, "Military System," 485, mostly because he eliminated non-Hessians from the counts in a manner more consistent with good demographic technique. I am grateful to him for pointing out the descrepancies and especially for letting me use his counts.

25. Fox, "Studies in the Rural History of Upper Hesse," 429–31. A least-squares regression equation was calculated on the basis of Fox's price series and used to produce predicted prices as recommended by Gutman, *War and Rural Society.*

Table 7. Comparative vital rates in Parish Oberweimar, 1700–1800

Period	Mean births per year	Mean weddings per year	Mean deaths per year	Mean natural increase per year	Number of cases
1700–1799	32.48	8.00	27.26	5.22	100
1700–1730	30.35	7.94	23.65	6.71	31
1731–1733	32.00	10.00	37.00	−5.00	3
1734–1746	33.15	8.61	28.31	4.85	13
1747–1755	33.33	8.44	27.89	5.44	9
1756–1762	29.00	7.14	42.57	−13.54	7
1763–1775	36.00	8.38	26.23	9.77	13
1775–1800	33.71	7.38	26.00	7.71	25
1677–1815[a]	30.02	7.96	26.63	3.40	48
1677–1815[b]	33.10	7.47	25.04	7.70	91

SOURCE: George Thomas Fox, "Baptisms, Burials, and Weddings in Parish Oberweimar" (unpublished, 1973); KaOw, Kp I–VIII, 1660–1830, Br, Hr, Tr.

[a] Years troops were absent

[b] Years troops were not absent

deaths than births. The parish suffered all of the effects of seventeenth-century warfare with the exception of wanton destruction and uncontrolled looting at the hands of ill-disciplined troops. Oberweimar frequently found itself between hostile armies descending on the town of Marburg. Usually through the routine of tax collection, its surpluses found their way into the coffers of the occupying armies. The presence of several different armies brought disease and disrupted agricultural routines, while fighting destroyed crops and buildings.

Although physical destruction recalled the wars of the past century, this time of trouble represented the effects of the new warfare rather than the old. Hessian involvement in the Seven Years War became a certainty when French diplomats failed to break the subsidy relationship between the Landgrave and the king of England. French generals could not attack Hanover without leaving a flank exposed to Hessian units; therefore their invasion of the Landgrave's territory came early in the war.[26] What is more, the use of Hessian subsidy troops to defend Hanoverian neutrality meant that French occupation of Hesse-Cassel was more easily accomplished, more easily sustained, and more difficult to dislodge.

26. Günther Hollenberg, "Landstände und Militär in Hessen-Kassel," *Hessische Jahrbuch für Landesgeschichte* 34 (1984): 107.

The intensity of the Seven Years War, and the subtler effects of the subsidy system had negative consequences for the Hessian countryside. During the forty-eight years before 1815 in which Hessian soldiers fought away from home, the mean yearly surplus of births over deaths in parish Oberweimar totaled less than half that during years they remained in the territory. (See Table 7.) A similar comparison of the same groups of years in eight rural parishes around Gießen suggested the same disparity between subsidy years and non-subsidy years but not nearly as sharp a one.[27] A reduced number of births, rather than any change in the numbers of deaths, accounted for most of this loss. The reductions in fertility, a predictable result of conscripting males of reproductive age for military service, meant that the parish had perhaps 17.7 percent fewer people in 1799 than it might have, had it not been for reduced growth during subsidy service years.

In a manner consistent with the Wrigley-Schofield model and with Gutman's findings about the effects of war, peasants overcame demographic losses in the years after troops returned home. For nine years after the Wars of the Spanish Succession, on average, the number of births remained roughly equal (33) to the mean number births for years in which troops stayed home. But in three of the nine years they surged beyond that mean (33.09). In the nine years after the War of the Austrian Succession four years also exceeded the means for years troops were home but the mean for those years was 1.5 births higher. For six of nine years after the Seven Years War births exceeded the baseline measure and the mean number of births for those years exceeded the baseline by 3.6. Similarly, four of eight years (mean = 2.2 more than baseline) after the American War but seven of nine (mean = 2 more than baseline) after the French revolutionary campaign saw similarly heightened fertility. For all of these groups of years, mortality continued to be somewhat of a drag on population recovery with means higher than the home years' baseline (25.79) varying between .3 after the Seven Years War to 6.5 after the intervention in the French Revolution. Thus heightened fertility more often compensated for population losses — most intensely at the end of the century.

Peasants matched the ravages of war on their home soil as well. The crisis of the Seven Years War produced a net deficit (109) of deaths over births. Yet ten years after it was over, the population of the parish had all but recovered (1029 in 1773) its pre-war numbers (1039 in 1747). What is more, this recovery occurred despite the two crisis years of

27. Imhof, "Die nicht-namentliche Auswertung," 1:119–21.

Table 8. Differences between mean vital rates for the eighteenth century and the period 1763–1775 in Parish Oberweimar

	For 13 years at century means	*Actual numbers for 1763–75*	*Difference*	*Total births gained from*	*Percent of change*
Total births	422	468	+46		78
Total deaths	354	341	−13		22
Total gain	68	127	+59		100
% births illegit.	9.1	10.9	+1.8		
Total births illegit.	38	51	+13	$13^{(28.1\%)}$	
Weddings	104	109	+5	$19^{(41.1\%)*}$	
Legit. births per wedding	3.69	3.82	+.13	$14^{(30.8\%)**}$	

SOURCES: George Thomas Fox, "Baptisms, Weddings, and Burials in Parish Oberweimar" (unpublished, 1973); KaOw, Kp I–VIII, 1660–1830; George Thomas Fox, "Studies in the Rural History of Upper Hesse" (Ph.D. diss., Vanderbilt University, 1976), 287.
  *Gain = difference in weddings (5) × legitimate births per wedding (3.82).
  **Gain = difference in legitimate births per wedding (.13) × weddings (109).

1772 and 1773 when hunger, disease, and crop failures pushed the number of deaths beyond the number of births. Growth beyond the post-war recovery launched a demographic revolution that continued well into the nineteenth century. Heightening the apparent paradox, this demographic revolution after 1775 began precisely when troops were absent for the American campaign.

During the crucial thirteen years after the conflagrations of the Seven Years War, the net mean yearly surplus of births over deaths was nearly 9.8. This was the highest growth rate of the century and was 1.9 times the mean for the century. Most (78 percent) of the difference between mean yearly surpluses for the century and the surpluses of the years 1763–75 can be accounted for by increases in fertility during the latter period. The rise in fertility may be attributed mostly to increases in weddings, but also to increased marital fertility, and births out of wedlock.[28] (See Table 8.) Thus, more than two-thirds of the enlarged

28. Fox, "Studies in the Rural History of Upper Hesse," 287, estimated vital rates for the parish which are inconsistent with my findings. Although Fox shows the crude birth rate for the parish at 31.6 per thousand per year for the decade beginning 1755 and an increase to 38.8 per thousand for the decade beginning 1765, his figures also show drops in the marriage rate (from 8.9 to 8.2) and marital fertility rate (3.96 to 3.42). This [descrepancy between my numbers and his] is probably the result of lagging births 5 years at a time when there were strong fluctuations. The increase in illegitimacy from 9.1 percent to 10.9 percent of all births still cannot account for increase in the fertility rate.

number of births during this period represented reductions in celibacy. They signaled important changes in the pattern of reproductive behavior and laid the ground work for the slower but revolutionary growth in the numbers of people experienced in parish Oberweimar after 1775. After 1775, the average yearly net surplus of births over deaths dropped closer to century means (7.2). This second change occurred because fertility dropped by 2.2 births per year on average and mortality increased by .37 death per year on average. (1776–84, 1787, 1792–94 were all subsidy years.) (See Table 8.) From this point increased fertility (65 percent) and decreased mortality (35 percent) made more equal contributions to growth. Even so, the natural increase of the parish (180) almost doubles the net gain in population between 1773 and 1793 (91). The figures suggest net emigration from the parish on a substantial scale. Emigration did not, however, keep the parish from growing at the rate of .4 percent a year — higher than most German parishes between 1680–1820 but less than half English population growth over the same period.[29]

The aggregate demographic data of parish Oberweimar show that the most prominent negative effects of the subsidy system on population size resulted from Hessian involvement in the Seven Years War — an involvement attributable, at least in part, to the Landgraves' participation in the subsidy market. Landgraves also diminished Hessian population growth when they ordered their standing armies to serve outside of Hesse-Cassel for subsidies in forty different years during the eighteenth century. Despite these large deficits, the rural population of Oberweimar grew anyway. Peasants adjusted marriage behaviors, produced a few more children per marriage, and engaged in more unsanctioned unions with illegitimate births. We must now consider whether these adjustments themselves represented the peasants' response to the subsidy system.

Recruitment Reform and the Breakdown of Intimate Authority

In September 1787, the landgravial administration in Kassel reissued a writ from 1714 which admonished children "to hold their parents in honor [*in Ehren*], and treat them with due respect and modesty [*Bescheidenheit*]."[30] In their preface to the renewal, officials expressed

29. Gutman, *Towards the Modern Economy*, 126.
30. StaM, HLO 24.9.1787.

growing concern for the erosion of parental authority. They referred particularly to parents who had given up farms to their children early and had subsequently experienced beatings and verbal abuse from their heirs. Authorities warned that such children were not only "offenders against nature, but transgressed against God's law and worldly legislation" as well.[31]

Official anxiety was not the only reflection of a general weakening of ties of authority among Hessian kin-ordered households. As we have seen, loosened ties between parents and children have also been used to explain social change and population growth in many eighteenth-century societies. The numbers of rural Hessians had begun growing in 1762 and this growth was driven by those increases in marriages, fertility, and illegitimacy which seemingly signaled the loss of control by parents over the reproductive behavior of their children. As official hysteria indicated, these changes appeared with new patterns of inheritance and marriage-making. Although parental authority seems to have weakened in the period between 1763 and 1787, it did not seem to represent the liberation some students of historical demography might have us believe.

Changes in marriage behavior and parental authority can be attributed directly (at least in part) to changes in the regulation of the recruitment process for the subsidy army effected by the Kanton ordinance of December 1762. In the law, Landgrave Frederick II carefully specified the conditions which rendered young men eligible for conscription. As the regulations became more transparent to the parents of potential recruits, the parents were able to manipulate bureaucratic recruitment practice. Responding to the new information, Hessian peasants adjusted to this law which targeted their sons for long-term involuntary military servitude by altering patterns of marriage and property devolution.

The law represented an attempt to exempt from military service all holders of viable peasant farmsteads as well as the heirs to substantial ones.[32] Viable (*anspannig*) meant farms which required a plow team to work them. The amount of military taxes paid on the holding defined whether or not it was substantial (*stark begütherte*). Officials assessed taxes on the potential income of the farm and so based their demand for payments almost entirely on the amount and estimated productiv-

31. Ibid.
32. StaM, HLO 16.12.1762.

ity of the land held by the farmer. Holdings on which peasants paid one Reichstaler per month earned an exemption not only for a male holder, but also for one male heir as well. Exempted farms included every estate in parish Oberweimar that possessed more than seventy-five Ackers or eighteen hectares.[33] In the year 1747, out of 166 households in the parish, 84 qualified as viable, and, of these, 54 had sufficient property for officials to exempt one of the male children of the owner.

If we assume, with Hessian regional officials (whom we saw worrying that the draft threatened population size) that the threat of conscription reduced the pool of marriageable men, we would expect the parish's fifty-four wealthiest households to provide an increased proportion of spouses in marriages contracted after the institution of the draft. Theoretically, these large estates, acquired exemptions for the heir and provided sufficient compensatory portions to prevent disinherited males from emigrating. Contrary to expectations, the percentage of Oberweimar spouses from exempted estates was at its lowest during the years 1763–1774 when peace-time conscription was in effect. (See Table 9.) Particularly noticeable was the low percentage of first-time grooms coming from these larger estates.

If we compare the three groups of marriages made at mid-century (Table 10), we see that the reduced proportion of spouses from farmsteads carrying exemptions resulted both from increased numbers of grooms from nonexempt households and decreased numbers from exempt ones. We can safely say that the higher number of grooms from nonexempt households after 1763 did not occur as a result of increased numbers of small and middling households because the numbers of such households did not rise in the parish until after 1775. Rather, the marital behavior of nonexempted households differed so dramatically from that of exempted households that we are compelled to look to the higher risk of conscription for sons of nonexempt households to help explain changes in marriage and reproductive patterns.

Two connections between conscription, or the threat of it, and marriage patterns seem possible. First, conscription created a tighter labor market and therefore higher wages. Consequently, the expectation of greater income might affect potential couples in the same way as protoindustrial development. That is, higher wages meant young couples need no longer pay much heed to parental or village controls over property and could marry with greater frequency and at an earlier

33. StaM, K/I Allna 1746, etc.

Table 9. Percentage of spouses from Oberhessian marriages with parents whose tenures conferred draft exemptions

Years	1722–1732	1742–1753	1754–1762	1763–1774	1798–1808	Overall
Grooms	27.4	28.6	41.9	14.1	24.6	25.3
Brides	28.6	34.3	38.7	26.8	29.2	30.7

SOURCE: Marriage database described in Appendix.

Table 10. Oberhessian grooms from exempt and non-exempt tenures

Years	From exempt farms	From nonexempt farms	From untenured households
1742–53	20	44	6
1754–62	13	17	1
1763–75	10	54	7

SOURCE: Marriage database described in Appendix.

age. Alternatively, the new marriage patterns may indicate a parental decision to provide several sons with property, and therefore draft exemptions, that otherwise might not have been available.

In Oberweimar, we have evidence of an increase in wages.[34] Both peasants themselves and officials who governed them complained about the increased cost of servant labor as a result of conscription. Problems became particularly acute between 1775 and 1784 when over twelve thousand men of the twenty-two thousand-man Hessian army served in America. The distant removal of these men meant that the system of extended leaves for half of each regiment which had been normal practice for the army could not mitigate labor shortages caused by involuntary military service.[35] But even before the American campaign, census data suggest that peasants in the parish adjusted to a tightened male labor market by increasing the number of females they hired as servants. (See Table 11.) The absolute numbers of male servants only recovered their 1747 levels after the draft was eliminated in 1794. More important, changes in the patterns of marriages came immediately with the institution of the draft, without the ten-year lag

34. Inge Auerbach, "Marburger im amerikanischen Revolution," *Zeitschrift für hessische Geschichte* 87 (1978/79): 321ff.; StaM, B/17e, Allna 18.

35. StaM, B/12 abN 8848, mL.

Table 11. Changes in the servant population of Oberweimar, 1747–1799

	1747	1773	1793	1799
Male servants	88	77	73	88
Female servants	94	109	105	97
M/F ratio	.936	.706	.696	.907

SOURCE: StaM, K/I Allna 1746 etc., B/23b ALb, Allna etc., B/17e Allna etc. B/5 2107, H/ 118.

characteristic of English responses to higher wages.[36] It is unlikely, therefore, that the opportunity of increased wages decisively impelled young peasants to liberate themselves from traditional restraints and establish new families. Nor, as we shall see, can the changes be laid to a pattern typical of recovery from demographic crisis (and irrelevant to conscription) where large numbers of new couples took over farms emptied of owners by the scourges of war.

Far from being a response to opportunities provided by death or higher wages, the increases in the numbers of grooms and brides from middling and poorer families indicated the use of marriage as a means of avoiding subsidy service. We find confirmation of this explanation in the behavior of Hessian peasants and in the testimony of government officials. Early marriage and settlement with an estate requiring a team of oxen theoretically exempted men from service in the standing army. Indeed, Hessian officials of the 1780s indicated that farmers had frequently settled sons on fragments of land not large enough to require the work of a plow-team, but purchased plow animals to acquire an exemption.[37] Such behavior helps to explain why the Landgrave instructed officials certifying the inheritance arrangements of rural dwellers to ensure that no marriages had been made to avoid the draft and that small estates with plow-teams actually required the animals.[38] It also helps to explain the rigid restrictions on the size of portions for disinherited youths which the Landgrave's officials imposed through the Hufen edict of 1773. The smaller the portion, the less likely it would be to support an independent existence and a draft exemption for a second son.

The artificially constricted labor market added its own element of

36. Wrigley, "The Growth of Population," 232.
37. StaM, B/4h 4072, von Keudel.
38. StaM, HLO 21.4.1786, 16.12.1762.

Table 12. Oberhessian couples from non-exempt farms who received full or fragmentary tenures

Decade beginning	Receiving full farms	Receiving fragmentary farms	Ratio
1742–53	37(4)	7	.189
1754–62	17(7)	0	—
1763–74	40(6)	14	.350

SOURCE: Marriage database described in Appendix. Numbers in parentheses are cases where couple received tenures of bride's parents. Excluded from this table are those couples whose parents were untenured. Inheritance data is simply not available for such couples. What is more, the access to land for both parents and couples was tenuous at best. It was illegal to hold land except on the basis of written leases. Parcels with such letters accounted for all available land in the villages. If the untenured had access to land it was as part of labor contracts or legally unprotected short-term rental contracts of one kind or another. Such parcels were not part of the inheritance paths here discussed.

compulsion to marriages among the children of middling and small peasants and helps to explain why the nonexempt behaved so differently than the exempt. Poorer households could less easily afford the increased costs of male labor and thus became more dependent on the work of family members. Yet, precisely these sons of middling and poor families became a primary target of the selective service legislation. Parents needed a way to gain their sons exemptions from subsidy service and to bind them to home and work.

For families hoping to save their sons from conscription and to keep them in the village, culturally and legally mandated strategies of impartible inheritance became dysfunctional and laden with heavy social strains. Table 12 suggests that some parents responding to these needs began dividing their estates among their children rather than follow past practices of impartible inheritance. The increase in the number of those receiving divided farms accounts for 70 percent of the increase in the number of couples coming from nonexempt families. (See Table 10.)

Traditionally, the division of estates is seen as a response to population growth rather than as part of its explanation.[39] What makes this construction less adequate in the circumstances under investigation is

39. Ladurie, *The Peasants of Languedoc,* 4–5; Conrad Vanja, *Dörflicher Strukturwandel zwischen Überbevölkerung und Auswanderung, zur Sozialgeschichte des oberhessischen Postortes Halsdorf, 1785–1867* (Marburg, 1978).

that parish population was lower between 1762 and 1774 than it had been in 1725 and 1747 and yet division occurred far more frequently in the later period than the earlier ones. The fact of increased division of properties also makes it unlikely that population increase after the Seven Years War can be seen as simple response of the demographic system to the losses of the wartime period as argued by Fox.[40] Normally, the burst of marriages in a recovery period would be couples taking over estates left vacant by the deaths of owners and so would not require this spate of division to take care of them.

As the 1763 marriage of Johannes Rau of Hadamshausen to Eliesabetha Laux of Hermershausen shows, the process of division among poorer families rarely occurred in a straightforward manner.[41] The couple settled in Hermershausen with a small shed, a cottage, and an Acker (.66 acre) of garden land. Eliesabetha's father, who died before the wedding, had long rented the house into which the couple moved. It was likely that even if he had never owned any property in the village, his business as a blacksmith made it possible for him to contribute to Eliesabetha's dowry and to help purchase the estate upon which the bride and groom lived.

However much of the father's resources went to making this marriage, the contributions of the groom's parents were decisive. At mid-century, cottages of the type Johannes and Eliesabetha bought usually cost 50 to 100 Reichstaler to build from scratch while those already in existence sold for Rt 28. The land, an Acker of prime garden land, sold for Rt 56 in 1746. Following general inflationary trends, the same estate probably cost somewhat more in the 1770s. In the year preceding the couple's purchase of the land and house, Johannes' father sold some of his medium-sized estate. It would seem that the lion's share of the purchase price for the couple's cottage came out of the Rt 95 received in 1770 by Johannes' father, Hans Henrich, for the sale of 1.75 Acker of prime crop land. The purchase price represented 25 percent of the assessed value of Rau's full estate and the sale documentation indicates that it was part of an inheritance transaction. Selling part of an estate to purchase more conveniently located or more functional property was a pattern typical of regions of Germany where partible inheritance was practiced.[42] It appeared then, that partibility

40. Fox, "Studies in the Rural History of Upper Hesse," 270.
41. KaOw, Kp, Hr, 1773; StaM, K/I Hadamshausen 1747, Hermershausen 1747; B/49d r M 186, Hermershausen; B/23b ALb, Hermershausen, Hadamshausen, 1773.
42. David Sabean, "Aspects of Kinship Behavior and Property in Rural Western Europe before 1800," in Goody, *Family and Inheritance*, 96–112.

was becoming a more frequent practice among Oberweimar's draft-vulnerable families.

The Rau couple had been bound to the parish by a parental promise to provide resources for the purchase, the direct record of which we no longer have. The couple lived in the neighboring village, within a ten-minute walk of Johannes' birthplace, rendering them theoretically available for work. Additionally, Rau purchased a team of oxen even though such a team could not effectively be used on his small garden plot. As recruitment nets spread wider and wider in the mid-1770s, Johannes Rau compounded any strategy to avoid conscription through marriage by later fleeing with his young bride and his parents. The couple left a young child in the purchased cottage with Eliesabetha's mother. Johannes returned only after the subsidy army departed for America in 1776, when recruitment needs of the state eased temporarily.

Although Johannes' father, Hans Henrich Rau, had not created or made possible any new farms on the land of his own estate in Hadamshausen, there is good reason to believe that the resources stemming from the sale of parts of this estate had created a new, much smaller one, in Hermershausen. The couple's cottage had belonged to the estate of Johannes Weyersheuser, one of two dwellings on his farm. It undoubtedly served as a retirement cottage before Weyersheuser sold it. Although the younger Rau became a property owner through this purchase, he did not possess the smith skills of his father-in-law, and so, he remained a member of the village's growing class of wage-workers whose property was as much a golden chain as a source of liberation from parental authority.

Another kind of marriage that was sharply limited during the first eleven years after the institution of the draft were those like the 1745 match of Anna Margretha Schneider of Rohnhausen and Henrich Iburg of Gisselberg. Anna's father, Ludwig, held a tenure on 32 Ackers which he passed on to a son. Henrich's father settled the newlyweds on his Gisselberg estate. The couple managed to increase this estate from 106 to 109 Ackers by 1747, suggesting that Anna brought substantial cash or movable resources into the marriage.[43] Anna came from a family that could not have exempted an heir after 1762, but married into one with an estate later eligible for exemption and three times the size of her father's marginally independent tenure. Table 13 shows that

43. StaM, K/I Gisselberg 1747, cites land purchase values varying from Rt 10 per Acker to Rt 35 per Acker.

Table 13. Grooms from exempted families marrying brides from non-exempted families

Years	Poor brides	Acquiring estate of groom's parents	Acquiring estate of both parents	Acquiring estate of neither
1742–53	8	3	2	2
1754–62	5	2	2	1
1763–74	2	1	1	0

SOURCE: Marriage database described in Appendix.

there were eight such upward marriages of women between 1742 and 1753, but only two after the institution of the draft.

The military system played an indirect role in this behavioral change. If middling farmers like Anna's father divided their estates to settle and exempt as many of their sons as possible, this meant sacrifices undoubtedly had to be made in their daughters' marriage portions. Such reductions made them less attractive matches for the sons of the wealthy. Concomitantly, as the capacity to attract wealthy males diminished, the need increased for poor brides to marry the growing number of poor men who were being settled to avoid the draft. More and more frequently, then, did marriage partners come from the same classes of wealth. The new pattern reduced the number of social ties across the chasms of wealth which were increasingly separating villagers from one another.

While families who could not exempt an heir frequently created new estates for disinherited sons, those who could protect at least one son responded to the threat of conscription much differently. These parents theoretically could have divided tenures and still kept them viable, yet they did not do so any more frequently than in the past. Tables 13 and 14 show that parents of this group ceased permitting their estates to pass through the hands of their daughters after the draft was instituted. After 1762, conscription made marriages where brides brought the estate less likely because its administration transparently increased the vulnerability of sons not receiving their paternal estate. The 1762 law defined disinherited sons as the household's most expendable (*entbehrliche*) people and made them another primary target for military recruiters.

As officials had noted, any soldier or potential draftee without property was a poor risk to parents who arranged the matches of their

Table 14. Oberhessian couples from exempt farms who received full or fragmentary tenures

Years	Receiving full farms	Receiving fragmentary farms	Ratio
1742–53	18(7)	2	.111
1754–62	11(2)	2	.181
1763–74	8(0)	2	.250

SOURCE: Marriage database described in Appendix. Numbers in parentheses are cases where couple received bride's family estate.

children.[44] If the match was made to provide additional retirement benefits for the parents or an influx of new capital for a farm from the inheritance portion of their in-marrying son-in-law, the legal status of soldiers and potential recruits rendered the attempt uncertain. Should the young groom be drafted, his inheritance portion and whatever other wealth he claimed were frozen by laws that prohibited soldiers from liquidating their assets. Additionally, soldiers could not even borrow money using these assets as collateral because the state attached a lien to them to prevent soldiers from deserting or fleeing.[45] Accordingly, these men could not sell their portions nor borrow against them, nor even consign them to some one else, which paralyzed them. In short, if the purpose of the marriage was to bring in new wealth to a family holding, the transfer might never occur once the young man became a soldier. Even worse, the groom's military liabilities might be attached to the property of his bride or her parents.

Tables 13 and 14 also show that fewer men from exempt families attained permission from their parents to marry. Parents of disinherited sons also had little incentive to provide them the resources necessary to marry. The chance that these resources would become bound up by the military service of their son also threatened them with potential legal and financial problems resulting from the failure to keep promises stemming from any such marriage. Allowing disinherited sons to be taken into the Landgrave's service even had potential benefits for parents who could afford to pay for labor to replace the absent adolescent. Such an alternative could easily prove financially less demanding than providing the undoubtedly large portion to match an heiress of independent stature. It is difficult to find anyone admitting

44. Chapter 5.
45. StaM, HLO 3.3.1786.

that such decisions were ever made, for they violated the notions of what parents owed children. A village headman tacitly admitted, however, that for one family a son's service in the army was a way of preventing conflict over the inheritance. Clearly his mother's favorite, Johannes Werner sought release from the army because she claimed he was inheriting the farm. This violated the wishes of the father who had tried to give it to his older brother. In this case, the headman could suggest keeping the boy in the army because he was not speaking of his own family but intervening to support the wishes of Werner's father.[46] Additionally, the army might be a place to put away a younger son discontented with his disinherited status, someone who frequently disrupted the work routines of the household with bickering and backbiting. Such a pattern was already established earlier in the century and apparently conscription strengthened it substantially.

If peasant parents responded to conscription by limiting their willingness to provide resources for upwardly marrying daughters and downwardly marrying and disinherited sons, then the severe disruptions of the rural credit markets after the Seven Years War almost certainly intensified their inclinations. Loans were commonly a necessary part of constructing a dowry, and acquiring them became more difficult because of currency manipulations by the Hessian Landgrave, further debasements of currencies in neighboring territories, and the loss of the right of creditors to seize livestock and other movables for bad debts.[47] Legislation which prevented the liquidation of soldiers' assets certainly contributed to the general crisis in credit reported by Hessian officials. Under these conditions, it is no surprise that a greater proportion of marriages occurred between partners within the different exemption categories. Not only were there more sons from nonexempt families in the marriage market but a smaller proportion of them found their spouses in exempt families. From 1742 to 1753, 29 percent of all first marriages of men from the nonexempt families were to women from exempt families. Between 1762 and 1775 this proportion had dropped to 18 percent. As fewer marriages were made across this bureaucratically-defined line, however, there was an absolute numeric reduction of ties across social boundaries. This shift represented at least a temporary sharpening of class boundaries.

Changes in the patterns of marriage and property devolution were

46. StaM, B/17e Gisselberg 7.
47. StaM, B/5 13446.

only part of the story. Yet another striking change in reproductive behavior was the increase in extramarital fertility from 6.8 percent of all births in 1745–54 to 10.9 percent in 1765–74.[48] A wide variety of sources over the course of the entire century connect illegitimate births to the unsanctioned unions of soldiers and local women. Not surprisingly, between 1773 and 1775 soldiers fathered two thirds of the babies born out of wedlock.[49] Between 1746 and 1748 they had been responsible for only two in eleven such births. As we shall see, this phenomenon resulted as much from the unwillingness of authorities at all levels to sanction soldiers' sexual unions as from any amorality on the part of soldiers.

Official attitudes revealed themselves in the frenzied tone of reports on soldiers' liaisons. As early as 1763, one official from Wanfried accused released veterans of dishonoring village girls, setting up illegal households with them on common land, illegally using common grazing areas for their livestock, and finally terrorizing village officials to prevent their behavior from being reported.[50] That such unions obviously went far beyond brief encounters to establishing permanent households suggests that soldiers and their lovers did not envision themselves as "living in sin."

The change in marriage patterns that represented the greatest threat to demographic equilibrium in the Oberhessian region was the increased number of couples, married or not, settled on fragmentary estates or without property. These couples represented a potential contribution to the population explosion in two ways. First, these couples were responsible for a nearly three-year decline in the mean age at first marriage for both men and women in the parish. (See Table 15.) As in Wrigley's Colyton, impoverished young couples represented a potential increase in marital fertility of one child per family.[51] Dependent on their own wages and those of their children, such people had strong incentives to have as many children as they could manage as one avenue to increase family income. Secondly, as each new couple began

48. Fox, "Studies in the Rural History of Upper Hesse," 287–88.

49. KaOw, Kp, Tr, 1660–1830. Compare Michael Mitterauer, *Ledige Mütter: Zur Geschichte illegitimer Geburten in Europa* (Munich, 1983), 90.

50. Otto Könnecke, *Rechtsgeschichte des Gesindewesens in West- und Süddeutschland* (Marburg, 1912), 63.

51. E. A. Wrigley, "Family Limitation in Pre-Industrial England," in Orest and Patricia Ranum, eds., *Popular Attitudes towards Birth Control in Preindustrial France and England* (New York, 1972), 53–99.

Table 15. Declining mean ages at first marriage in Parish Oberweimar, 1722–1799

	Males marrying 1720–60[a]	Females marrying 1720–60[a]	Males born 1743–48 not drafted[b]	Males born 1743–48 drafted[b]	Females born 1743–48[b]
Mean age at first marriage	29.5	29.1	24.5	37.0	25.1
N =	130	154	18[c]	12[c]	28[c]

[a]From George Fox, "Studies in the Rural History of Upper Hesse" (Ph.D diss., Vanderbilt University, 1976), 309.

[b]Marriage database after 1760 described in Appendix.

[c]Numbers are too small to be entirely confident about means but they are consistent with other evidence of marriage patterns. Final confirmation awaits full reconstitution of the Oberweimar parish register.

having children they increased both peasant and official pressure on village authorities to grant the new household official status. As villages gave in to these pressures, they established new permanent niches for reproducing couples in the villages.

Initially, however, this feature of marriage behavior resulted only in increased numbers of complex households in Oberweimar. As we have seen, the census taken in the parish during 1732 revealed only 20 complex households (more than one couple with children) out of 151.[52] All but one of these were three-generation family arrangements typical of regions of impartible inheritance customs which also required the heir to provide both retirement for his parents and compensation for disinherited siblings. A census of the same villages in 1773 showed 71 complex households out of a total of 171.[53] Many of the new complex households did not reflect the typical structure of the three-generation family. Rather than consisting of elders, inheriting couples with children, and servants, new combinations included two couples of the same generation or single mothers and their children living with relatives or with unrelated couples. Also, we find couples with children who had no prospect of inheriting the farm on which they were living. Such combinations suggest that, at first, the new establishments created by the fragmentation of estates did not constitute independent units. Their demographic significance would not

52. StaM, B/40d r 29, 76, 1732.

53. StaM, B/17e Allna unnumbered, Kehna 9, Gisselberg 3, Cyriaxweimar 10; B/23b ALb, Hadamshausen unnumbered, Niederweimar 7, Oberweimar, Hermershausen, Weiershausen all unnumbered.

Table 16. Occupied cottages and full
farmsteads in Parish Oberweimar, 1726–1799

Year	Farmsteads	Cottages
1726	91	58
1747	109	57
1775	112	58
1799	113	78

SOURCES: StaM, K/I Allna 1746 etc., B/23b ALb,
Allna etc., B/17e Allna etc. B/5 2107, H/ 118.

be long-term unless the establishments created to support them became both permanent and truly separate from the households and
farms out of which they were carved. As long as fragments of land did
not become associated with their own cottages and as long as couples
who held them lived with one set of parents or another, it was easier for
them to be reabsorbed into original holdings.

The new niches did become permanent, to some extent, as a direct
consequence of the Hessian military system. One factor, concern to
settle veterans, seemed particularly strong after the army returned
from the American campaign in 1784. For the first time we see regional
and territorial officials supporting the petitions of veterans who wished
to build cottages on village common lands.[54] Nine new cottages were
built in the parish between 1784 and 1790. Of these, six were built by
veterans of the American campaign. By 1799, there were twenty-one
more households in the parish than there had been in 1775. All but one
of these occupied small cottages with marginal amounts of land. (See
Table 16.) Moreover, financing this building spurt was possible because of payment to veterans of accumulated wages kept in military
treasuries as a surety against their desertion.[55] Abolished in 1794, this
policy of enforced savings apparently resulted in the influx of much
money after the American campaign. The viability of marginal households was further enhanced by the higher wages born of the labor
shortages caused by conscription.

Any account of social change in Hessian realms has to take into
consideration the adjustment of peasant kin-ordered enterprises to the
realities of the military system and its conscription policy. Conscrip-

54. StaM, B/17e Kehna 8, 1785.
55. StaM, B/4h 4159.

tion required such changes in the family because some families sought to gain exemptions for sons and keep them near to home. The military system reduced the supply of male labor in the countryside and thus changed the relative advantage of partible and impartible inheritance. On the one hand, households with sufficient land to exempt an heir became less likely to allow their estates to pass through the hands of their daughters or to allow their sons to marry women of lesser standing. On the other hand, families not able to acquire exemptions for heirs seemed to marry their children earlier and more frequently, giving up some control over their reproductive lives. To do so, they divided their estates, making those sons property holders who were not eligible to serve in the subsidy army. The same decision bound young couples to wage work through permanent poverty and dependence. The new patterns of heirship probably contributed to increased numbers of children for each marriage, an increased number of establishments to support reproducing couples, and increased numbers of extramarital unions. By all official reports, the new establishments subsisted on the margins of village society and increased in numbers even more quickly after the inheritance reforms of 1773, so that when population growth came after 1775 it resulted in increasing numbers of desperately poor people. The Hessian selective service system helped to create the very expendable people it hoped to draft at the expense of parental and village authority so important for kin-ordered production. Not a liberation, the dissolution of intimate authority in Hesse-Cassel was accomplished by, and in the end, favored the further establishment of the rationalized and distant authority of the Hessian mercenary state.

The Decline of Patrimonial Authority in the Countryside

By 1772, peasants had evaded conscription and abused tax collecting authority for at least a decade. In response to such conditions, Frederick II began a second wave of reform which included the institution of Landräte to manage recruitment and to oversee tax accounts in the villages. Additionally, he instituted a policy of tax farming. Most important of all, he attempted to intervene directly in the processes of social reproduction through the Hufen edict. We have already seen how officials, particularly the Landräte, responded to both recruitment and inheritance legislation in an extremely critical way and connected both with the absence of troops fighting in America after 1776 as causes of crisis in rural society. But how did the directors of kin-ordered enterprises respond to this second wave of reform which, in part, was a response to their own earlier evasions?

At least temporarily, and probably very fitfully and carefully, peasant mediators began withdrawing some of the services they provided to tributary authorities. As I have remarked, evoking obedience in early modern Germany involved unequal exchanges between authorities (both official and unofficial) and subjects. While subjects offered obedience in the form of material wealth and other services, the service offered by authorities was protection. Within the context of a patrimonial officialdom and the patriarchal relations of a peasant commune or household, protection was a personal relationship and necessarily involved the preferential treatment of friends over enemies. To the extent that recruitment policy proceeded rationally, that is without respecting "friendship or other moving causes," it foreclosed this kind of preferential personal protection.[56]

Similarly, when officials intervened in peasant inheritance as the Hufen edict required, they acted on the basis of objective and quantified standards. The rigid way the law constructed inheritance possibilities meant that enforcement favored heirs over both their parents and their siblings. While dispossessing siblings may have served some purposes of the military system, it tended to thwart those parents seeking to use inheritance settlements to vault into retirement status by making such moves illegal. These elders were the very people who mediated authority through credit, through their village offices, and through their position as church leaders. Their collaboration was crucial to military recruitment and tribute collecting, and to the functioning of demographic restraints. Under the new conditions, noble officials and their servants could not protect village officials and village officials could not, in turn, protect their own household members and friends within the commune. Obedience, based as it was on protection, necessarily became harder to evoke. This crisis of legitimation manifested itself in increasing disorders and social strain within the structure of officialdom and in rural society in general.

Though we have substantial evidence of disintegrating parental authority, we have no obvious signs that the Landgrave's patrimonial

---

56. This is precisely the formulation used by Max Weber, *Economy and Society* 2 (Berkeley, 1978), 959, to characterize how a "rational" bureaucrat may be distinguished from a "patrimonial" one, and we find it in StaM, HLO 16.12.1762.

officials suffered similarly. There was no widespread peasant violence and so we must look instead for subtler forms of erosion. It appears that initially peasants used the normal channels of authority to petition for special dispensation from military service and from the Hufen edict.[57] One might expect that such a response to the tightening screws of regulation would enhance patrimonial authority by making protection more necessary, but apparently local and regional authorities were unable to grant sufficient numbers of special favors to acquire the beneficial effects of dispensing official grace. This we can tell from the bitter complaints of the Landräte who received peasant petitions and constantly had to say no — circumstances which intensified beyond measure during the American campaign.[58]

Even this apparent order disintegrated after officials used the apparatus to fill the ranks of units designated for service in America by the subsidy treaty of 1776. Certainly contributing to any decline of legitimacy, the Landgrave's decision to use garrison regiments to fill two thirds of the troop requirements under the treaty also frustrated many peasant strategies which centered around garrison service to avoid service in the standing army. This meant many peasants needed to take more drastic action. The most obvious disorders came in the form of large-scale emigration by draft-eligible males. Beyond even these desperate acts, Landräte reported the flight of whole families and village populations on the approach of recruitment officials.[59] In Oberweimar, population figures in the last quarter of the eighteenth century never fully reflected the substantial surpluses of births over deaths in the parish register; emigration seems the only reasonable explanation.

Flight was not nearly as significant as a general failure of official and village authority. After the departure of the first two divisions of subsidy regiments in the spring of 1776, the court records of the Landrat von Schenck zu Schweinsberg showed an upsurge in the number of fines for delicts, obviously linked to the effectiveness of the authority of his own officials. In Oberweimar between 1776 and 1784, von Schenck's Amtschultheiß, Karl Kroeschel of Fronhausen, levied, on average, more than twelve fines a year for failure to appear before or participate in the business of quarterly court sessions. Attendance at

57. Charles W. Ingrao, *The Hessian Mercenary State* (Cambridge, 1987), 119 n. 112; StaM, B/17e; B/23b ALb.
    58. StaM B/4h 3700, von Baumbach 1776.
    59. Ibid.

these village courts sessions was required of all householders in his jurisdiction. Twelve fines a year represented a doubling of the rate from the previous fifteen years (disregarding Kroeschel's first year, 1768, in which they soared over forty).[60] Such absences were even more important because they frequently involved village officials responsible for reporting local misdemeanors. The noncooperation of such men threatened the very capacity of the village courts to do business and thus to provide the normal incomes for the structure of jurisdictional authority and to maintain order.

Even when court sessions did proceed, they were punctuated by violence and rough language more often than in the past, further suggesting a growing tension and lack of order.[61] Although the records of fines do not permit a direct connection between the tyranny of conscription and this breakdown of authority, village headmen and other officials did blame the draft and its consequences for their own growing unwillingness to serve the Landrat further.[62] Village offices, which proliferated over the course of the eighteenth century to satisfy the status demands of villagers, now became so difficult to fill that the Landgrave began ordering them abolished.[63]

The most obvious case of breakdown in the processes of patrimonial authority came when the Landgrave ordered that villagers accept the returning veterans of the American campaign with open arms. Villagers, remembering the bad experiences with veterans of the Seven Years War, simply refused to allow veterans to establish themselves.[64] Veterans represented problems for village finances as well, because they were usually poor and became welfare cases, and because the Landgrave exempted them from rents for commons privileges (*Beisitzergeld*). Their veterans' benefits also exempted them from Kontribution payments for which villages picked up the bill.

In mediating the Landgrave's decision to encourage resettlement, Landräte once again could not protect the people who were the basis of their authority. Village councils protested against the Landgrave's policy citing the potential overuse of village pastures and woodlands by these new households. Communes also accused veterans of immoral and rough behavior, an accusation they believed would bring official

60. StaM, B/340, von Schenck zu Schweinsberg 1 A 10, 1760b–1790b.
61. Ibid.
62. StaM, B/17e Allna 18.
63. StaM, HLO 20.2.1775.
64. Könnecke, *Rechtsgeschichte*, 69.

support for keeping these men out. In parish Oberweimar, the resistance of villagers did not prevent a spate of cottage building on
the commons. (See Table 16.) Landrat von Schenck zu Schweinsberg
brought them the bad news in several cases in which the General
Directory ordered villages to allow veterans to settle.[65]

Landgrave William IX judged the authority of the Landräte to be so
compromised by the beginning of his reign that he simply stopped
replacing them when they died or resigned.[66] By 1797, no Landrat held
office, and local administration returned to what it had been before
but, unlike the past, the Landgrave's regional officials directed it more
closely. Rather than rely on the patrimonial Landräte, William increasingly extended and further rationalized his central military bureaucracy in the hopes they could better direct village officials.[67] Whether
this rational authority had better luck in articulating with kin-ordered
authorities is a story for someone else to tell.

The Recovery of Intimate Authority after 1793

After the completion of William IX's military and inheritance reforms
in 1793–94 and the return of troops from the counterrevolutionary
coalition against France, the directors of Hessian kin-ordered enterprises made some attempts to reestablish the basis of intimate authority. The impressions left by Tables 17 through 20 that marriage makers
turned away from the equal matches of the years 1763–74 is confirmed
by the regression analysis of Tables 21 and 22. This represented a
return to the pre-Seven Years War regime — qualified by an apparent
strengthening of a trend toward male-line inheritance. The wealth of
the groom's family predicted the couple's wealth somewhat better than
it had before 1756.

The return to unequal marriages was led by the wealthy. Young men
from these families entered the marriage market much more frequently
than they had under Frederick's recruitment regime and they more
frequently married brides of lesser stature than themselves. (See Tables
19, 20, and 22.) Wealthy parents apparently let their daughters make

65. StaM, B/17e Kehna 4.
66. Kurt Dülfer, "Fürst und Verwaltung. Grundzüge der hessischen Verwaltungsgeschichte 16.-19. Jahrhundert," *Hessisches Jahrbuch für Landesgeschichte* 3 (1953):
219; Ingrao, *The Hessian Mercenary State*, 205.
67. Chapters 2 and 3; Dülfer, "Fürst und Verwaltung," 219–20.

Table 17. Wealth and marriage matches III, 1763–1774

	None (0 Ar)	Poor (<17 Ar)	Independent (<75 Ar)	Wealthy (>75 Ar)	Total N	Missing
Total spouses	36	61	49	34	188	8
% Brides	18.9	22.2	34.4	24.4	98	8
% Grooms	21.1	45.6	20.0	13.3	98	8

SOURCE: Marriage database described in Appendix.

Table 18. Wealth and marriage matches IV, 1763–1774

		None (0 Ar)	Poor (<17 Ar)	Independent (<75 Ar)	Wealthy (>75 Ar)	Total N	Missing
% Spouses = match		38.9	26.2	24.5	47.1	108	—
% Grooms	down	0	14.7	26.5	8.8	34	—
	up	27.8	32.5	4.1	0	74	—
% Brides	down	0	11.8	27.0	17.6	74	—
	up	27.8	14.7	5.9	0	34	—
Missing		2	7	3	2	—	—

SOURCE: Marriage database described in Appendix.

Table 19. Wealth and marriage matches V, 1798–1808

	None (0 Ar)	Poor (<17 Ar)	Independent (<75 Ar)	Wealthy (>75 Ar)	Total N	Missing
Spouses	33	55	28	40	162	4
% Brides	19.8	34.6	17.3	24.7	81	3
% Grooms	21.8	34.6	17.9	25.6	81	3

SOURCE: Marriage database described in Appendix.

Table 20. Wealth and marriage matches VI, 1798–1808

		None (0 Ar)	Poor (<17 Ar)	Independent (<75 Ar)	Wealthy (>75 Ar)	Total N	Missing
% Spouses		42.4	47.2	28.6	40.0	64	—
% Grooms	down	0	5.5	17.9	27.5	19	—
	up	30.3	16.4	17.9	0	24	—
% Brides	down	0	9.1	25.0	25.0	24	—
	up	24.2	14.5	10.9	0	19	—
Missing		1	2	0	3	—	—

SOURCE: Marriage database described in Appendix.

Table 21. Regression analysis: wealth of bride's family, groom's family, and couple, 1763–74 (one-tailed test of significance)

	Bride's family	Groom's family	Couple
Bride's family	—	.439	.483
	—	(<.001)	(<.001)
Groom's family	.439	—	.720
	(<.001)	—	(<.001)

SOURCE: Marriage database described in Appendix.

Table 22. Regression analysis: wealth of bride's family, groom's family, and couple, 1798–1808 (one-tailed test of significance)

	Bride's family	Groom's family	Couple
Bride's family	—	.292	.273
	—	(.005)	(.009)
Groom's family	.292	—	.641
	(.005)	—	(<.001)

SOURCE: Marriage database described in Appendix.

matches with young men of lesser stature once again. The wealthy, through these means, extended their influence over the landed wealth of the parish's lesser families.

Also qualifying this reestablishment of ties of dependency between classes was a growing inclination on the part of the parish's poorer families to marry amongst themselves. These marriages, however, did not receive the same support as did those between equals during the Fredrician period. Parents of this strata virtually ceased dividing their estates for their children, dropping well below pre-1756 levels of partition. (See Table 23.) Perhaps productive units belonging to the poor had suffered as much division as they could bear. Surprisingly, wealthier parents seemed more inclined to support the downward marriages of their children than ever before, dividing their estates twice as often as during the 1763–74 period.

The partially restored pattern of marriage and devolutionary behavior failed to stem the long-term trend toward increasing numbers of dependent families in Oberweimar's villages. During the Fredrician period more than 70 percent of all couples had received insufficient means for independent existence. Though this proportion dropped to

Table 23. Changing marriage and property devolution patterns, 1762–1808

Couples receiving estates:		Full or more	Fragmentary	Ratio
Grooms from families	1763–74	40(6)	14	.350
with <75 Ar	1798–1808	26(8)	2	.076
Grooms from families	1763–74	8(0)	2	.250
with >75 Ar	1798–1808	10(1)	4	.400
First time couples	1763–74	17 of 71		.239
receiving no land:	1798–1808	20 of 65		.307

SOURCE: Marriage database described in Appendix.
Numbers in parentheses indicate couples receiving estate of bride's parents.

somewhat more than 59 percent after 1798, much of the drop was accounted for by reduced numbers of marriages. The number of couples receiving nothing at all from their parents actually increased from 17 to 20 between 1763–74 and 1798–1808. Finally, the 59 percent figure was still higher than 47 percent dependency rate for couples during the pre-1756 period.

The reduction in the percentage of couples receiving insufficient resources to subsist within the parish community actually represented a moral and social disaster of tremendous proportions. Throughout the period after 1793 the population of both Oberhessen and Oberweimar continued to grow. At the same time, the reconstruction of intimate authority reduced the number of first-time marriages and increased the share of those marriages made by spouses from wealthy families marrying down. This meant that parish couples sustained population growth by increasing marital fertility and also by increasing the rate of illegitimate births. According to Fox's figures for the parish of Oberweimar, marital fertility increased from 3.85 children per marriage for 1785–94 to 4.6 children per marriage for the decade after 1795.[68] Given infant and child mortality rates still around 41 percent, this increase probably represents two extra pregnancies in a married woman's life. For the same periods illegitimate births jumped from 10.4 percent to 14.3 percent, climbing in the next decade to 18 percent of all births. On the one hand, the socially and legally approved sexuality of women in marriage was put to more intense use with all of the dangers inherent in multiple pregnancies. On the other hand (as we shall see) for poor women and men (particularly veterans), sexuality

68. Fox, "Studies in the Rural History of Upper Hesse," 287.

was delegitimized and put in the realm of persecuted behavior. Some soldiers and others might find an establishment on the margins of the village with their mates but apparently many other matches went without such resources or protection, a burden which inevitably fell more heavily on the women involved. Given the reentry of the wealthy into an increasingly constricted marriage market, it seems reasonable to suggest that the children of matches made to avoid conscription in the 1760s and 1770s were limited in the expression of their sexuality and further limited in their general life chances and their capacity to realize their life plans. The soldiers of the American campaign era, some of their male and female siblings, and their children, appear, then, to be the "system-necessary victims" to which we must turn our attention in the next chapter.

Population growth continued on the margins of families and villages in Hesse-Cassel. Increased marital fertility meant more dispossessed children and smaller portions for them. More marriages of couples receiving no land or buildings meant a growing dependent sector which was observed by many who commented on Hessian rural life in the nineteenth century.[69] The development of the fabled rural poverty in the region was given a strong push by Fredrician recruitment and inheritance policy. These policies were inspired and coupled together by the needs of Hessian military-fiscalism to provide both tax incomes and personnel for the subsidy army. Rural poverty deepened in the nineteenth century and was exacerbated by the imposition of the Napoleonic system which brought a brief free market in land and at the same time foreclosed the international markets for the Hessian rural linen industry.[70] After 1815, all need for a subsidy army disappeared as the British chose to intervene on the continent economically rather than militarily and the army ceased to represent even a diminished form of alternative employment.

The Landgrave's reform of the rural guild system after the Restoration contributed to the further destruction of rural industry and closed

69. Vanja, *Dörfliche Strukturwandel*, 90–107; Kurt Wagner, *Leben auf dem Lande im Wandel der Industrialisierung. "Das Dorf war früher auch keine heile Welt." Die Veränderung der dörflichen Lebensweise und der politischen Kultur vor dem Hintergrund der Industrialisierung — am Beispiel des nordhessischen Dorfes Körle* (Frankfurt, 1986), 54–72.

70. Dascher, *Das Textilgewerbe*, 156–60.

more doors to those on village margins.[71] Apparently, the abolition of feudal tenures and dues (*Grundlastenablösung*) merely intensified the conditions of poverty in the Hessian countryside.[72] Rural Hessians finally voted against chronic underemployment and poverty by emigrating, mostly to America, in three massive waves — one in the early 1850s, one in the late 1860s and early 1870s and finally one in the mid 1880s.[73] Neither the Hessian Landgraves nor their Prussian successors ever allowed Hessian youths many alternatives to being soldiers.

71. Uhlrich Möker, *Nordhessen im Zeitalter der industriellen Revolution* (Vienna, 1977), 43–48.
72. Eihachiro Sakai, *Der kurhessische Bauer im 19. Jahrhundert und die Grundlastenablösung* (Melsungen, 1967), 105–8.
73. Möker, *Nordhessen,* 33.

Part IV

The Culture and Class Experience of System-necessary Victims

In identifying the victims of the Hessian military system with "masterless servants and loafers," or the "household's most expendable people," or with disinherited or partially disinherited sons and daughters of peasant directors of kin-ordered production, we have identified what Max Weber called "market positions" or what Karl Marx called a "class in itself" (*an sich*). However, as E. P. Thompson has suggested, class is more than a position, it is a set of lived historical relationships. For Thompson, it is out of lived experience and symbolic materials available to them that people fashion a culture to give new meanings to common experiences with those in similar conditions. A sense of these commonalities gives them a tool to begin making their own history as a "class for itself" (*für sich*), a conscious corporate actor on the stage of history.[1] However, even the superficial position analysis thus far provided should show the reader that the essence of being a victim in Hessian society was to occupy many positions at the same time. The purpose of this section is to suggest that the experience of class for these victims was sufficiently ambivalent that any vision of class that is univocal and monadal cannot account for its complexities. Rather, we must apply a notion of class which allows for articulation between "modes of production" to occur within the "persons" who participated in them.[2] Ambivalence in experience resulted from "persons"

1. E. P. Thompson, *The Making of the English Working Class* (New York, 1966), 9–12.
2. Eric R. Wolf, *Europe and the People without History* (Berkeley, 1982), 73ff.; David Warren Sabean, *Power in the Blood* (Cambridge, 1987), 137–38.

occupying positions in more than one "mode of production" simultaneously. To be a victim was to bear the contradictions between systems and within them at the very core of the self.[3] Ambivalence itself damaged these lives leaving the victims as outsiders who lived within a kin-ordered mode of production.

The group for which this task is most easily carried through is that of the soldiers. Their different identities had widely separated spatial and temporal dimensions. Less easily accessible was the experience of divided selves for soldiers' sisters, lovers, and wives who acted out their identities more simultaneously on fewer stages. For this reason, my analysis in Chapter 9 will emphasize soldiers and speak of women when the material allows me to do so. The problem of culture and "consciousness" we will leave to the last chapter.

3. Hermann Rebel, "Cultural Hegemony and Class Experience: A Critical Reading of Recent Ethnological-Historical Approaches (part two)," *American Ethnologist* 16 (1989): 131ff.; Fredric Jameson, *The Political Unconscious: Narrative as a Socially Symbolic Act* (Ithaca, 1981), 23–58, 88–98.

9   The Ambivalent Class Experience of
Soldiers and Their Sisters, 1742–1809

Because peculiarities of the Hessian military system were combined with the subsidy business of the Landgraves, the identities of drafted soldiers were formed in three different arenas. They began their military life in their own villages and often spent most of their terms of service there. Immediately after soldiers were sworn in, however, they became part of the military hierarchy and the company management business of their commanding officers. Occasionally they were called upon to fight in one of the Landgrave's subsidy corps outside Hesse, or outside of Germany, or even away from the European continent, as with the treaty of 1776. Roles played in each arena eventually influenced the position and permanence with which they occupied roles in each of the others.

Insiders Out: On Becoming a Soldier and a Commodity

The process of transformation began at yearly spring musters held in each village. According to one regional official visiting the villages of his area, the muster "made a terrifying [*schreckende*] impression" on the village male population. Many village youths — married or single, and particularly the poor — were "convinced that their measurement and enrollment on lists has no other purpose than to induct them at the first opportunity and to send them to foreign places." Moreover, after visiting their first muster, youths became sullen (*Mißmütig*) and depressed (*Niederschlagen*) because "from the time they are measured until they are conscripted all comes to a standstill," for they were not permitted to marry, take over estates, or borrow money.[1] Though the process recalls the Russian custom of holding a funeral when a village youth was conscripted, it was by no means as extreme. But that in itself held disadvantages.

Draftees irrevocably crossed the social boundary from civilian life by executing an oath administered to them by their parish pastor and the local representative of their patrimonial jurisdiction.[2] It was usually between their eighteenth and twenty-fifth year that newly inducted Hessian youths bound themselves to the orders of their commanders "in service, discipline, and subordination, directly or indirectly." The new recruit also swore to be "true, favorably disposed, and obedient" to the Landgrave himself, protecting his property from "harm, disruption, and disadvantage."[3] Where before the recruit was connected with Hessian tribute-takers indirectly through the authority of his parents, his village, and his parish, now he became direct participant in the Landgrave's tribute-taking apparatus.

A soldier's oath from 1780 invoked supernatural sanctions as well as worldly ones. Soldiers took the oath with the thumb and first two fingers raised to symbolize the trinity. The oath specified that violators should be excluded body and soul from the Christian community. Moreover, the inductee asked God to take the digits used to swear the oath if he should deviate from its conditions.[4] Terrors, both physical and otherworldly, were appropriate to an important rite of passage between two social worlds. Its seriousness would not have been lost on the fifteen-year-old boys who had just confirmed their own connection to the Christian fellowship and, at the same time, had begun to attend the yearly spring musters in the parishes.

Despite the fear, distaste, and emotional disruption with which peasant youths faced the prospect of military service, Table 24 shows that a group of 108 soldiers who served from Oberweimar between 1768 and 1793 came from households in every category of landed wealth to be found in the parish. What is more, the distribution of soldiers does not differ appreciably from that of a group of 113 chil-

1. StaM, B/5 16,622, Lahnstrom.
2. StaM, HLO 16.12.1762. Compare David Warren Sabean, *Power in the Blood* (Cambridge, 1987), 20–27.
3. StaM, HLO 12.7.1780.
4. Ibid.

Table 24. Household of origin for soldiers and their contemporaries in Parish Oberweimar

Households with	< 17 Ar	< 75 Ar	< 140 Ar	> 140 Ar
% Soldiers from (N = 108)	54.8	19.2	17.3	8.7
% Cohort members from (N = 112)	53.2	18.0	15.3	13.5

SOURCE: Soldier and comparative parish database described in Appendix.

dren born in the parish between 1742 and 1749. Only the households with 140 Ackers or more of land provided a somewhat lower percentage of soldiers than of children in the cohort. Such underrepresentation is only surprising because it does not extend to those families with more than seventy-five Ackers but less than 140, who did not exempt their children even though the draft law of 1762 made it possible for them to exempt their heirs as well. The pattern seems to indicate a failure in the selectivity of the Hessian selective service system.

Such an impression is confirmed by Table 25, which shows that soldiers came from large estates with increasing frequency as time passed, while households at the bottom of the social scale provided a diminishing proportion of soldiers even though the numbers of such households grew during the same time period. This trend may be attributed to the recruitment crisis brought on by the strenuous requirements of the subsidy treaty of 1776–83. If such strains on the apparatus had continued, perhaps even the parish's richest parents would have seen their sons march off to the Landgrave's wars with greater frequency. Pressure of this kind, keenly felt by local administrators, was at the root of the successful attempts to reform the recruitment system in the late 1780s and early 1790s.

Beside holdings of land, another important indicator of social position in rural Hesse was the means by which the household earned its

Table 25. The changing impact of military recruitment on the Parish Oberweimar, 1763–1793

	1763–72	1772–82	1783–93
Recruits	44	38	26
Mean property of recruits' parents	28.9 Ar	43.1 Ar	57.6 Ar
% poor recruits	61.4	60.0	46.2

SOURCE: Soldier and comparative database described in Appendix.
Households with less than 17 Ar of land were poor households.

daily bread. Very roughly speaking, one could rank occupations on a scale of wealth in the following order: innkeepers and millers, peasant farmers, artisans, livestock herders, meat processors, cattle traders, servants, day laborers, beggars.[5] This picture was complicated considerably because many households included people with more than one occupation. As a result, we often find combinations of farmers and artisans, herdsmen and farmers, artisans and day laborers in the same household.

Despite this complexity, the distribution of occupations for households from which soldiers came varied little from the general population. The exception, the sons of millers and innkeepers, represented 6.2 percent of the population but only 3.2 percent of the soldiers. Artisans were also underrepresented among draftees with 19.8 percent but 23.9 percent of the population.[6] Though village power may have protected the sons of millers and innkeepers, low proportions of artisan offspring may have been the result of the geographic mobility permitted by the traditional wandering of journeymen (*Wandersjahr*).[7]

Donning uniforms more frequently (3.6 percent of soldiers) than their numbers in the parish population (1.9 percent) would suggest were children whose father's only occupation was listed as "soldier" and those whose parents herded livestock (5.4 percent to 1.9 percent) for a living.[8] These parents tended to be mobile, and we cannot reject the possibility that they may have been invited into villages so that their children would make the children of the wealthy less vulnerable to conscription. This certainly seems to be what happened to Ludwig Brehmer who entered the parish when he married the daughter of Johann George Rauch.[9] Brehmer was one of the few individuals from Oberweimar serving in the army before the institution of the draft for whom we have much documentation.[10] He lost all means of support when his wife's father went bankrupt. He was released from regiment von Kospoth in 1773. The village officials gave him the job of cowherd

5. Ranking for Oberweimar StaM, K/I Allna 1746, etc., figured by crosstabulating net worth and occupation informally.

6. Peter K. Taylor, "The Household's Most Expendable People: The Draft and Peasant Society in Eighteenth-Century Hessen-Kassel" (Ph.D. diss., University of Iowa, 1987), 364.

7. StaM, B/4h 4072.

8. Taylor, "The Household's Most Expendable People," 364.

9. StaM, B/17e Allna 9, 1778.

10. StaM, B/12 abN 8848, mL, von Ditfurth.

and suffered with his inadequate performance until his first son was recruited. He was replaced in 1776 and the recruited boy, Conrad, died as a peacetime soldier in 1788. Apparently, his brother Jost was expected to take his place. Jost was somewhat more fortunate. Although listed as a deserter in 1789, he, unlike his father, was able to find a permanent place in the parish by associating himself with its most acquisitive citizen, Magnus Dörr. Part of one of Dörr's land management consortiums, Jost married twice, once in 1797 and again in 1811. Before he died, he acquired a tenure from Dörr that rendered him independent.

Passing from civilian to military authority did not mean that the new recruit necessarily spent a lot of time away from home. Eleven Oberweimar draftees ended up serving exclusively in garrison regiments which obligated them to only six weeks of active duty a year plus one or two two-week stints of guard duty.[11] The period of active duty (coming in mid-July just after the first hay harvest) was theoretically timed to provide minimum disruption to the agricultural cycle. The Hessian agricultural cycle was in the process of change, however, and one cannot tell whether a timing based on traditional cycles still worked with new, more intensively farmed crops.

Some members of Hessian line regiments also spent a lot of time in their home villages. The furlough policies of such regiments reduced the amount of time soldiers spent on active duty. For ten or eleven months of the year, nearly half to just over half of the nominal members of regiments were on leave. Even regiments such as that of Colonel von Ditfurth sometimes attended Spring exercises at only 70 to 80 percent of full strength.[12]

Soldiers began to be important parts of the Hessian military machine even before leaving home for the barracks or the drill ground. The struggle for financial and bureaucratic success in which the officers were involved largely determined what the soldiers experienced.[13] In financial terms, a soldier had more value to his superiors the longer he remained at home with his name enrolled on the regimental and company lists. Doing so, he represented no expense to the company treasury because he lived at the expense of his kin. Nevertheless, his wages

11. StaM, HLO 12.7.1765.
12. StaM, B/12 abN 8848, mL, von Ditfurth.
13. Taylor, "The Household's Most Expendable People," 65ff.; Otto Büsch, *Militärsystem und Sozialleben im alten Preussen* (Frankfurt, 1981), 113–33 and 152–56.

flowed into the treasury and were held there under a policy of enforced savings (*Lohnwacht*), and thus, he remained a source of income for the company proprietor (*Chef*).

Even in garrison, a draftee could benefit his Chef financially as a source of labor.[14] Regimental reports show that soldiers worked on a variety of construction projects.[15] For example, Colonel von Ditfurth regularly dispatched up to sixty men per month to work building fortifications and palaces for the Landgrave in Kassel.[16] If Hessian commanders were similar to their Prussian counterparts, they found a way to extract some financial advantage from such activity.[17]

An officer's success also depended upon his capacity to balance the needs of the unit treasury with the Landgrave's requirement that he produce well-trained, efficient, and good-looking military units for the subsidy business. To this latter end he needed to change Hessian farm boys into replaceable parts that would fit into an army based on mechanical "Enlightenment" models.[18] Unlike financial management, this task demanded the presence of the young men in garrison so that the discipline characteristic of eighteenth-century armies could be applied to them. Military training of the time featured frequent beatings and turned common soldiers into the whipping boys (*Prügelknaben*) of their officers.[19] As Michel Foucault has observed for eighteenth-century French armies, officers used fear to control the most minute gestures of the soldier and required him to perform standardized and machinelike maneuvers without flaw or hesitation.[20] A Hessian drill manual lists forty-three standard steps used to load, fire, and reload a musket within the ranks, each with its standard command. It took 130 steps to form the ranks and numerous others to move them.[21] Such manuals provided the objective standards upon which military units were judged on the practice field by the Landgrave and probably by

14. Büsch, *Militärsystem,* 115.

15. StaM, B/12 abN 8849, von Ditfurth Rapporte.

16. StaM, B/12 abN 8848, mL, von Ditfurth.

17. Joachim Fischer, "Eiserngespartes aus Amerika 1776–1783," *Aus Geschichte und ihren Hilfswissenschaften: Festschrift für Walter Heinemeyer* (Marburg, 1980).

18. Hans Delbrück, *Geschichte der Kriegskunst* 4 (Berlin, 1962): 162–63, 292, describes the mechanistic models of eighteenth-century military tactics.

19. StaM, HLO 12.2.1789, 12.7.1780; Büsch, *Militärsystem und Sozialleben im alten Preussen 1713–1807,* 27–41, Jürgen Kuczynski, *Geschichte des Alltags des deutschen Volkes 1650–1810* 2 (Berlin, 1981): 346–49.

20. Michel Foucault, *Discipline and Punish: The Birth of the Prison* (New York, 1979), 135–36.

21. StaM, B/4h 3518.

those who wished to use them in the subsidy trade. Furthermore, it was probably the machinelike nature of the enterprise that required the more directly exercised form of authority between officer and soldier characteristic of the Enlightenment and expressed in its extreme by the Prussian Army's demand for zombielike obedience (*Kadavergehorsamkeit*). The brutality of this new order of discipline came from a general belief by officers that peasant boys made poor raw material for the human machines they hoped to create. An officer's advancement, and thus his opportunity for financial success, depended upon the performance of his units on the drill ground where the general staff evaluated them and issued favors accordingly.[22]

Seventeenth-century military reformers and their successors well into the eighteenth century believed that military discipline served positive pedagogic purposes for the rural population.[23] However, late eighteenth-century critics of "puppet factories," as the armies of the time were characterized, pointed out that the numbing monotony of the drill, punctuated by the petty brutalities of officers, drained the soldier of any spirit, courage, or sense of honor.[24] These same critics claimed that a man placed in the context of a military machine and separated from other social contexts lost any sense of morality, and calculated his actions carefully only so as to avoid the punishments rained on him by watchful officers.

The moral climate experienced by a soldier differed sharply and negatively from that in his home village. At times, the newly formed barracks of the eighteenth century appeared, even to the officers in charge of them, to be dens of iniquity frequented by gamblers, prostitutes, and pornographers. One general became sufficiently desperate about the moral climate of his barracks that he sought to ban all females, seeing them as the source of difficulty.[25] These problems thus belied the hope that military discipline could spread a more austere and productive morality among the general population.

Judging from such conditions, the chronic depressive mentality of

22. StaM, B/12 abN 8849, von Ditfurth Rapporte.

23. StaM, B/17e; Eugen von Frauenholtz, *Entwicklungsgeschichte des deutschen Heerwesens*, "Die Heere in der Zeitalter des Absolutismus," 4 (Munich, 1940), 11.

24. Johannes Kunisch, "Das 'Puppenwerk' der stehenden Heere," *Zeitschrift für historische Forschung* 19 (1990): 50–83.

25. StaM, B/12 abN 8849, von Ditfurth Rapporte; Gunther Thies, *Territorialstaat und Landesverteidigung: Das Landesdefensionswerk in Hessen-Kassel unter Landgraf Moritz* (Marburg, 1970); Hans Georg Böhme, *Die Wehrverfassung in Hessen-Kassel im 18. Jahrhundert bis zum siebenjährigen Krieg* (Kassel, 1954).

the eighteenth-century soldier reported by Fritz Redlich comes as no surprise.[26] If, as David Sabean has suggested, the "persons" of peasant boys were shaped on a grid of "friendship" and "enmity" through the gossip of fellow villagers, the new grid in which draftees found themselves placed was of a different order. Here the axes were meaningless petty rules enforced by torture and an underworld morality in which the soldier was stripped of any sense of accountability to anything but survival and stolen pleasures. The psychological resolution of these contradictions between one social arena and the other can hardly have been an easy task.

The financial and bureaucratic success of officers depended not only on training but also on physical appearance. Eighteenth-century military commanders and their princes placed a premium on physical stature as a sign of strength, health, and military effectiveness.[27] Frederick William I of Prussia sought tall men from all over Europe for his regiment of tall fellows (*langen Kerle*). Military commanders so came to value soldiers and potential recruits by their height that bounties paid for the return of deserters were calculated on the basis of stature.[28] Such evaluations led to a kind of internal trade in soldiers in which military commanders bartered with civilian officials and the heads of peasants households to acquire or hold onto the tallest men for their units.[29] Human flesh they judged and treated as they did horseflesh.

The rigors of peacetime military service had measurable effects. Until the reforms of the 1790s, the extended duration of service expected of Hessian soldiers intensified the risks of an early death. For example, in 1787 the noncommissioned officers and common soldiers of the von Ditfurth regiment averaged over seven years of service and close to half (46 percent) of the troops had served over ten years. Moreover, terms of service already longer than fifteen years were not unusual (13 percent).[30] The common soldiers of this regiment died at the rate of 8.1 per 1000 per year between 1785 and 1788.[31] General mortality rates for Oberweimar during the last quarter of the eigh-

---

26. Fritz Redlich, *The German Military Enterpriser and His Workforce* 2 (Wiesbaden, 1964–65): 188; Kuczynski, *Geschichte des Alltags,* 340–49.
27. StaM, B/11 MRb.
28. StaM, HLO 8.2.1793.
29. StaM, B/17e Kirchvers 28.
30. StaM, B/11, MRb, vacantes Bataillon, 783.
31. StaM, B/12 abN 8848, mL, von Ditfurth.

teenth century were 21.7 per 1000 per year.[32] During the decade between 1785 and 1795 males aged 15 and 30 years had a much lower rate of death, 6.2 to 6.7 per 1000.[33]

Though these differences are small, they become more significant when one considers that soldiers were supposed to be the healthiest and strongest members of the population and, further, that records understated deaths because they failed to include those of deserters or soldiers on leave. The heightened risk of death for soldiers was probably the result of a combination of poor sanitary conditions in the barracks, poor food, exhaustion from constant exercise, and the brutalities of military discipline. For example, in the barracks at Ziegenhayn human excrement was piled near sleeping quarters, there was much sickness, and little medical care.[34] In addition, bringing together people from all parts of Oberhessen in one barracks probably increased the risk that men would catch an infection for which they had not yet developed a resistance.

Ultimately, the needs and desires of the very few buyers (mostly England, France, and the Netherlands) who entered the international soldier trade determined the standards in the internal soldier trade and on the drill ground. The Landgraves of Hesse-Cassel depended on the subsidies acquired through this commerce. Thus, as tiny parts of a very well-oiled machine, the soldiers of Hesse-Cassel were essential to the financial integrity of the Landgrave and the Hessian state, and were engaged in virtually every major European conflict of arms during the eighteenth century. It was rare that these soldiers played the role of defender of the hearth and home to which we, in our more nationalistic times, have become accustomed. More often, they defended the interests of other princes in other lands and toward the end of the century gained a reputation as one of Europe's finest armies in the service of counterrevolutionary powers.[35]

Despite the fact that soldiers of subsidy armies won praise as "brave Hessians" serving "the liberties of Englishmen," this role had its emo-

32. George Thomas Fox, "Studies in the Rural History of Upper Hesse" (Ph.D. diss., Vanderbilt University, 1976), 287.

33. KaOw, Kp, Br, 1776–1876. The high end of the range used the census of 1780 as a baseline while the low end used the census of 1793 in StaM, B/5 10,597 and 2,107.

34. Erich Kaiser, "Nachschub für die hessischen Regimente in Amerika," *Zeitschrift für hessische Geschichte* 86 (1976/77): 185–95.

35. Rodney Atwood, *The Hessians: Mercenaries from Hessen-Kassel in the American Revolution* (Cambridge, 1980), 247ff.

tional and physical pitfalls. Separation from home apparently created some emotional difficulty, serious enough for one soldier sent to serve in America who was reputed to have died from "homesickness" (*Heimweh*).[36] The officers, anticipating difficulties on the long journey to America, increased rations of food and drink, presumably to dull the sensibilities and quiet fears among their recruits. Along with separation came the emotional experience of becoming an outsider and an enemy. Americans feared Hessians as "barbarous strangers" whose foraging activities (still normal for eighteenth-century armies) local citizens perceived as looting and pillaging.[37] Should such activities go even slightly awry, the soldiers could be executed or beaten by their own officers. In a more positive and somewhat contradictory light, Hessian soldiers found themselves working for American farmers in areas that their regiments occupied or when they became prisoners of war. Beyond wages earned, this prospect offered opportunities for some to stay behind as deserters when the Hessian army left to return home after a campaign. It also offered the opportunity for serious role conflict should an employer become a target of military operations in the process of foraging or campaigning.

Military operations abroad threatened the physical well-being of soldiers as well. Of the fifty-one draftees from the parish of Oberweimar who served the King of England in America 1776–1783, sixteen never saw their homes again. Ten died of sickness or wounds and six more were listed as missing or deserters.[38] This figure is somewhat lower than the 43 percent which Rodney Atwood's figures show did not return. Atwood included many non-Hessians recruited into Hessian service whom we may consider already permanently alienated from their homes.[39]

Any evaluation of the situation of the soldiers drafted under the law of 1762 must conclude that being under military authority was a disadvantage for the farm boys of Hesse-Cassel. Their role in the markets of the soldier trade and on the drill grounds of Hesse-Cassel reduced them to objects and even commodities whose value was measured in terms of the objective standards of a bureaucracy and a

36. Inge Auerbach, "Die hessischen Soldaten und ihr Bild von Amerika," *Hessisches Jahrbuch für Landesgeschichte* 35 (1985): 139.

37. Atwood, *The Hessians*, 171.

38. Inge Auerbach, et al., eds., *Hessische Truppen im amerikanischen Unabhängigkeitskrieg* 1–4 (Marburg, 1976).

39. Atwood, *The Hessians*, 254–56.

marketplace. The multiple arenas of experience and identity formation were neither internally consistent nor were they consistent with one another.

Insiders Out: Sisters, Lovers, and Wives

While soldiers' multiple roles and positions were highly formalized, legally recognized, spatially separated, and ritually celebrated, this was less frequently the case for the female victims of the Hessian military system. As sisters of soldiers and potential conscripts, they were required by inheritance arrangements to sacrifice their dowries and marriage prospects. The absence of their brothers required them to perform new roles in the kin-ordered economy. As lovers and wives of soldiers, women were scourged by moral authorities and fretted over by bureaucrats. These women frequently saw their children labeled illegitimate and suffered many attempts to cast them out of their communities. Even recognized wives of conscripts often became poverty-stricken outcasts and were made to bear the entire responsibility for their children.

Quantitative evidence from the parish register of Oberweimar shows that between 1762 and 1775, women of the parish married as if they received smaller marriage portions than they had in the past or would in the future. (See Tables 13 and 14) I have suggested that parents may have required their daughters to sacrifice dowry and inheritance portions in order that brothers could be rendered exempt from subsidy service. These interpretations seem supported by materials from Hessian oral tradition which suggest that in such sororal sacrifice lay the key to liberating brothers from military service.[40] This functional, if partial, exclusion from a family community of property to which they had undoubtedly contributed labor, was confirmed by the Landgrave when the 1773 Hufen edict drastically reduced the portions of non-heirs. As the official complaints about this reform suggest and as Table 26 illustrates, many women, along with their disinherited brothers, apparently emigrated to seek employment and marriage prospects away from home.

40. Peter Taylor and Hermann Rebel, "Hessian Peasant Women, Their Families, and the Draft: A Social-Historical Interpretation of Four Tales from the Grimm Collection," *Journal of Family History* 6 (Winter 1981): 367–70.

Table 26. The likelihood that a soldier or cohort member would be an heir or do better

	% Soldiers (N = 108)	% Cohort (N = 112)	% Cohort males (N = 58)	% Cohort females (N = 54)
Heirs/better	27.8	38.9	44.6	29.1
Left parish	24.1	38.9	36.2	40.0

SOURCE: Soldier and comparative database described in Appendix.

The new mobility of women combined with the absence of so many men in military service resulted in an increased use of women as servants in the households of Hesse-Cassel. Table 11 from the previous chapter showed that peasants compensated for reductions in the number of male servants by hiring increased numbers of females. This adjustment may not have been so significant if it had not come at a time when labor regimes were shifting toward more intensified agricultural practices. The altered ratio of male to female labor at this time virtually ensured that women came to perform the new intensive tasks while men, when they returned to the servant labor market after 1793, remained associated with older, less intensive forms of work. Sabean points out this process was occurring anyway but military service certainly must have encouraged it.[41]

Joining the mobile populations of seasonal agricultural laborers, itinerant artisans, herders, and milkmaids did not mean that these young women did not marry. Nearly 40 percent of all couples apparently never acquired land after the Seven Years War (compared with less than 30 percent before that time). Landlessness enhanced the probability that their death entries would read like that of Anna Cathrein Hopf, who wandered for years with her husband, Joseph, who collected paper for a living. In her life she changed religion twice, married a Pole, and lost her husband nine years before her death in April 1799. As a widow, she moved among the villages of parish Oberweimar and "honorably earned her living by knitting."[42]

Even when the sisters of soldiers married into more settled conditions they brought with them the seeds of chaos and disorder. For example, when the daughter of Anna Gertraut Binzler married in

41. David Warren Sabean, "Small Peasant Agriculture in Germany at the Beginning of the Nineteenth Century: Changing Work Patterns," Peasant Studies Newsletter 7 (1978): 218.
42. KaOw, Kp, Br, Oberweimar 1775–1825.

1781, her mother felt it necessary to appeal to the Landrat von Schenck zu Schweinsberg to confirm the marriage contract and the inheritance portions in it.[43] She fretted that when her son returned from military service in America he would lay claim to the estate and cause serious trouble. Indeed, the young groom's parents insisted on the confirmation she requested.

Conflicts between married sisters and unmarried soldiers remained the least of problems for the female victims of the Hessian military system who managed to marry into stable farmsteads. Those who negotiated marriage contracts in the 1780s frequently wrote into those contracts that veteran siblings of the couple "shall receive free room and board in the house for the rest of" their lives.[44] Although these clauses sometimes required the soldier to work, to behave in orderly manner, and to maintain religious observance, for women they established a strong structural conflict between the welfare of their brothers and that of their children whose inheritance and community property diminished with welfare demands made on the estate.[45] They had been asked to cannibalize the inheritance portions of their children. The same conflict of interest existed for any woman who accepted a reduced dowry in an effort to protect her brothers from recruiters. Commonly mothers' dowries and inheritance portions (*mütterlichen Gut*) helped fund the portions of the children who did not acquire the farm. Reduced portions and dowries meant that the disinherited could expect less from their mothers.

The same structural conflict had psychological dimensions which are illustrated by a case of assault in the village of Rossberg.[46] One night in January 1785, a young woman of twenty years, Anna Margreta Hämmer, received a head wound from a piece of wood thrown at her as she emerged from a village spinning bee. As she lay in a coma for several weeks, the testimony elicited from villagers by the authorities indicated that two soldiers on leave, Johannes Becker and Conrad Stahl, had done the deed. Becker was the uncle of the injured woman (brother to her mother) and lived with his sister, her daughter (Anna), and her husband in the same house.[47] Becker apparently performed

---

43. StaM, B/23b ALb, Sichertshausen 490, 1781.
44. StaM, P/II Caldern and Reizberg, Ep, 30.4.1783.
45. StaM, P/II Caldern and Reizberg, Ep, Jost Mathai and Kathrein Dörr.
46. StaM, B/23b ALb, Rossberg 1516.
47. We know of Becker's relationship to Margretha Hämmer only because his brother-in-law (*Schwager*), Johann Dietrich Hämmer, gave important testimony in the

chores such as cleaning out the night soil (*Hauserde*) and cutting wood. Frau Hämmer's blood relationship demanded that she protect Becker as she had by bringing him into her house in the first place. But as her daughter's mother her position in the village grid of kin, friends, and enemies demanded that she seek justice and revenge for her daughter's injury.[48]

The psychological tension this woman faced was revealed in her contradictory and twisted testimony. Initially, when the boys returned to the house after the incident she attacked the other culprit, Conrad Stahl. Calling him a rogue (*Schelm*), a rascal (*Spitzbube*), and a bastard (*Scheißkerl*), she accused him of instigating the entire incident and of throwing the wood himself. Later, under questioning from village authorities she testified that "the soldiers didn't care whether it cost thirty or a hundred Gulden, they were going to throw wood at the girls." When her brother, Johannes Becker, denied that he had any part in throwing wood at the women emerging from the spinning bee, both she and her husband backed his story.[49] But Conrad Stahl claimed all along that Becker started the trouble with his sister's daughter and suggested that they throw the wood at her and others as they left the evening work and entertainment. After Becker left him to take the rap, Stahl could only point to the relationships which bound the members of the Hämmer household together and suggest that they were protecting the comrade who had betrayed him. Stahl's participation thus provided a convenient escape from what might have been a double bind. Anna's mother could deny to herself and to others that her brother caused the difficulties, against all evidence of her fellow villagers, and thus fill her obligations in her own mind.

Peasant women also became entwined with soldiers sexually. One of

---

case. Although we know of Johann Dietrich's relationship to Becker, the sources don't tell us whether he is so related because he married Becker's sister or because Becker's sister married his brother (presumably Johann Henrich Hämmer, the girl's father). Becker himself is obviously single. In short, we don't know whether Becker belongs to the parental generation or that of the injured girl.

48. If Margretha's mother is not protecting Becker because he is her brother then she may be doing so to protect the connection established by Johann Dietrich's marriage to Becker's sister.

49. Despite the ambiguity of the relationship between Becker and the injured girl's mother, either possible position creates irresolvable kin-based ambivalences which help to explain her twisted testimony. Given that no mention is made of Johann Dietrich's wife in the entire transcript of the case, I have concluded that she doesn't exist and therefore that Johann Dietrich is the brother of the injured girl's father.

the striking changes in the patterns of fertility revealed by the parish register of Oberweimar in the last chapter was an increase in extra-marital fertility. Beginning at 6.8 percent of all births in the decade before the Seven Years War, the percentage of illegitimate births climbed sharply after the war, reaching 18 percent by the turn of the century. Much of this illegitimacy was attributed by authorities and villagers to relationships between "licentious" soldiers and village girls.[50]

Hessian evidence, however, suggests that illegitimacy stemmed as much from the unwillingness of authorities to sanction the unions of military veterans and soldiers as from any licentiousness of soldiers or their lovers. Civil and military law required soldiers who wished to marry to have permission from parents, village religious authorities, and civil officials as well as their unit commanders. The commanders charged fees for such permissions if they granted them. Officers abused the practice frequently enough that the Landgrave felt compelled to intervene several times in attempts to regulate it.[51] Certainly soldiers found it more difficult to acquire appropriate sanctions for their sexual unions than did their civilian brothers.

This difficulty inevitably meant that impregnated women were not being taken to the altar, but were victims of broken promises, as in the case of Johann Peter Herpel's brother. Living in Kehna as an honorably discharged veteran, he fathered two children out of wedlock and still could not get permission to marry the woman even when she became pregnant a third time.[52] Difficulty getting permission to marry stemmed both from civil authorities who did not think highly of soldiers as well as from military authorities. One regimental commander complained to the Landrat von Schenck zu Schweinsberg "that your highness cannot imagine the terrible consequences the marriages of soldiers have" because "the chap is spoiled as a soldier" for without long-term leaves "his wife falls into poverty [*Noth*]."[53] From the late seventeenth century, armies had been trying to reduce the size of baggage trains and the population of camp followers and soldiers' wives as matter of logistical policy. Added to these considerations, commanders strongly desired to hold on to well-trained and tall men for whom they had had to bargain vigorously with civil officials.

50. KaOw, Kp, Tr, 1660–1830: Michael Mitterauer, *Ledige Mütter: Zur Geschichte illegitimer Geburten in Europa* (Munich, 1983), 90.
    51. StaM, HLO 31.4.1786.
    52. StaM, B/17e Kehna 11, 1775.
    53. StaM, B/17e Kirchvers 28, 1787.

Clearly, despite the difficulty, many soldiers simply flaunted regulations and established fundamentally illegal households with their lovers. In 1763, one official from Wanfried reported this practice, accusing many soldiers of violating the honor of village girls. He claimed, further, that the women would acquire cows and illegally graze them on the village common lands. When village officials tried to report the illegal grazing, the soldiers intimidated them by physical attacks and broken windows.[54] Here, liaisons between soldiers and village girls led to the illegal diversion of common property and to assaults on village notables.

The flavor of the official attack on women who had unsanctioned sexual relations with soldiers also emerges from a 1775 entry in Oberweimar's parish register which reported the death of an illegitimate child born to the lover of a soldier. Pastor George Friedrich Wilhelm Usener wrote that her "father was presumably a soldier, but [her] mother is nothing but a licentious whore."[55] Apparently the mother, abandoned by her lover whom she had followed to the garrison, left Kassel to face the wrath of the parson and her parents alone. Under these conditions the woman could easily have been labeled one of those "careless girls whose depraved behavior [*Aufführung*] led them first to pregnancy and frequently then to infanticide" and who, for that reason, the Landgrave subjected to strenuous investigations.[56] The widespread belief in this combination of circumstances lent plausibility to the scene in Friedrich Schiller's play "Conspiracy and Love" in which a Valet describes "a frantic mother [who] ran to spit her suckling infant on [the] bayonets" of subsidy troops departing for America.[57]

Abandoned women who bore the children of soldiers were not without all recourse. In 1783, Anna Barbara Pfingsten received compensation and child support from her lover's regimental treasury.[58] The amount was taken from the soldier's inheritance portion and his garnished wages when he deserted his unit.

Villagers perceived women who became entwined with soldiers as sources of disorder. They labeled them whores, depraved or fallen

---

54. Otto Könnecke, *Rechtsgeschichte des Gesindewesens in West- und Süddeutschland* (Marburg, 1912), 63.

55. KaOw, Kp, Br, 10.5.1775.

56. StaM, HLO 10.5.1765.

57. Friedrich Schiller, "Conspiracy and Love," in *Plays*, ed. Walter Hinderer, trans. Walter Passage (New York, 1983), Act 2, Scene 2.

58. StaM, HLO 17.7.1783.

women, and their children bastards. Should these babies die, the authorities subjected the aggrieved mother to investigation on suspicion of infanticide. But the illegitimate nature of these unions and their issue was as much a product of official obstacles placed in the way of soldiers' marrying as it was any licentiousness of men or women involved in them.

Despite all attempts to keep military men separated from women, many married men ended up in the Landgrave's regiments. For example, in 1792 the von Hanstein regiment recorded that 134 of its 686 troops had wives. Only ten of these women accompanied their husband to the barracks while the remainder stayed at home to care for 135 children.[59] These latter women stayed with their parents, their husbands' parents, or even tried to survive alone.

Such relationships seemed sustainable as long as the Landgrave sent no regiments on subsidy campaigns, but when the troops left to fight, poverty became the rule of the day. Within a month of the departure of the first troops to America, the Landrat von Schenck of Schweinsberg reported soldiers' wives in dire straits, indebted and relying on the help of relatives and the labor of their eight- and nine-year-old children.[60] The absence of husbands also left some women vulnerable to robbery and other violence.[61] As their difficulties deepened, some women fled with their children to garrison towns in hopes that officials there would provide the legally required support.[62]

Even when women and soldiers received official sanctions for their marriages, villagers perceived them as disorderly, or as portals to disorder in their kin-ordered communities. In May 1775, Landrat von Schenck zu Schweinsberg gave the village headman of Möln permission to evict Johannes Wisker and his wife from their small houses.[63] When the headman failed in his task, the Landrat complained to the General Directory that too many soldiers married women who possessed small houses. Like the partners in illicit liaisons already discussed, these couples were accused by villagers of misusing the commons. The couple had earned a reputation as "disorderly marginals" (*unruhigen Beysitzer*). The Landrat also pleaded with Wisker's com-

59. StaM, B/11, MRb 792, von Hanstein.
60. StaM, B/4h 3700, von Schenck 1776.
61. StaM, B/17e Brungershausen 4.
62. StaM, B/5 14740, 1778.
63. StaM, B/17e Möln 175, 1775.

manding officer to order him to move out, but Wisker was sent to America, mooting the issue.

The village council raised the issue again in 1785 when Wisker's brother-in-law, Wilhelm Opper, once again tried to transfer to him the title of the house. Not only did Schenck relent at this point but he actually took up the couple's cause when Opper reported that past resistance to Wisker on the part of the community had been largely fraudulent. Schenck's change in position may well have been related to the need to settle many American war veterans. The community based its continued resistance to the couple on Wisker's reputed abuse and the claim that he kept a disorderly house by boarding some of his military companions. Although the Landrat granted Wisker's application to live in Rossberg, he and his brother-in-law petitioned for further intervention because "should any more spiteful neighbors behave as before by erecting new difficulties it depends upon your graceful orders" to get them removed.[64]

Marrying a soldier could also open the door to family difficulties. In a tragic story from 1780, Johannes Wienant, a recently married soldier, set off from his mother-in-law's house where the couple was living to obtain a dismissal from military service. On the way he became involved in a squabble with an innkeeper in which he was beaten senseless.[65] The beating he received rendered him insane and his subsequent behavior resulted in several more beatings. As it turned out, his own violent behavior began before he had run afoul of the innkeeper. Coming home on leave he had been so abusive that his own father disinherited him. When he moved in with his wife he beat his mother-in-law as well. His treatment while in jail for confronting the innkeeper rendered him incapable of further military service and the military court which tried him subsequently released him to the custody of his parents. Here the violence of military training had clearly impinged upon a domestic environment in a way that inspired repeated complaint.

Despite all of the potential for disaster and disorder, one group of women — widows — seemed particularly attracted by the prospect of celebrating nuptials with soldiers. When old soldiers themselves appealed to their commanders for release because of an impending marriage, they usually wed an even older widow. Soldiers frequently

64. Ibid., 1785.
65. StaM, B/4h 3472, von Stockhausen.

brought their pensions and accumulated savings to marriages like these. Widows might be looking for male labor and infusions of capital. Technically, children from such unions had no claim on the widow's estate, which would go to children from the first marriage before any from the second. Soldiers received a place to live and a managerial position, and, perhaps, a comfortable retirement.

As wives, lovers, and sisters, women experienced their disadvantaged position more intensively when they became connected with men doing military service. They came to be seen as portals of crime, disorder, and diversion of property in their families and communities. As if to confirm their outsider status, in 1774 the Landgrave ordered that wives of soldiers be assimilated to the same special legal status as their husbands.[66] Now, like their husbands, they became directly connected to the tributary system. Nevertheless, they continued to live, for the most part ambivalently, within kin-ordered households, lineages, and communities shaped by a double grid whose contradictions they had to reconcile or compose in their own hearts.

Outsiders In: Soldiers and Their Relations with Other Kin-ordered Producers

Soldiers became outsiders whose identities were formed in many arenas but who, for most of their lives, remained in home villages in contact with the kin-ordered society they entered as children. During the eighteenth century, Hessian line regiments served outside the territory in only forty years. Even at home, line regiments kept only a half complement of men in garrison for all but two months of the year. Soldiers in garrison or militia regiments served six weeks of every year after the first hay harvest and then might do a week or two of guard or police duty during the remaining months. This limited active duty actually made it possible for the Landgrave to rely so heavily upon his own population for recruits. Other German princes tended to rely on recruits dragooned from the roads and cities of the Empire outside of their own territories.

Though the soldiers were frequently physically present in their home villages, their legal and social position rendered them socially absent. As I have suggested, the most obvious legal and social disability for a

66. StaM, HLO 1.8.1774.

soldier stemmed from the requirement that he have his commander's permission to marry — something both difficult to acquire and expensive to purchase. But the disabilities extended even further than this. A landgravial order from 1752 forbade soldiers to "sell immovable property or borrow money using it as security."[67] Moreover, "no one may loan, purchase, or make the least payment" to soldiers on their inheritance portions without permission from their officers. William VIII had made this provision explicitly to prevent soldiers from having the resources to desert and leave the territory. Military authorities used similar concerns to justify the policy of enforced saving (*Lohnwacht*), in which the regimental commander held the wages of soldiers as surety against their return from leaves or their desertion from garrison. Soldiers thus possessed no resources with which they could participate independently in social and economic relationships.

Legal and financial disability combined, unfortunately, with a widespread opinion that soldiers made poor workers to further wall off soldiers from those with whom they had grown up. Landrat von Pappenheim reported the general belief that "no employer will have anything to do with such people" because they "take advantage of their military relationships" or they are "taken away at the most inopportune times."[68] Moreover, military men, accustomed as they were to the demoralizing physical brutality of eighteenth-century training regimens, made ungovernable workers without the application of similar techniques which were legally foreclosed to peasant employers. Pastoral authority suffered as well as that of employers and parents.[69]

The demoralizing nature of barracks life and military training, combined with the legal and financial incapacity to form everyday social relationships, transmuted soldiers into sources of sexual danger and familial chaos in the eyes of people who lived with them. Illustrative of the perceived sexual danger posed by soldiers was the incident which resulted in the assault on Anna Margretha Hämmer by her uncle cited earlier in the chapter.[70] Becker and Stahl became angered by their treatment in the spinning bee at the home of Andreas Mahr, which they had attended along with Becker's niece. In the sexually charged atmosphere of teasing and play so characteristic of these village occasions,

67. StaM, HLO 10.2.1752.
68. StaM, B/4h 4072, von Pappenheim.
69. StaM, HLO 15.1.1791.
70. StaM, B/23b ALb, Rossdorf 1516, 1785.

Becker placed his pipe in the bed of Mahr's daughter.[71] The implication that a sexual relationship existed between Becker and Mahr's daughter outraged her father, who accused him of sullying her honor. The young men fled the house to avoid a fight but their anger suggests that the man's response was unexpected.

If they had not expected it they probably should have. Implied relationships led to implied promises which soldiers could not legally keep. Behavior that might have been encouraged or tolerated had Becker not been entwined with military service became threatening in the way a soldier's advances threatened Andreas Krieger's wife. Landrat von Schenck zu Schweinsberg fined Frau Krieger because she attacked and brutally clubbed a soldier in her village. She appealed the fine, claiming the soldier had tried to seduce her because "he thought I would be receptive and even tried to get my attention by throwing clods of earth at me."[72] She claimed that she clubbed him when "the very name of the soldier became disgusting to me and like an insult." We must be careful not to discount this woman's voice or her self-defense, but throwing clods of earth seems a signal for a sexual advance only if the person initiating it was already marked by his uniform as a seducer or rapist. Such an attitude makes sense only if soldiers themselves were signs of sexual danger and what they did carried an impurity which she tried to remove by "shaking this wicked filth [*böshafter Schmutz* (the clods of earth?!)] from my dress." Such an attitude squares with official statements which attributed upsurges in unsanctioned unions and consequent illegitimate births to "licentious" soldiers and their "whores."

Soldiers also opened the door to family chaos: as we have seen, resources were diverted to the care of veterans, violent persons were introduced into family settings, labor routines were disorganized, and conflicts over inheritance arose. To these disruptions we must add the ongoing expenses of supporting young men in the army, as well as the incessant interventions by authorities in peasant inheritance, marriage arrangements, and retirement arrangements. Soldiers became financial burdens to their families because the army did not provide all that a

71. Edward Shorter, *The Making of the Modern Family* (New York, 1977), 101–5; Hans Medick, "Village Spinning Bees: Sexual Culture and Free Time among Rural Youth in Early Modern Germany," in David Sabean and Hans Medick, eds., *Interest and Emotion* (Cambridge, 1984), 317–27.
72. StaM, B/340, von Schenck zu Schweinsberg A 10, 1800b, 680–81.

soldier needed to subsist even while he was in garrison. Soldiers paid for substantial parts of their own uniforms and equipment. Apparently their burdens were great enough that Landrat von Baumbach argued that "many subjects" made, in effect, "continuing tribute payments" when they had "to support their sons in the military estate" because soldiers "were unable to live on their wages."[73] One family head, Johann Conrad Laucht of Allna, faced particularly sharp costs, as he had three sons serving the Landgrave at the same time. Both his eldest and his youngest he supported without complaint, but he disowned his middle son, Antonius, who was running up substantial debts in the military. Whether Antonius simply could not feed and clothe himself or whether he ran up gambling or other debts to which his father objected on moral or economic grounds is not clear from the sources.[74] The reluctance of peasants to hire people with military connections certainly made soldiers more rather than less dependent on their families' means, as did the policy of Lohnwacht. These circumstances may well have combined in Antonius's situation to require him to borrow illegally.

Because of their control over soldiers and over the levers of conscription, regimental and civilian authorities became more deeply implicated in the timing of devolution and the selection of heirs than they had been in the past. Regimental commanders affected the timing of marriages by holding on to the largest men even after they became eligible for release. Civilian authorities intervened in such situations as well. For example, in February 1780, the Landrat von Schenck zu Schweinsberg suggested (contrary to law) that the second son (not the first!) of the linen weaver Philip Lemmer be released to take over his aging father's tenure.[75] Here von Schenck selected Lemmer's heir for him and in the process condemned two other sons to long-term military service.

Just how far local and regional officials went in using the military system to intervene in peasant households becomes clear from the experience of Johannes Werner. In September 1774, Werner, a soldier from Gisselberg, appealed to the Landrat von Schenck zu Schweinsberg for release from military service. His father had died recently and he claimed he had come into the tenure and was paying the taxes on

73. StaM, B/4h 4072, von Baumbach.
74. StaM, B/17e Allna 15.
75. StaM, B/17e Leidenhoffen 25.

it.[76] When requested to testify by the Landrat, the Bauermeister of Gisselberg, Dietrich Elmshauser, told a different tale. According to Elmshauser, the farm belonged not to Johannes, who was the youngest of five siblings, but to the eldest brother who was already married and had children. A check of the village tax rolls suggests that, in fact, none of the Werners owned the estate in question but were renting it or managing it for an absentee peasant landlord.[77]

Elmshauser's testimony should have been enough to ensure that Johannes Werner did not get his release from military service. Perhaps because Elmshauser could not produce supporting documentation from the tax rolls the Landrat requested further testimony from him. This time the headman swore that the widowed mother had excluded three daughters and an older son with his family from her table. She kept company only with young Johannes at meal times. Although all of these people lived under one roof, the elder son, his wife, and his sisters had been forced to sacrifice and live together in a single room as if they were boarders. Moreover, the widow required them to work on other farms to support themselves. The chaotic condition of this family's life together — an extreme version of the patterns of sibling sacrifice we have previously seen — Elmshauser blamed on the mother's affection for her son. He asserted that "the entire household rests upon the Grenadier Werner alone, and without him the mother would not [let] the house [come] to these circumstances."[78] He appealed to the Landrat to end these conditions by revoking Werner's leave and forcing him to live permanently in garrison.

The Bauermeister's second story seems fuller and closer to the truth. However, he still concealed the actual tenurial relationships involved and his intervention remained unsupported by available documentation. Nevertheless, support of his position by one of the Landgrave's officials, Syndicus Uhlrich of Marburg, meant that it was successful. It is unclear from the sources whether Elmshauser was defending the integrity of an inheritance contract negotiated by Werner's dead father or whether he was simply trying to thwart Werner's mother's disorderly attempts to protect her son from further military service. Whatever his stance, he certainly did not want the young man to remain in the village.

76. StaM, B/17e Gisselberg 7.
77. StaM, K/I Gisselberg 1747ff.
78. StaM, B/17e Gisselberg 9.

The special position of soldiers sometimes entailed privileges but even then it did not always work in their favor. Most privileges came from the legal recognition of common soldiers as belonging to a military estate (*Stand*).[79] Some of the most important concessions made to them included special jurisdictional status, exemption from church fines, tax abatements, and pensions. Although the special jurisdiction (*judicious mixtus*) subjected soldiers, their wives, and their children to the fundamentally harsher system of regulations entailed in military justice, many times they parlayed it into an escape from local criminal charges. Both Johannes Becker and Conrad Stahl, whose assault case we examined above, escaped all punishment when their commanding officer intervened to demand the joint hearing in front of military and civilian officials required by law.[80] The commanding officer went beyond even this requirement when he insisted that Stahl be compensated for the damage to his honor he suffered when the injured girl's mother called him names. Finally, he addressed barely veiled threats to village officials complaining that he got "more complaints about my troops from this jurisdiction" than he got "from the entire district." He was sure "that many trivialities have been made into something more than they really are" and warned officials he would, in the future "not let the least trespass go unpunished."[81] Thus, at times, the very ambivalence of soldiers' legal and social condition could be played for advantage.

Just as often their privilege became a burden. This seems particularly true of tax abatements and fee reductions which soldiers gained in proportion to the amount of military service they performed. In 1763, Landgrave Frederick II renewed the ordinances of 1739, 1741, and 1742 which gave soldiers a fifty percent reduction in military tax payments, exemptions from citizenship entry fees, and other onera related to the corvee.[82] This exemption made them attractive marriage prospects for widows seeking relief from such burdens for their estates. For a soldier to settle in a village as an official marginal citizen, however, represented a certain liability for the community. Villages continued to pay the same total tax whether they had few or many such men living in their midst. This meant that non-veterans automatically had their tax liabilities and corvee burdens adjusted upwards every

79. StaM, HLO 2.12.1730, B/4h 3734.
80. StaM, B/23b ALb Rossberg 1516.
81. StaM, HLO 30.9.1763.
82. StaM, B/17e Kehna 8, 1785.

time a soldier took over the former place of a taxpayer in the village. Moreover, villages could not collect from soldiers the entry fees which compensated villages for the use of the common properties that these households represented.

This unfortunate set of circumstances helps to explain the nearly universal resistance met by soldiers coming home from the American campaign when they attempted to settle in their own villages or in those of their wives. Such community considerations almost certainly entered into the willingness of the villagers of Möln to use fraud and slander to prevent Johannes Wisker from settling there in the case cited above. It was explicitly the case when Johann Peter Herpel sought to overturn the decision of the council of Kehna to deny him a place to build a house.[83] The Landrat, as he did with increasing frequency in the 1780s, supported the soldier's position in the matter. The village council retorted that there was simply no room for the house, the commons were already overused, and tax burdens too high. To add a moral dimension, they appealed to the stereotype of the "licentious" soldier, claiming that Herpel lived a loose and disorderly life. According to their claim he and his brother had avoided military service and currently lived in sin together with "loose" women with no visible means of support. When the village was finally ordered to allow the Herpels to build, Syndicus Uhlrich specifically cited their loyal service to the Landgrave's army. But could this recommendation overcome lingering resentments on the part of villagers?

Perhaps one of the most striking ironies about being forced to participate in that most manly art of war was that soldiers in very important respects experienced life in ways much more similar to those of the women they were born with than the men. Like the image of Eve portrayed in many catechisms and from many pulpits, the soldiers were seen as open doors to moral temptation and social chaos. Not surprisingly, this position affected their social fates in the village context. Table 26 shows quite clearly that females and soldiers settled equally infrequently on estates the same size or larger than that of their parents. Both groups endured substantially more hardship than a group of males who never experienced military service. This frequent disinheritance, along with long terms of military service, helps to explain why soldiers on average married for the first time almost

83. StaM, B/12a 489–90, 1831.

thirteen years later than their counterparts who did not do military service. (See Table 15.)

For females, such hardship meant frequent moves from the parish, the consequences of which we have discussed above. Mobility had similar consequences for soldiers. Impoverished veterans sometimes appealed to past military commanders to be able to continue their service in regiments of invalids designed for such purposes. Pensions were provided, particularly for American war veterans, and applications for them elicited stories of tremendous hardship continuing long after service had ended. Even with pensions, the chances were great that many ended up like one whose death entry appears in the parish register of Oberweimar in the year 1767.[84] Born in Marburg and released from his regiment in 1745, this man spent the last twenty-two years of his life in the Oberweimar region and in neighboring Hesse-Darmstadt wandering and begging. Pastor Usener guessed that "his brutal poverty had for a long time kept him from communion [*Abend-mahl*] in the various places that he had lived." No one knew him well enough to vouch for him. Nevertheless, he was buried in the cemetery in Oberweimar.

Apparently, soldiers ended their lives in the parish of their birth more frequently than did their sisters. Table 26 shows that while 60 percent of females died in their original parish and 64 percent of all males did so, 75 percent of those who served in the Hessian military died near home. Geographic mobility for men and women usually stemmed from marriages in nearby parishes so that the larger number of those who had moved reflects their better prospects compared with those for soldiers. Soldiers certainly wandered during their lives but their return home at the end signaled failure rather than success. Some of soldiers' difficulties in completing their lives successfully showed in death registries and pension applications. A Zimmerman drowned blind and drunk in a field drainage ditch in circumstances suggesting suicide. Another veteran was murdered by shady characters with whom he had business transactions. If the higher percentage of military men staying home did not result from happy circumstances perhaps it reflected an increased dependency or even emotional or physical damage that developed from their military experiences.

Considering the common experiences of war and the general disadvantages of performing military service, it is no surprise that soldiers

84. KaOw, Kp, Br, 10.5.1767.

developed a rudimentary group consciousness. Johann Gottfried von Seume reports to us that some soldiers in the Hessian army actually developed their own language.[85] Veterans and soldiers selected one another as godparents for their children.[86] They married the widows of their comrades-at-arms as well.[87] When they became involved in legal conflicts in their villages, they reminded authorities of the service they had rendered without contradiction or complaint.[88]

This self-consciousness was also manifest in the collective participation of veterans in the rebellion against King Jerome's Westphalian kingdom in 1809.[89] Under the leadership of an English spy, Colonel Emmerich, and patriotic professors in Marburg, former officers organized off-duty soldiers and veterans from rural areas to the south of Marburg and sought to press other elements of the peasant population into the service of the rebellion. Those with military connections were plied with liberal helpings of brandy and beer at local taverns. In turn, soldiers used more violent methods, including beatings and barn burnings, to press substantial farmers into the rebellion. The rebellion would not have happened without a group of men who knew and understood one another because of their military experience. Though peasants in the area had long been willing to apply such violent coercion to fellow villagers to get them to participate in political protest, that these same sanctions were applied by soldiers, who in the past were used to suppress disorders, was high irony.[90] Finally, some military men had pensions to lose and feared the wrath of the Landgrave who threatened to have their heads if they did not participate.[91]

When underprivileged, the position of soldier rendered him a source of impurity and chaotic danger. Legal strictures associated with military status meant that soldiers spent considerable time in their villages where they could not be full social participants. Physically present, a soldier was socially absent and only partially included in the grid of

85. Redlich, *The German Military Enterpriser,* 2:207.

86. KaOw, Kp, Tr, 1675–1875.

87. KaOw, Kp, Hr, Johannes Hilberg, 1786.

88. StaM, B/23b ALb, Ebsdorf 433, 1781.

89. Willi Varges, "Der Marburger Aufstand des Jahres 1809," *Zeitschrift für hessische Geschichte* (1892): 350–60.

90. Werner Troßbach, *Soziale Bewegung und politische Erfahrung: Bäuerlicher Protest in hessischen Territorien, 1648–1806* (Weingarten, 1987), 82–100.

91. Varges, "Der Marburger Aufstand," 350–60.

friendship, enmity, and work that defined the person in early modern German communities. Other grids with which he became associated made him even less desirable as a community member and fashioned his new identity through the process of violently elicited obedience and a struggle for personal survival. Even as privileged veterans, soldiers returned from war bringing with them fiscal and environmental strain. This chaotic and ambivalent set of roles and identities extended not only to soldiers but to the women who, out of choice or compulsion, became associated with them. The internal dimensions of this chaotic class experience and the ways in which peasant culture gave meaning to this suffering and pointed to possibilities beyond itself are the subjects of the next chapter.

10 Peasants Tell Tales: Soldiers and Sisterly Love in Hessian Oral Tradition, 1809–1815

Until recently most history and, indeed, a good deal of conventional social history has used the language of the bureaucratic sources it relies on so heavily. Indeed, in this book I have relied on what bureaucrats and historians have said about Hessian peasants and have given peasants little opportunity to speak in their own language about their own experiences. My account remains fundamentally unbalanced because the language of recruiters named the system's necessary victims first "masterless servants and loafers" and then "the household's most expendable people" or distinguished them sharply from "completely indispensable people." In the related but tangential inheritance law of 1773, victims became "demanding co-heirs" whose claims threatened to encumber peasant tenures with debt or force the division of closed estates, rendering children dangerous to the fundamental basis of fiscal stability in the Hessian state. In such ideological language the state became the victim and the actions of its officials merely redressed a balance by turning "loafers" and "expendables" into valuable resources in the army or reduced their threat by eliminating their claims as co-heirs. The systematically distorted communication of this dramatic reversal of responsibility renders all historical accounts which rely exclusively on the language of bureaucratic discourse unbalanced in crucial ways.

To redress the balance, to provide a more critical account of the system's costs, and to examine the beliefs of the people most affected by the system as well as those who adjusted to the conscription of their sons, brothers, and nephews we must turn our attention to peasant voices. Few people, however, recorded peasant conversations and those who did mediated them through the same distorted official language we hope to get beyond. Peasants spoke what James C. Scott called a "hidden transcript" because their complaints always threatened to embroil them in difficulties.[1] The terms of this largely oral "hidden transcript" of peasant tradition are still only poorly understood because peasants hid their meanings and bureaucrats rarely cared about them.

Until recently, many scholars believed that an important source of texts coming from the Hessian plain people was the Grimm collection of fairy tales, *Kinder- und Hausmärchen,* but recent literary scholarship has called both the German and the lower-class origins of the texts into question.[2] Coming at a time when historians and ethnographers have begun using such materials to try to give poor people a voice in historical accounts, the attack on the integrity of the Grimms as collectors of tales threatens permanent laryngitis to the unheard. At the same time, the necessity of finding these voices and understanding them remains compelling, and in the absence of anything better some effort to use carefully selected tales collected from Hesse-Cassel in the early nineteenth century must be made.

Recorded Oral Tradition as an Historical Source

Although the Grimms' statements about "collecting the tales as faithfully as possible" became programmatic for the "scientific collection of folktales," their dubious methodology, their "improvement" of published versions, and their passionate concern to give Germans a culture separate from the Frenchified culture of the Enlightenment made it

1. James C. Scott, *Domination and the Arts of Resistance: Hidden Transcripts* (New Haven, 1990), xiff., 8–10.
2. John M. Ellis, *One Fairy Story Too Many: The Brothers Grimm and Their Tales* (Chicago, 1983); Heinz Röllecke, "Die Marburger Märchenfrau," *Fabula* 15 (1974); and "Die stockhessischen Märchen der 'alten Marie'; Das Ende eines Mythos um die frühesten *KHM* Aufzeichnungen der Brüder Grimm," *Germanische-Romanische Monatschrift* 25 (1975); but compare Jakob and Wilhelm Grimm, *Kinder- und Hausmärchen* (Berlin, 1812); Wilhelm Schoof, *Zur Entstehungsgeschichte Der Grimmischen Märchen* (Hamburg, 1959), but most important Herman Rebel, "Why Not 'Old Marie' . . . or Someone Very Much Like Her?" *Social History* 13 (1988): 1–27.

inevitable that their tales would not stand up to latter-day ethnographers' standards of collection.[3] Because of flawed collection and reproduction procedures, most recent scholars want to suggest that the tales did not become part of German culture until the Grimm collection made them so. Thus, in her introduction to a recent edition of the collection, Ingeborg Weber-Kellermann speaks of a nineteenth-century "domestication" (*Verheimatung*) of the tales.[4] Other critics point out that versions of many of the tales can be found written in sixteenth- and seventeenth-century collections like Perrault's and the Italian *Pentameron*.[5] Heinz Röllecke, for example, even suggests that because many of the Grimms' informants were of Huguenot origin, the tales were French rather than German.[6] In addition, Röllecke casts doubt upon the Grimms' access to much material from ordinary people.[7] He concludes that many of the *Kinder- und Hausmärchen* came from a Frenchified middle-class circle of persons who told the tales to one another — perhaps in the spirit that led Marie Antoinette to pretend to be a peasant.[8]

Though I wish to make no defense of the Grimms, whose misappropriation of the tales for their own purposes is an old and oft-repeated story, I do believe that the suggestion that their collection has no relationship to the oral culture of rural Hesse rests on a misapprehension of what recorded oral texts are. Linda Degh has argued that to understand folktales one must understand them as something performed before an audience. She describes a typical performance situation from the Balkans in which a tale-teller was constantly interrupted by ongoing audience interpretation and comment.[9] Following Millman Parry and others, Walter Ong has argued that this is generally how performances occur in a culture dominated by orality.[10] Thus the interaction between the performer and the audience creates the shared meanings in this form of peasant culture. Story texts can come from

3. Grimms, *KHM*, 1812, cited in Ellis, *One Fairy Story Too Many*, 13–16.

4. Ingeborg Weber-Kellermann, ed., Jakob und Wilhelm Grimm, *Kinder- und Hausmärchen gesammelt durch die Brüder Grimm* (*KHM*) (Marburg, 1981), 15.

5. Ellis, *One Fairy Story*, 26–31.

6. Röllecke, "Die Stockhessischen Märchen," 74–76.

7. Röllecke, "Die Marburger Märchenfrau," 87–93.

8. Heinz Röllecke, *Die älteste Märchensammlung der Brüder Grimm* (Konstanz, 1976), 341–45; and also "Die stockhessischen Märchen," 74–80.

9. Linda Degh, *Folktales and Society* (Bloomington, Ind., 1962), 119–21.

10. Walter Ong, *Orality and Literacy: The Technologizing of the Word* (London, 1988), 20–22.

anywhere, but are likely to have been constructed in performance from a broad range of possible materials, by professional and sometimes highly mobile raconteurs.[11] More important, story meanings are likely to be rooted firmly in the context of particular performances. Thus, for texts, the boundaries between oral and written, between different languages, between different classes, and between different ethnic groups can be extremely fluid. For the social historian interested in what peasants believed rather than community ownership of the text itself, a reconstruction of meaning in performance becomes important.Such a reconstruction can be created by confronting the texts of professional tale performers with contexts of likely audiences in specific social and historical circumstances. Beyond the familiar operation of confronting texts and contexts, the historian must also establish the availability of at least textual elements of stories to the audiences whose social context is used in the interpretive process. Finally, it is important to remember that "folk tales are more than simple stories; they function as conceptual tools."[12] Thus their language is condensed and our access to it is always problematic and partial.

We must lay some groundwork before using the texts of the Grimm collection as a key to peasant beliefs about the consequences of military and monetary policies in the countryside. We must first establish that the texts are at least gross facsimiles of tales told in rural Hessian regions at the time the Grimms were collecting (circa. 1806–15) and in the fifty previous years. Given the recent assertions by Heinz Röllecke, John Ellis, and other literary scholars that the Grimms' informants were overwhelmingly urban and middle-class, this would seem to be a difficult task.[13] Even if one grants that Röllecke is correct (I do not) in arguing that Dorothea Viehmann and "alte Marie" (two crucial informants for the collections) were solidly middle-class and not really German, the assertion that the tales and their meanings were limited to similar class and French ethnic contexts cannot be made because it assumes hermetic seals between classes, linguistic groups, and nationalities. There is no doubt that elements of fairy-tale texts traveled

11. Peter Taylor and Hermann Rebel, "Hessian Peasant Women, Their Families and the Draft: A Social-Historical Interpretation of Four Tales from the Grimm Collection," *Journal of Family History* 6 (Winter, 1981) 4: 356.

12. Ibid., 355.

13. Ellis, *One Fairy Story*; and Röllecke, "Die stockhessischen Märchen." For an effective criticism of these ideas upon which I rely heavily in the following section see Rebel, "Why Not 'Old Marie,'" 1–27.

and that they entered the repertoire of traveling storytellers throughout Europe and thus became the property of any who cared to listen. Thus one needs to find points of contact where transmission of oral material did occur, either formally or informally.

Such points of contact between classes and ethnic groups did exist in the Hessian countryside where the Grimms did so much of their collecting. Huguenots were not Hutterites, and the fact that the Grimms married into and lived on the edges of a Huguenot community in Kassel shows that ethnic boundaries were not sharp. Landgrave Carl's Huguenot colony program, which his successors extended, established French-speaking villages throughout Hesse-Cassel. But such villages could not be sealed hermetically, for they needed to buy and sell in regional markets; the days when economic self-sufficiency was possible had long passed. Moreover, with the interspersal of different ethnic communities, successful traveling raconteurs needed to perform in both French and German and to take textual materials between both communities. The Huguenot presence in Hesse-Cassel may have explained the appearance of certain textual materials, but the way storytellers constructed them in performance and the way audiences contributed to meanings must be directly related to the social context.

Women provided an important point of contact between classes. In sifting through the material that comes to us about the Grimms' informants, we see that thirty-seven of the fifty-four tales in the Brentano manuscript were identified as having originally female sources. In addition, this collection is notable for the near absence of males as informants. Male sources became more frequent in the 1812 and later editions of the *KHM*, but females continued to provide a large amount of material.[14] Why did women — middle-class or otherwise — have particular access to the materials and techniques of story construction in the Grimms' Hessian haunts?

One of the clearest descriptions of the process of collecting tales concerns a woman known to us only as the Marburger Märchenfrau, an older woman living out her years in the poorhouse of Saint Eliesabeth's Hospital in Marburg. The Grimms came to know of her through their fellow romantic Clemens Brentano, who had heard stories told by her but had failed to record them. The woman would

14. Röllecke, *Die älteste Märchensammlung*, 390ff.; Johannes Bolte and Georg Polivka, *Anmerkung zu den Kinder- und Hausmärchen der Brüder Grimm* 1–4 (Hildesheim and New York, 1982).

Otto Ubbelohde, *A Hessian Storyteller*. Source: Bildarchiv Marburg; by permission of N. G. Elwert Verlag.

not tell them her tales and so they were forced to acquire what material they could through the mediation of the wife of the hospital director. When men approached her she demurred, fearing that having a reputation for spinning yarns would ill serve a poor old woman already at the mercy of a welfare bureaucracy. Approached by a woman, however, she loosened up sufficiently to provide two or three tales.[15]

The exclusively woman-to-woman discourse in this anecdote of the Märchenfrau and the wife of the hospital director is consistent with what we know about female participation in oral traditions performed in village spinning bees. Hans Medick described the *Lichtstube* or *Spinnstube* as one important arena for the performance of folktales.[16] According to him, rural women and girls gathered in the home of a wealthy householder to spin flax or wool into yarn and to carry out other chores related to the sexual division of labor. This labor was done communally, both because it saved the tallow of candles used for light and because it provided an atmosphere of entertainment that eased the insufferably dull work of spinning. Living in households where their parents held frequent spinning bees undoubtedly provided an excellent foundation for young women who subsequently needed to find alternative occupations because they married no heir nor inherited family property themselves. These had become overwhelmingly female gatherings because state officials sought to exclude males for moral reasons and accepted gender norms. The Lichtstube remained part of the Hessian rural experience well into the nineteenth century.[17]

A primarily rural, lower-class female oral tradition could enter the households of the Hessian urban bourgeoisie in at least two ways. Medick pointed out that the eighteenth-century Spinnstube often became a rationalized arena of production.[18] Moreover, "enlightened" opinion, which had previously opposed peasant institutions of this kind on moral grounds, came to regard them as places where habits of industry could be taught. Authorities now regarded those who managed Spinnstube, the Lichtherr and his wife, in this new version of the institution as mediators of elite values to the peasantry.[19] However,

15. Schoof, *Zur Entstehungsgeschichte*, 68–72; Rebel, "Why Not 'Old Marie,'" 1–27.

16. Hans Medick, "Village Spinning Bees: Sexual Culture and Free Time Among Rural Youth in Early Modern Germany," in David Sabean and Hans Medick eds., *Interest and Emotion* (Cambridge, 1984), 317–27.

17. StaM, B/23b ALb, Rossberg 1516, 1785.

18. Medick, "Village Spinning Bees," 317–27.

19. Ibid.

influence could travel both ways because Lichtherrn and their wives heard the tales and songs of rural women whether they were peasants or not. The transmission of peasant culture to the elites under these circumstances was no less probable than the imposition of elite values on peasants. One of the Grimms' informants, Dorothea Viehmann, could have been involved in story performances either as a participant or a manager whether she were an innkeeper's daughter, the wife of a tailor, or a simple peasant woman from the village of Niederzwehrn. Because her husband had been a tailor, her contact with textile production in a Spinnstube environment was that much more probable. In light of this possibility, Röllecke's attempts to seal her from lower-class sources would seem to be a failure.[20]

Yet another manner by which lower-class oral material passed into the *Kinder- und Hausmärchen* is illustrated by the story of the Grimms' informant "alte Marie." Until Röllecke's recent attempts at revision, scholars believed this storyteller was Marie Müller, a servant in the household of the Kassel apothecary Rudolf Wild. Many stories from the Grimms' collection they attributed not only directly to Marie but also to Dortchen and Gretchen Wild, who had grown up under her supervision. That lower-class nannies propagated folktales as children's tales is something widely accepted apart from the Grimms' use of material from the Wild household. Servants of urban households early in the nineteenth century usually came from rural environments, traveling some distance and using a wide variety of connections to find their positions.[21] This experience of mobility put them in a position to acquire and dispense an even broader body of folklore than even women who were associated with a Lichtstube.

Even if "alte Marie" turns out to be a mythical figure herself (again something I do not concede), she represented a way in which elements of lower-class oral traditions became part of the experience of bourgeois girls. We can assume that the Wild girls built stories from some materials transmitted by the many servants that passed through their household. Whether or not a given story reveals lower-class concerns must be decided on the basis of its own history, its own content, and in some circumstances, its own language. In short, we must ask whether

20. Compare Ellis, *One Fairy Story*, 30–35.
21. Rebel, "Why Not 'Old Marie,'" 1–27. See also Rolf Engelsing, "Das häusliche Personal in der Epoche der Industrialisierung," in his *Zur Sozialgeschichte deutscher Mittel- und Unterschichten* (Göttingen, 1973), 225–35.

the tales fit with what we know about the experience of lower-class people in the social contexts from which they come. It is to the task of relating some stories of the Grimm collection to the experience of the military system in the Hessian countryside that we now turn.

The Ideology of Connectedness

Anthropologists, among them Eric Wolf and Claude Lévi-Strauss, have observed that ideologies of groups practicing kin-ordered production center on the fundamental distinction between groups whose members are connected by descent (consanguines) and members of groups who may become connected through marriage (potential and actual affines).[22] David Sabean has found these categories at the center of much peasant discourse recorded in the villages of Württemburg in the three centuries before 1800.[23] Peasants spoke of these categories in terms of enemies (*Feinde*), friends (*Freunde*), and relatives (*Verwandte*). Enemies and friends were, respectively, affines and potential affines, that is, the group of marriageable people. Relatives, or in the nomenclature of Hessian peasants, blood friends (*Blutfreunde*), were covered by the incest taboo enforced by religious authorities. Peasants expected certain kinds of danger from nonrelatives including intentional aggression and envy which seemed appropriate to competition among equals. The danger represented by relatives and recognized in peasant discourse could only be unintentional — a kind of genetic pollution — because the opposite of hatred (we may say love) was appropriate to relations between members of this group. Peasants saw marriage as a way to (only) partially diminish the dangers of enmity by converting enemies into friends from whom one could expect support. In discourse, as in the practice of kin-ordering production, marriage played a central role for German peasants.

The usefulness of the categories of enemy, friend, and relative shall become clear as the analysis of selected stories proceeds. As with any set of ideological categories, however, limitations and blind spots obscure or paper over experienced social tensions within the contexts in which peasants tell stories. As Wolf has suggested, the language of affinity and consanguinity — the language of connectedness — has great

22. Eric R. Wolf, *Europe and the People Without History* (Berkeley, 1982), 389.
23. David Warren Sabean, *Power in the Blood* (Cambridge, 1987), 31, 94–112.

difficulty with the groups of people we call orphans and strangers.[24] The bureaucratic process of recruitment, the legal status of soldiers, and the concrete experiences of military life that changed connected peasant boys into soldiers also changed them into disconnected strangers and even functional orphans. Compounding the direct operations of the military bureaucracy, related state intervention in the process of peasant inheritance extended the difficulties to soldiers' sisters. I have selected certain tales because they seem to provide both an exploration of the meaning of disconnectedness related to the military and some suggestions for relieving it.

Images of Disconnectedness and the Military System

Three tales that have already received substantial attention from Hermann Rebel and myself present themselves as obvious candidates for interpretation.[25] Although the account I give here closely follows what we have written in the past, the new focus offered by Wolf and Sabean appears to offer further clarity and enables me to connect our past work with the present one. The tales, "The Three Ravens" (*KHM*, 1812, nr. 25), "The Twelve Brothers" (*KHM*, 1812, nr. 9), and "The Six Swans" (*KHM*, 1815, nr. 119), all share the same fundamental structure — young brothers magically transformed from human to animal form and then rescued by their sisters' performance of a magical ritual of renunciation. The similarity of structure suggests they are improvisations on the same chord progression, the earliest and sparsest version of which appears in an 1810 manuscript sent by the brothers Grimm to Clemmens Brentano.[26] These handwritten versions appear to be the closest to the original ones provided by informants who were more carefully designated by the Grimms than were those for some other materials. These designations allow us to locate textual materials in geographic and social space as well as in time. This oldest of the three recorded texts, "The Three Ravens," the Grimms attributed to old Marie Müller ("alte Marie"), supposedly a servant in the Wild and Grimm households who came from the Main river valley near Hanau. Wilhelm Schoof believed the woman had lost a husband to the Hessian

24. Wolf, *Europe*, 289.
25. Taylor and Rebel, "Hessian Peasant Women."
26. Röllecke, "Die stockhessischen Märchen."

military campaign in America.[27] Her version of the tale, along with version titled "The Six Swans," appeared in the first (1812) edition of the *Kinder- und Hausmärchen der Brüder Grimm*. Dorothea Viehmann, a marketwoman and the daughter of a Huguenot innkeeper from the village of Niederzwehrn, contributed "The Twelve Brothers." At the time the Grimms did their earliest collecting (1809–14) both women were old enough to put them in that generation most deeply affected by the savagery of the Fredrician military system.

The structure of the tales juxtaposes two worlds: one of normal family life and one the state of transformation where "people become . . . birds, 'unstable male cosmogones,' whose destiny is to be socially disconnected."[28] Performers connected this particular state of social death and disconnectedness with military status through the symbolism of the birds into which the boys are transformed.[29] In Muller's versions, the boys become ravens or swans and in Viehmann's they fly away as ravens. In Teutonic mythology, ravens accompany Odin, god of war, to the field of battle to feast off the dead, while swans are the Valkyrie, another soldier symbol. With these similarities and connections in mind, we turn to the variations in the tales which appear to be meditations on the reasons for disconnection, the processes by which it occurs, and finally on the meaning of existing in the world of the socially dead.

In all three versions of the tale, magical transformation comes out of the context of family conflict, anger, and fear. In the oldest extant text an angry mother curses her three sons for having played during Sunday church services and as a result "they were turned into ravens and flew away."[30] It is difficult to tell from the language of the tale whether the transformation of her sons was a punishment of the woman for her anger, or whether it was punishment of the boys for violating sacred ritual. The use of passive construction in the quoted sentence enhances the belief that the woman did not intend to transform her sons and that they became functional orphans not because of the enmity of a relative but because of pollution of either kin relations or sacred ritual. The lack of harmful intent is even more explicit in the 1819 version of the tale ("The Seven Ravens," *KHM*, 1819, nr. 25) in which a father curses

27. Schoof, *Zur Entstehungsgeschichte,* 60–64; Rebel, "Why Not 'Old Marie.'"

28. Taylor and Rebel, "Hessian Peasant Women," 365.

29. Compare Orlando Patterson, *Slavery and Social Death: A Comparative Study* (Cambridge, 1982), 39.

30. Röllecke, *Die älteste Märchensammlung.*

his sons for breaking a pitcher they were supposed to use to carry baptismal water for their newborn sister. Although the father wishes out loud for the transformation in the moment of anger, the tale implies immediate and deep regret over the consequences of that expression. Further, the parents' own shame at what has occurred leads them to conceal the existence of the brothers .from their sister. She discovers them only through the gossip of neighbors who blame her for what happened to them. But here again, the change is treated as a kind of misfortune that lacks any intent on the part of those responsible. These narrative constructions just barely stay within the rule that consanguines may not intentionally harm one another.

In a far more complex variant, "The Six Swans," old Marie told of the magical metamorphosis as the result of a premeditated act of a stepmother who saw the children of a past marriage as a threat. Though the wicked woman converted the six brothers to swans by throwing magic shirts on them, their sister escapes notice, remains unharmed, and is left to cope with the consequences of the militarization of her brothers. The success of the stepmother represents the failure of the father's attempts to protect his descendants from her maliciousness. Though the result of an intentional act and conscious enmity, this orphanage remains within the boundaries observed by Sabean because a stepmother was seen as no real relative. In this view, her action is structurally determined from the stance of the children because she is neither an affine nor a potential affine (she is already married) and so her enmity cannot be converted to friendship. The aid expected from affines was the reason the father married the woman in the first place. He needed his present mother-in-law's aid to help him find his way out of a dark forest. She, in turn, extracted the promise that he marry her daughter, something which made him deeply uneasy. Though the father of the boys was helped by his marriage to the stepmother, his children were not. Such an interpretation seems indicative of the strain that military orphanage placed upon the cultural materials available to women hearing these tales. Faced with a choice between denying depth to the loving power in a blood relationship or denying the same quality to the relationship of marriage or parenthood, this storyteller ultimately chose to deny efficacy to the latter rather than the former.

Where Marie's stories stayed barely within the boundaries of the ideology of connectedness, Dorthea Viehmann's treatment did not, and finessed the issue in another way. In "The Twelve Brothers," a father actually expresses the intention to kill his twelve sons so that his newborn and long-awaited daughter may inherit his patrimony; yet, he neither kills the boys nor does he transform them into avian form. The boys' mother warns them and they flee to hide in the forest. When their sister later discovers their existence and searches them out, her act of picking flowers out of their garden accomplishes their transmutation into ravens. Unlike the father, the girl in this circumstance has nothing but the best intentions. Though Frau Viehmann touched upon the ideologically dangerous idea that disinheritance (orphanage) and military service were related to choices parents made between children, she does not carry through an analysis in which blood-kin can be fatally and intentionally divided by interest and emotion. The sister's unintentional act is made to bear the burden of tragedy.

In all versions of this story, boys are cast out of families and, orphaned, become strangers to their relatives. The position of these narrative characters replicates many aspects of the experience of Hessian draftees dispossessed by inheritance practice and later law and, as a result, subject to military service as the household's most expendable people.[31] Although it is clear that parental decisions to advantage one child over others played crucial roles in the process of subjecting some to involuntary military servitude, none of the stories can finally confront this terrible fact directly. Story texts contain ambiguous language about intent, or ambiguous constructions of consanguinal and affinal relationships to avoid the issue. Even when the harmful intent of choosing between children enters Viehmann's variant directly, she finessed it and gave it no large role because another blood relation intervened to deflect that intent. Through avoidance, the hegemony of connectedness reigned, giving no conceptual handle to transform social relations of the kin-ordered mode of production.

Though the tales failed to provide the conceptual apparatus to face and transform relationships between kin, they do provide insight into the meaning of disconnectedness for those who suffered it. The avian symbolism of the transformations, the dark forests, or glass mountains in which the transformed male children live each provide insights into the ways military orphanage might be perceived. In Germanic culture, birds were not only symbols of soldiers but also of outlaws. Medieval

31. Taylor and Rebel, "Hessian Peasant Women," 367–76; Peter K. Taylor, "The Household's Most Expendable People: The Draft and Peasant Society in Eighteenth-Century Hessen-Kassel (Ph.D. diss., University of Iowa, 1987), 125–33.

and early modern legal sentences proclaimed traitors and other serious criminals to be "free as birds" (*Vogelfrei*), meaning that they no longer enjoyed the protection of law and might be killed with impunity. This freedom condemned the disconnected to live in the social forest of family trees (*Arbores Consanguinitas*) in "The Twelve Brothers" and "The Six Swans." As birds, they might fly among the trees, perch in them briefly, wander among their trunks, but they could never be of their substance or draw upon their resources for protection. The condition of being physically present in a society of families but without connections to or membership in one is most clearly symbolized in Marie's story "The Three Ravens." The transformed children are condemned to live not in the forest but locked in a glass mountain. Thus imprisoned behind walls through which they may see and be seen but through which no human contacts can be made, they exist in a state physically present but socially absent. No better representation of social victimization can be made and no clearer tie between the two hegemonic ideologies of "marginality" and "connectedness" may be drawn.

Rescue Operations

Although the discourse of peasant folktales did not directly confront the culpability of the directors of kin-ordered production in the victimization of peasant children, it did address issues related to rescuing the boys from the state of disconnectedness. In all three stories their sisters reconnect them to the world of families through manipulation of the rules of property devolution and marriage. Sisters perform symbolic transfers of property, undertake vows of silence, and marry to effect the salvation of their brothers from military servitude. Such acts seem to reflect some of the shifts seen in peasant marriage and devolutionary behavior in response to the extremes of the Fredrician military system. As the mother of Anna Margretha Hämmer suffered in the previous chapter, each woman in these tales suffers substantially for her decision to help her siblings. (If Margretha's mother was Becker's mother-in-law rather than his sister, she still faced conflicts between justice for her own daughter and the relationship created by her son's marriage to Becker's sister.) Though these women become heroines through their acts of self-sacrifice and renunciation, so constructing their acts blurs the source of their own victimization and reveals a tension between the

value of loyalty to parents' and lineage and loyalty to siblings. However, the stories are clear that women are to bear and reveal — more
fully than even their brothers — the ideological contradictions of the
Hessian military system.

In "The Three Ravens," the self-sacrificing heroine was aware of her
brothers' plight when it happened and she was motivated to rescue
them because she was depressed (*betrübt*). Other versions have her
discover her brothers' military or dispossessed status by accident or
from neighbors. In any case, the way to retransformation was fraught
with danger for the girl who traveled to the ends of the earth to find a
solution for her brothers' removal from normal human existence.

Before she literally found the key to her heart's desire, the girl
confronted the sun and the moon, both of whom were consumers of
human flesh and who offered no help. Were these veiled symbols of
Germany's petty sun-kings who drafted their subjects for fiscal purposes? For peasants to see their lords as cannibals consuming their
flesh was as old as the central European legends of Count Dracula. The
sun and moon consumed the flesh of children in behavior that seemed
very reminiscent of those rulers who took young boys to serve involuntarily in their armies. It also seems particularly appropriate that the
solution to the boys' retransformation did not lie in appeals to those
higher authorities but in the symbolic manipulation of devolutionary
rules. The stars forced the moon to give the girl a finger bone (*Hinkel-
beinchen*) that unlocked the glass mountain in which the boy-ravens
were imprisoned. Taylor and Rebel have already pointed out how
joints of the human body had long been used to calculate devolutionary paths in Germany.[32] It seems reasonable to assume that this tale
suggested the manipulation of inheritance as a key to releasing the
brothers from their condition. The sister of the Brentano manuscript
simply went to the glass mountain and unlocked it with the bone key
and left a ring on the ravens' table. The retransformation of the brothers occurred when the ravens recognized their sister and her love. In the
ritual exchange of weddings, the ring was a sign of what each member
of the couple brought to the marriage and gave to the other. In giving
the ring to her brothers, it is unclear whether the woman renounced
marriage or simply her dowry.

In the 1819 variant of the tale under discussion, "The Seven Ra-

---

32. Jack Goody, *The Development of the Family and Marriage in Europe* (Cambridge, 1983), 136–46.

vens," Marie's symbolism is much less opaque. First, the bone key is not the gift of "the stars" but of "the morning star," Venus. This clearly associates it with the Germanic custom of "the morning gift" (*Morgengabe*) which, in the nomenclature of Germanic inheritance custom, was provided by the groom's family to the bride the morning after the marriage was consummated. Second, the sister loses the gift and instead of unlocking the glass mountain with it she must cut off her own little finger to perform the task. Losing the gift stands as a loss of the benefits of marriage itself while cutting off the finger meant renouncing the claims to a marriage portion from her own family. This latter renunciation is consistent with our study of marriage in the previous chapter. Some parents diminished their daughters' opportunities for a good match in order to pursue conscription avoidance strategies. In some cases, the renunciation of dowry resources meant that the prospects for marriage itself became seriously restricted, if not lost. But once again, it appears that causal agency is blurred. Though heroic acts of self-sacrifice were not inconceivable, it seems more likely that they were required by those who arranged the patterns of property devolution and, ultimately, through the inheritance law of 1773, the Landgrave himself.

In the other versions of the tales under scrutiny, renunciation does not mean the end of marriage prospects but rather becomes the opportunity to meditate on another range of problems created by reduced inheritance portions. The heroic sisters of "The Twelve Brothers" and "The Six Swans" both renounce their portions by undertaking long vows of silence which they begin by sitting in trees in the forest. In both cases, they are found by hunting kings who fall in love and marry them. In both cases, the king's mother disapproves of the marriage. In "The Six Swans" she complains, "This slut who can't talk. . . . Who knows where she comes from? She's not worthy of a king." In this manner women marrying with little or no dowry are associated with the promiscuous or with prostitutes. The inheritance portion stands as a marker of personal worthiness, the sign of the strength of kin connections, of having a known past.

Ultimately, because the new bride makes no claims on her own kin through her silence, she does not possess the resources to convert the enmity of the king's mother to friendship. As a result, she suffers an attack which further elaborates the dangers of renunciation and the distortions of marital exchange wrought by military servitude on the process of ordering production through kinship. In "The Twelve

Brothers," the attack merely takes the form of constant slander by the mother-in-law, "Even if she's dumb and can't speak, she could laugh once in a while. Anybody who doesn't laugh has a guilty conscience." In "The Six Swans," the attack is more elaborate and more revealing. The king's mother steals the children of the marriage, accuses the queen of eating the babies, and manufactures evidence for her charge by smearing the queen's mouth with blood as she sleeps. The mother-in-law's dishonesty pointed out that not bringing in a portion, not uniting the fortunes of two families in marriage is tantamount to cannibalism of one's own children. This crime went far beyond the polluting danger that kin usually represented to one another. The mother-in-law has accused the silent girl of enmity against her own descendants — of practicing witchcraft against them. Anna Margretha Hämmer's mother similarly faced a choice between her descendant, (Anna Margretha) and her brother (Johannes). Anna Margretha's mother had to resolve the contradiction in her heart and adopt a strategy that had a chance of punishing someone for her daughter's injury, and, at the same time, rescuing her brother. The storytellers resolved it as conflict between new bride and mother-in-law. As in "The Twelve Brothers," where the crime remains unspecified, the new bride is sentenced to be burned as a witch for her (alleged or real?) crimes.

The heroism of the sister is not punished, rather at the last moment the term of the vows of silence expire, her brothers return to human form, she is able to tell her story and the mother-in-law is punished in her stead. This resolution is not as straightforward as it would appear, for though the sham cannibalism is exposed, the girl's innocence is not established in any symbolic sense. Instead, the conditions of her guilt may now be revealed and explained as she regains her voice. The problem of her descendants is simply ignored as the [mother-in-law] is executed and the tale is resolved in favor of sibling love.

If viewed from the point of view of the executed mother-in-law, though, the sister may not be guilty of literal cannibalism, but she is guilty of sacrificing the welfare of her own children to that of her brothers. The common interest in descendants converts affines into friends as much as do contractually shared resources. But here the sister's failure to contribute is a sign of lack of common interest — in fact, a sign of conflicts of interest between two different groups of consanguines (brothers and children). This conflict of interest is structural in the predominantly patrilineal and patrilocal inheritance and marriage practices of most Hessian regions. To increase portions of sons is to decrease those of daughters and their children and vice versa. In medieval Germanic epics, this structural conflict is ideologically and perhaps practically blurred by assigning brothers as protectors of their sisters' male children.[33] In these stories children, but mostly the sisters, and mothers-in-law, bear the burden of such tensions — again a structural necessity because brothers (Johannes Becker) needed protection more immediately than their potential nieces or nephews (the unborn Anna Margretha Hämmers).

In Hesse-Cassel, the intensified need for protection of this kind grew out of the victimizations of conscription and the inheritance reforms of 1773 which intentionally dispossessed and enslaved. But these practices dispossessed women too, both directly and through peasant adjustments to conscription, and the tales fail to render that process fully transparent. As the contradictions of kin-ordered groups are blurred at the beginning of the tales by insufficiently specified causal agency, so also are they blurred at the end by too much agency wrongly attributed. The victimization of women is masked to the extent that tales picture suffering as the result of intentional acts of other women. The heroic self-sacrifice of sisters and the attempts of mothers to maintain the value of the patriline cause both to suffer. It seems unlikely that women, in the real living conditions to which the tales obliquely refer, frequently experienced a dominant role in the arrangements of marriage and inheritance that caused their suffering.

Women as Mediators through Illicit Love

As we have seen, Fredrician military reforms were associated in the minds of officials with the beginning of substantially increased rates of illegitimate births in Hessian rural society. The illicit liaisons of soldiers and village women appeared in Hessian oral tradition as well. In the tale "The Three Surgeons," a woman's love is shown as the key to other more tenuous forms of connection than that afforded by sisters. Because of the dangers of such connections, storytellers seemed to caution young girls against making them.[34]

33. David Sabean, "Aspects of Kinship Behavior and Property in Rural Western Europe Before 1800," in Goody et al., *Family and Inheritance: Rural Society in Europe 1200–1800* (Cambridge, 1976), 108.
34. Grimm, "Die Drei Feldscheer," *Kinder- und Hausmärchen* (Berlin, 1815), 32.

In the tale that the Grimms collected from the village of Zwehrn in 1813 (through Dorothea Viehmann?), three doctors staying at an inn want to show off their newly acquired medical skills to the patrons. Using a magic salve, one cut off his hand, another removed his eye, and the third took out his heart. The body parts they placed on a platter which they put in the innkeeper's cupboard. As the doctors slept, the serving maid let in her lover, a soldier, to feed him. She unlocked the cupboard and while she trysted with the soldier a cat stole the surgeons' organs. The maid was beside herself with anxiety when she discovered the theft but the soldier calmed her by promising to put things right. He replaced the hand with one cut from a thief dangling on the gallows; a new eye he acquired from the thieving cat; and the heart he stole from a pig's carcass hanging in the innkeeper's larder.

In the morning, the surgeons placed the new body parts in their bodies and went on their way only to discover that the thief's hand continued to steal, the cat's eye saw only mice in the dark, and the pig's heart caused its new owner to root and snuffle like a pig. Returning to the inn, the surgeons threatened to burn it down if the innkeeper did not compensate them. Upon seeing them, the poor maid fled never to return and the furious innkeeper paid the surgeons off.

The relationship between soldier and serving girl led to two crimes that cost the unfortunate girl her position. First, she had misappropriated her master's property to feed the soldier, illicitly mediating resources from a "respectable" world to a questionable one. In more obviously military versions of the tale, ravens or even soldiers eat the body parts from the innkeeper's cupboard.[35] More importantly, the soldier/servant dyad mediated a kind of pollution between a criminal/animal underworld to the surgeons' world costing both the girl and her master position and wealth. No peasant woman hearing a story like this at a spinning bee could feel entirely comfortable about a liaison with a soldier. Connection could have its antiheroic aspects too.

Soldiers, Self-Help, and the Experience of Betrayal

Tales the Grimms collected from soldiers also indicated that these hapless men recognized their marginal and mediating roles between an underworld and a more everyday social and family life. Soldiers caught in this twilight existence portrayed themselves both as victims of be-

35. Bolte and Polivka, *Anmerkung* 2:553–54.

trayal and betrayers as they fought to preserve some connection with the better side of their lives. Particularly important for our purposes are two tales collected in 1812 from Friedrich Krause, a poor Hessian veteran who lived in the village of Hof. Krause was part of the generation of soldiers recruited under the Kanton ordinance of 1762 and the Grimms considered his tales characteristically Hessian soldiers' tales.[36]

Krause's version of "Old Sultan" appeared only in later editions of the Grimm's published collection but is relayed to us through the work of Johannes Bolte and Georg Polívka.[37] In the tale he told, dog (Sultan) overheard his master complaining to his wife that the dog was old and toothless, no longer of any value as a watch dog, and it was time to do away with him. The sympathetic wife pointed to the dog's loyal and effective service, but her husband replied that he had paid for that with the dog's food. Now the animal could no longer hunt or even keep watch over his flocks.

The unhappy dog went to one of his old friends, a wolf, and bemoaned his fate. The wolf slyly proposed a trick which offered the opportunity to prove the dog's value in his master's eyes. The wolf would steal the master's child and allow the dog to rescue it. They carried out the ruse to perfection and in gratitude for the rescue Sultan's master promised him porridge and bed for the rest of his days. Later, when he again spoke with the dog, the wolf pointed out how glad he was that the trick had worked. The wolf further suggested that the dog might now be willing to turn the other way when the wolf tried to make off with one of the master's sheep. Sultan demurred, saying that he must remain loyal to his master. Unfortunately, the wolf did not take him seriously and attempted to steal a lamb. The dog betrayed the thief and as he escaped the wolf promised revenge.

Later the wolf sent a pig to the dog proposing that they settle their differences by fighting in the woods. The dog could find only a three-legged cat with a stiff tail as an ally in this matter of honor. Nevertheless, the invalid cat and the toothless dog went forth into the forest to meet the wolf and his friend, the boar, at the appointed place. As they approached, the wolf saw the cat's upright tail and mistook it for a saber. He further took the cat's limping gait as the act of collecting stones to throw at the wolf. Upon reflection, the wolf and the boar decided to hide themselves from the approaching pair. The pig however, failed to hide completely, leaving an ear exposed which the cat

36. Ibid. 2:19ff.
37. Ibid.; also Grimm, *Kinder und Hausmärchen* (Marburg, 1981), 2:15–16.

mistook for a mouse and immediately bit. The boar, assuming he had been attacked, screamed and ran off pointing to the wolf's hiding place. The wolf, ashamed of his cowardice, made peace with the dog.

Krause's story points to an anxiety which many old soldiers may have experienced. As we have seen, even bureaucrats worried that long terms of military service left old veterans ill-suited for a return to civilian life. Return to social life is pictured in this tale as death itself and the result of the soldier's condition as a used-up object. To relieve this condition the dog (soldier) must resort to self-help because the mediation of a helping female fails. Help does come in the form of his friendship with the wolf, a dual symbol of soldier and outlaw which pointed to the belief that many dismissed soldiers ended up in the bands of robbers that frequented the wooded and hilly border lands of Hesse-Cassel.[38] The mutually plotted crime is followed by betrayal and reconciliation, repeating the theme of misappropriation associated with soldiers in the tale of the surgeons but more importantly indicating the tension between the soldier's legitimate role and his military friendships. Though the dog is reconciled both with his master and the wolf on the basis of martial values and comradery, the pain of the double betrayal is left for the marginal wolf to bear as his own "cowardice."

Krause's version of "The Queen Bee" reflected the anxieties that soldiers faced upon their dismissal from service but at the same time suggested that a soldier's shadowy connections could serve a master's interests as well as be used to trick him.[39] The protagonist, a dismissed soldier called Fix-und-Fertig (Spit-and-Polish), sought employment as a lackey in the house of a great lord. Though he immediately acquired a position by anticipating his employer's desire for a pipe and tobacco, the master made his permanent employment conditional on Fix's capacity to win the hand of a beautiful lady for the lord. To accomplish his task Fix asked that his master provide a coach and finery to make a rich show; a retinue of servants over which he had authority; and clothing fit for a prince.

Setting off with these items on his mission, the veteran found himself confronted with several conflicts of loyalty in which he misappropriates his master's resources. First, he diverts the coach from its course to

---

38. Hermann Bettenhausen, "Räuber- und Gaunerbänden in Hessen," *Zeitschrift für Hessische Geschichte* 75/76 (1964/65): 107.

39. Bolte and Polívka, *Anmerkung* 2:19 n. 2. Krause's version is called "Spit-and-Polish" (*Fix-und-Fertig*).

avoid disturbing a flock of birds in the woods. Fix justified his act saying the birds were praising the creator in their own way. Second, he killed one of his master's horses to feed some starving ravens. Finally, he rescued a fish in a stagnant pond, going far out of his way to find a freshly flowing stream.

In diverting his master's resources for acts of charity, the former soldier took terrible risks. These risks had their rewards as the beneficiaries repaid Fix's kindness in their own way. They also represented a vision of how a soldier viewed the operation of initiative in the context of clientage networks. To win the princess for his master, the king required him to perform three tasks which he could not have completed without the animals' help. The birds helped him collect a quarter of poppy seeds strewn on a field. The fish recovered a ring the princess had lost in the stream that was his new home. Finally, the ravens — as symbolic soldiers might — helped Fix attack and defeat a dangerous unicorn. The veteran soldier won the hand of the princess, became the new prince's first minister, and gave positions to those servants who had helped him.

This fantasy, told by a dismissed soldier who was so poor that he traded his stories to War Secretary Jakob Grimm for a warm coat, shows us a protagonist soldier who could profit from his marginal position between civilian life and a military existence. Was Krause suggesting that his own capacity to mediate between a world of "unstable male cosmogones" and more normal social states was something which might prove of value to a future employer such as Grimm himself? We can never know for sure whether this attempt to render necessity a virtue was anything more than fancy, but it nevertheless points out how one soldier told tales showing veterans walking the thin line between two worlds trying to serve them both and themselves as well. Like the tales of peasants, Krause's tales sought the means to reestablish "connectedness"; to blur and to dissolve the boundaries of the social monads created by bureaucratic theory; and to alleviate the consequences of marginality. In his tales, self-preservation, not self-sacrifice, was the issue.

A far more pessimistic assessment of the meaning of marginality than Krause's may be garnered from yet another tale which the Grimms claimed they published "following the telling of a soldier."[40] "The King from the Golden Mountain" repeats the themes of marginality and betrayal which we find in Krause's tales but ultimately rejects

40. Ibid. 2:318.

the possibility of connectedness between civil and military life. This story begins when a merchant, who had risked nearly all of his wealth on the contents of single ship, heard that it had been lost. He was left with nothing but his small acreage outside the city walls. One day as he worked his plot of land he was approached by a small man dressed in black who asked him what his heart desired. The skeptical merchant said what he most wanted was a new beginning. The man in black promised him the necessary capital if the merchant would give him that which first struck his (the merchant's) leg when he returned home that evening. Delivery was to occur in twelve years and a contract was to be drafted, signed, and sealed.

To these conditions the merchant agreed, thinking that the man was after his dog. He had forgotten his young children — a boy and a girl. The merchant was deeply shocked when it was his young son who first grabbed his leg. His worry grew when he later found the promised money. However, the money provided new opportunities and the merchant once again became a prosperous man.

Eventually, the time to fulfill the contract came and the man, heavy of heart, took his son to the appointed place. The son asked where they were going and when his father told him of the signed and sealed contract he replied optimistically that the small man dressed in black had no power over him. He tried to fortify himself with the blessings of a pastor but when the hour finally arrived, the boy was placed on a boat in a river and the merchant himself was required to push the young lad off the bank. The boat immediately turned over and the merchant gave his son up for dead.

However, the son continued to float down the stream standing in the boat. Head down and feet up, he had entered a world turned upside down. He floated to an unknown bank where he climbed out. There he saw a beautiful castle which was obviously bewitched because every room he entered was completely empty of man or beast. However, in the last room he discovered a coiled snake. The snake was a bewitched maiden who had been waiting twelve years for someone to rescue her. The lad asked how this might be done and discovered that all that was required was that he remain silent as he underwent three nights of torture by little men in black. The maiden promised that each night after the torture she would come to rescue him with the water of life. And so it went and the maiden returned to her original form as a beautiful princess. The two married and the lad became king from the golden mountain.

This story did not end happily, for the birth of his first son reminded the king of his own former connection with his father and he longed once again to see his home. His wife, unhappy with this turn of affairs, nevertheless gave him a magic ring with which he could wish himself anywhere he wanted to be. She made him promise only that he not use it to bring her and her son away from the kingdom of the golden mountain. The king immediately wished himself to the city where his father lived and he appeared before the city gates.

Things did not go well after that. Because his clothing was rich and strange, he was not granted entry into the city. He had to trade clothing with a shepherd on a nearby mountain before he could enter. When he appeared before his father, his father did not recognize him until he showed a birthmark that his mother remembered. Despite this belated recognition that the young man was his son, the father would not believe that the lad was king with a wife and child. The king, without thinking about his promise to his wife, used the ring to bring them there. The angry queen promised revenge for this betrayal, ignoring the protests of the king that he had had no evil intentions. Retribution came when one day as the king slept, the queen stole the ring from him and wished herself and her child back home again.

When the king awoke and found his family gone, he realized he could not go home without coming under suspicion of being a witch. His only alternative was to return to the golden mountain. On his way, he tricked three giants out of their inheritance and acquired from them a pair of magic boots that would take him wherever he wished, a coat that would make him invisible, and a sword that would do its work by voice command.

Using the boots to return to the golden mountain, the king found his castle filled with guests celebrating the remarriage of his wife. He used the magic coat to disrupt his queen's marriage feast. Standing at her side, invisible, he removed everything she put on her plate. The queen fled the room in tears, pursued by the king. As she pleaded to be rescued from the power of the devil, the king revealed himself, struck her, and reminded her of his past service. He then returned to the wedding party declaring it was over. When the guests tried to attack him he killed them all with the magic sword. As the bloody heads of the guests rolled away, he knew that he was once again king of the golden mountain.

This retelling of the legend of Dr. Faust may be interpreted on two levels, each revealing soldiers' attitudes toward the meaning of the Hessian military system. First, it is possible to see the merchant as the

Landgrave himself signing a contract with the king of England which involves the transfer of his male subjects (*Landeskinder* or, literally rendered, "children of the territory") to relieve the poverty of his household. It is important to note that the story denies that the merchant intended his son harm, thus protecting the relationship from the pollution of enmity. On another social plane, the same deal was made by Hessian fathers who accepted the recruitment bounties of their sons as household resources. In this version, the Landgrave is the recruiter, associated by his stature and black clothing with the devil.

Transition to military life, to life on the margins, is evoked by the image of the boat and world turned upside down, an existence where normal rules governing human relationships do not apply. This military realm, not without its rewards, is a realm in which violence and torture reign and where people are treated as means to an end. In such a realm, self-preservation dictates betrayal and counterbetrayal, kind acts are not returned in kind, and finally estrangement is ultimately permanent.

Perhaps the most poignant image of the impossibility of overcoming the estrangement comes as the tale recognizes the fundamental incompatibility of the two social realms. A king in one world, the merchant's son must become a shepherd in order to return home — perhaps a transition soldiers (particularly noncommissioned officers who had some authority) experienced when returning home on leave. Even when he is recognized, he may not stay within the civil realm because his relationships formed in the other world evoke suspicion and disbelief. Then caught between two worlds and striving for connection with at least one, the king becomes a criminal using fraud to acquire the weapons necessary for his survival. The tragedy of living in-between is sharpened as he is rejected even by the wife of the other world who sees him as a devil as well.

This soldier's tale belies the fantasy of one Hessian bureaucrat who argued that, "The brave Hessians are . . . so commonly raised and educated by one-time soldiers that . . . in most cases the soldiers' oath makes their youth vigorous and cheerful."[41] Far from a cheerful experience, Hessian military service was portrayed as fearful and alienating by both the peasants and the soldiers. Peasants hinted at and soldiers made explicit the feeling that military service came as the result of a betrayal by kin and their territorial father (*Landesvater*). Though most

41. StaM, B/4 4072, von Stockhausen.

of the peasants' and soldiers' tales here examined suggested that the intervention of women or questionable acts of self-help might rescue soldiers from their social marginality, this final tale suggests that this was not the case. The transparent barriers of social exclusion in this tale were read as permanent and unalterable. A soldier must remain locked within a world where torture, violence, and betrayal constituted a grid in which an individual fought for survival beyond the possibility of connection. In this text, the performer does not blur, ignore, or finesse the fundamental contradictions within and between victims' worlds and victims' actions. This soldier seems to face more squarely the terrible ways in which the hegemonic kin and tributary cultures of Hesse-Cassel interlocked to require victims to participate in and reproduce their own victimization by defeating the possibility of human love.[42] Such insight carried with it a forlorn and forsaken opportunity for transcendence. Is it any accident, then, that the family world from which soldiers became disconnected was later to be re-imagined as a "haven" from such heartless worlds, thereby continuing the hegemonic obscurity from which one soldier momentarily and partially escaped.[43]

42. Hermann Rebel, "Cultural Hegemony and Class Experience: A Critical Reading of Recent Ethnological-Historical Approaches (part two)," *American Ethnologist* 16 (1989): 126: "The real question for hermeneutical analysis concerns the additional splitting by and social penetration of an inherently split self required to perform, in life-and-death historical time—which includes theatrical time—incomplete and irreconcilably split texts." Also Fredric Jameson, *The Political Unconscious: Narrative as a Socially Symbolic Act* (Ithaca, 1981), 23–58, 206–80.

43. Christopher Lasch, *Haven in a Heartless World: The Family Besieged* (New York, 1977); Ingeborg Weber-Kellermann, *Die deutsche Familie: Versuch einer Sozialgeschichte* (Frankfurt, 1981), 107.

Postscript

Hessian military practice and its concomitant social relations were a necessary dark side of a fiscal-military state that defended the "liberties of Englishmen." Some Englishmen saw from the beginning the paradox of using the possibly tyrannical institutions of fiscal-militarism (primarily standing armies) to defend the liberty that grew out of their tributary order. To be acceptable to a party of skeptical country gentlemen, the institutional arrangements of taxation, state finance, and a permanent professional military establishment had to be fashioned in a way that was consistent with an idea of liberty which had little place for them. The practice of subsidizing or leasing trained military units recruited by petty European princes seemed one arrangement justified by this constellation of needs. The entire ensemble of practices of the English fiscal-military state of which the subsidy system was a crucial part formed the historical basis for a new capitalist mode of production within the interstices of England's tributary and kin-ordered social formation. Thus, German conscripts died indentured to defend English liberty both in its older tributary form and in a newer market form.

Responding to the color of English money, the Landgraves of Hesse-Cassel mirrored the fiscal-militarism of English speakers with a military-fiscalism of their own. British subsidy money allowed these princes to build more elaborate states, more "rational" bureaucracies, and more intensely articulated tribute-taking institutions than they otherwise might have built. In this process, they altered significant aspects of the political and social lifeworld, establishing a social militarism in their territories which might well have evoked Alderman Bull's suggestive hyperbole about German slaves.

Programmatic "rationalization" as it appeared in the Kanton law of 1762 and the Hufen edict of 1773 fundamentally undermined an administrative system based on "patrimonial" politics. In practice, it intensified the ideological contradictions of the cameralist theory of the household economy (*das ganze Haus*), producing a bureaucratically reified language that defined increasing numbers of Hessian children as marginals and as targets for recruitment and other state administrative action. Ultimately, the subsidy-financed dynamism of the landgravial state brought the subsidy system to a state of crisis during the American Revolutionary War. At this time, and for later historians, Hessian subsidy practice entered into an ideological and practical juxtaposition with English "liberties" and so became a fabled part of the German Problem.

For the bulk of the Hessian peasantry, however, "liberty" was not as important as "kinship" or "connection" through blood, marriage, and property. Rural agricultural producers practiced a kin-ordered mode of production which organized work around marriage, property devolution, family labor, and kin-based communal politics as did most other European peasant societies. Thus peasants, their tributary lords, and the landgravial state struggled to bind and unbind labor locked up in "rights in persons" which like land and movable wealth flowed to particular positions in the discursively or symbolically defined grid of inheritance and kinship. Through control of marriage and inheritance, an elite group of Hessian peasant men and women occupied those positions that not only allowed them to control the work of others but to order the grid itself. From this position, they directed unprivileged children to positions in which they only had indirect access to land or none at all, and thus prevented the poorest from marrying or reproducing. Crucial distinctions such as heir and non-heir, married and unmarried, housed and unhoused counted as class distinctions in this society.

When such class distinctions entered the discourse of Hessian bureaucrats as they began to regulate family production, the language of kinship acquired new harsher meanings. Through the Kanton law of 1762 and the Hufen edict of 1773, recruiters first targeted the disconnected and then disconnected the targeted younger male children of Hessian kin groups in order to "unlock" their labor for military purposes. Caught up in the general expropriation of the latter act and asked as a result of the former to sacrifice their dowries, peasant women too became entangled in social military relations. From less privileged members of kin groups, male and female children became the system-necessary victims of both a Hessian and an international social militarism. As their parents experienced a crisis of intimate authority, the experience of their own positions in kin groups, in and of themselves, as they conflicted with their roles in Hessian social militarism, and English fiscal militarism constituted a multivalent class experience which at times could be overwhelmingly painful. This divided experience, and the strained attempts to recompose it, appear in the folk tales of Hessian peasants which only intimate the social and psychic costs of split identities.

Subsidy wealth in the Landgraves' hands provided opportunities to rationalize, centralize, and extend their own networks of tribute taking. This wealth helped to increase the subordination of local and regional tribute-takers (Diet and nobility) to central authority, and it further helped to unlock the labor of peasant boys chained in the symbolic grids of the kin-ordered mode of production practiced by the Landgrave's rural subjects. Both processes tended to break and rearticulate the webs of kin-ordered production and thus contributed to a demographic revolution and intensified social conflict among rural dwellers. And so we may see how costs paid by peasants in an area considered "backward" by many contemporary standards contributed to the historical context which brought capitalism into the world. In Alderman Bull's terms, we begin to specify how this use of German "slaves" helped to convert the terms of slavery from "rights in persons" to "labor as a commodity." Further, we may begin to see how English "liberty" in this social formation was purchased at the cost of German "love." Finally, we see the origins of Germans' problems, both as experienced and as written, in an intimate embrace with the historical experience and writing of Anglo-Americans. Liberties, tyrannies, loves, and hatreds are all children of that embrace.

It has occurred to me that my story, which connects the trials of Hessian farm children with the development of English power and English capitalism, may be read as a brief in favor of national isolation — that is, that "German" problems may be solved by successful disarticulation and disconnection from broader world communities. In my view, such a reading would be a perverse misapprehension of what is possible. Internally homogeneous and externally bounded categories simply cannot become part of experience except as analytic and political fictions. To attempt to impose them on the social tapestry leads only to the monstrous unraveling of the social cloth that we see represented by Nazi attempts to define and enact a pure "Germanness" using bureaucratic and military murder. No borders are impermeable, nor should we wish them to be, for any hope of human survival is rooted in a human connectedness that gets beyond what Freud called civilization's discontents by the ongoing processes of contamination.

APPENDIX
Data Sets

Marriage Data

Marriage data set: Marriages from the parish register of Oberweimar

For years beginning	Total marriages	First marriages of men	As percentage of total
1722–32	85	63	72.4
1742–53	99	70	70.7
1754–62	69	31	44.9
1763–74	98	71	72.4
1798–1808	80	65	80.2
Totals	431	300	69.1

All 431 marriages in this sample come from Kirchenarchiv Oberweimar, Kirchen-Protokolle, Heirathsregister volumes 1–8, 1660–1830, and they represent all marriages from the designated years except those of the pastors' families and those of local nobles. G. T. Fox, in "Studies in the Rural History of Upper Hesse," has discussed the reliability of this register extensively and concluded that although the first volume, 1660–1760, was a copy of a preexisting set of records of undeterminable character, it was probably substantially complete. The one exception was a period between 1749 and 1755, when the parish had no pastor and was being cared for by a number of pastors from neighboring parishes. During this period in particular (but also occasionally during others), entries for the Lutheran parish in Marburg also found their way into the register. The pastor was formally required to preside over that parish on certain Sundays throughout the year. During the period of study, records were kept by only three different pastors, George Buchsen (to 1749), Friedrich Wilhelm Usener (1755–77), and Phillip Conrad Usener (1777–1820). The register entries represent a document of incredible detail until the death of Pastor Buchsen. Marriage entries included birthplaces of bride and groom, their names and both parents' names as well as spouses' ages. Often it was noted whether the couple paid a fornication fine. The first pastor Usener was not nearly as rigorous, frequently leaving out the age of spouses, names of female parents, and on occasion a birthplace when it was outside the parish. Within the limits of a 1776 law which required standardized entries, the second Usener was more diligent.

Although the marriages came from the register of a single parish of nine villages, many of the spouses did not. More than sixty different place names from outside the parish appear as birthplaces of the spouses. Most of these are from the region of Oberhessen and neighboring areas of Hesse-Darmstadt, but some are from places as far away as Vienna. This broad scattering makes these marriages more representative than they might at first appear.

The groups of marriages were selected for the following reasons. The years 1722–32 represent the last years of population growth associated with the recovery from the Thirty Years War. There was only one subsidy treaty during these years (1726) and no troops were sent abroad. The years 1742–62 correspond roughly to a period of population stagnation. Troops were absent on subsidy duty for the first six years of the period between 1742 and 1753. Although all who left were technically volunteers, many were recruited from militia units in which participation was required. Between 1754 and 1762, troops were absent on subsidy duty for the last seven years. In addition, the parish was under occupation from 1756 to 1760 and lay between two opposing armies. Significant fighting occurred there during this period. Between 1763 and 1774, there were no troops away on subsidy duty but these were also the first years the Kanton ordinance was in effect. After 1773, the number of marriages in the parish shrank, probably as a result of confusion concerning the Hufen edict. This shortfall was probably the reason why the number of marriages from 1763–74 was virtually the same as that during the eleven years of stagnation, 1742–1753. Nevertheless, it is through comparison of the periods 1742–

1753 and 1763–1774 that the relative effects of the draft, subsidy treaties, and military activity can best be separated. During the years between 1798 and 1808 the country returned to a militia-based military system that did little or no fighting outside the territorial borders. After 1806, Hesse-Cassel was incorporated into Napoleon's Westphalian Kingdom, which he created for Jerome. This was also one of those periods in which the population explosion took a brief pause in this parish.

The weddings from the parish register were painstakingly linked to the landholding records in the cadasters of 1725; StaM, B/17e Ortsrepositur, Reizberg 61; and K/1, 1747. These documents were used not only for the villages of the parish, but where possible, for all villages in the Oberhessian region for which they existed. Thus, spouses could be tracked to their home villages when they came from outside the parish. The linkages between these sources were not made by computer although the computer aided the process by constructing alphabetical lists. Most people on these lists had three names, a village of birth, parents' names, ages, and sometimes other collateral data. Eighty percent or so of the matches were relatively straightforward. The remaining twenty percent required consideration of difficulties such as variations in spelling of names and villages and imprecise data in the cadasters concerning timing of property transfers. Under these conditions phonetically similar spellings were accepted as matches. It also became clear from the sources that the first name "Johann" in combination with a second name such as "Henrich" could frequently be set equal to "Henrich" because this was done in everyday speech. Apparently peasants believed that the name "Johann" or "Johannes" protected the bearer from lightning strikes but did not use it if the person had another name. When there was a timing problem, matches were considered plausible within the time span of a decade of a known date. Other sources were also called upon. Records of fines, petitions, census worksheets, and reports of conflicts in villages often helped pinpoint people in time and space, giving more confidence to matches I made. Inevitably, I made some matches that perhaps should not have been or did not make matches that I should have. I believe there were more of the latter than the former.

For most of this book, I have limited myself to first marriages of men because they were the most transparently affected by the intertwining calculations of generational transmission and conscription. This smaller group also excludes all sixty-five marriages with spouses from outside Oberhessen. These marriages were distributed fairly evenly for three of the five groups — 1722 (fourteen marriages), 1742 (thirteen marriages), 1763 (fifteen marriages), representing between 13 and 16 percent of marriages for those years. During the Seven Years War, the proportion swelled to nearly 25 percent (seventeen marriages) and after 1798 fell to less than 8 percent (six marriages). These data in themselves suggest that significant changes in the pattern of marriage behavior took place during wartime years. The later changes suggest the efforts that peasant producers had begun making after the end of the draft to reestablish control by closing their communities to outsiders more stringently than they had before.

Soldier Data

Soldier data set: Soldiers from Oberweimar who served in the Hessian army, 1763–1793

Soldiers found in all documents	Soldiers found in parish register	Born in parish	Born outside parish	Found in parish cadasters
115	111	100	11	45

Construction of this data set began with the military muster lists of the von Ditfurth regiment to which Oberweimar was assigned as part of its recruitment district: StaM, B/11, MRb 770–79, 1768–75, 1783–84; 781, 1786; 783, 1787; 801, 1790; 803, 1792. I also used a muster list from the von Knoblauch garrison regiment, *ibid.*, 836, 1786, which had been assigned the same district. These sources provided full names, ages, sizes, and places of residence for seventy-nine soldiers from the nine villages of parish Oberweimar. To this list of soldiers, I added those I found in Inge Auerbach et al., *Hessische Truppen in amerikanischen Unabhängigkeitskrieg* 1–5 (Marburg, 1976–84), which used similar sources to list all soldiers thought to have served in the subsidy army sent to America. This source thus provided a better cross section of the Hessian army and added another fourteen Oberweimar residents to the list. The remaining twenty-two names came from a variety of Oberweimar records including the parish register, reports of local officials to the Landrat, and monthly lists of the von Ditfurth regiment (StaM, Best 12, monatliche Listen Regiment v. Ditfurth, 8849, 1768–85).

Names from this list were linked to parish register entries, cadastral entries, and census entries. Four of the names on the list were eventually eliminated because they appeared in only one source. Crucial for the linkage algorithm was the fact that the military lists always included age. This information permitted a linkage with a birth entry in the parish register to be made with relative certainty in all cases for which the soldier was born in the parish, and the register in turn provided data on parents and established the possibility of further links with cadastral and census data. For fourteen of eighteen cases in which there was no birth entry, there were other parish register entries such as confirmation, marriage, burial, or a mention as a godparent. Frequently, even these soldiers had multiple entries in the register so that linkages could be made with a high degree of confidence. This data set permitted the construction of the rough collective biography that appears in Chapter 9 as well as the quantitative analysis that accompanies it.

Comparative Data

Comparative control group from Oberweimar parish register born between 1743 and 1748

Total births	Peasant births	Male births	Female births	Two or more entries	Male	Female
206	201	95	106	112	58	54

Part of my task has been to show how soldiers differed from the rest of the Hessian rural population. To do so it was necessary to construct a comparative control group. I began with birth entries in the parish register for the years 1743–48. These years were chosen because they provided an age group that was roughly similar to that of the bulk of the soldiers in my study. Indeed over a third of the males (21) in this group also were members of the soldier group. This overlap had the unfortunate effect of blurring the differences. When differences do show up, we must therefore take them more seriously. Soldiers were left in the study because I wanted a cross section of the whole population of the generation.

Eventually all non-peasants (nobles and pastors' children) were eliminated from the group because they were not subject to the same regulations as others in the village. I also eliminated from the study all children who failed to have at least one entry in the parish register besides the registry of their baptism. To include the victims of infant mortality would mean that the group could not be compared to soldiers who by definition survived to at least their fifteenth year. Most second entries were found in confirmation lists, though few were seconded only by a burial or wedding entry. Confirmations normally occurred in the fifteenth year of life and immediately preceded a male subject's entry on recruitment lists.

The list was finally winnowed down to 112 names and the process of nominal record linkage was applied to that list to connect them with cadastral and household census records. This procedure worked with a high degree of confidence with men on the list. Women's names did not appear frequently in either census or tax records. In these circumstances marriage and burial entries in the parish register were helpful if they provided the names of husbands and, thus, indirect links. If a woman had no parish burial entry and she did not marry in the parish, or if her husband's name appeared in no other record, then I assumed that she moved out. Such a set of assumptions was also made with males, but with greater confidence, because males were more likely to appear in other sources than were females. This data set did provide a crude basis for comparison, but I do not wish to push it too far until a large portion of the movers can be located in parish and tax records of neighboring parishes. Such a task is probably too difficult and time-consuming to warrant any added confidence that might accrue by doing it.

Index of Concepts

Index of Persons

Index of Places